a cure for those who think they should have success and fame in sports handed to them, Coste is your kind of guy."
—*Sports Book Review Center*

"An enjoyable read . . . One . . . roots for [Coste] a little harder as each year passes without an invitation to 'the show.' . . . [*The 33-Year-Old Rookie*] offers a glimmer of hope. As James Earl Jones intoned in *Field of Dreams:* 'It reminds us of all that once was good and that could be good again.' "
—*The Free Lance-Star* (Fredericksburg, Virginia)

"What amazes me most about Chris Coste's unlikely career is that he did it playing the hardest position on the field, grinding out the daily barrage of nicks, bruises, and head-on collisions that are the life of a catcher. *The 33-Year-Old Rookie* is a great story of a man's triumph over adversity, not to mention the quirks of baseball players (you'll have to read the book to find out why Chris sniffs and burns his bats), but it's also a fascinating account of the view from behind home plate."
—TIM MCCARVER, Fox Sports

"Chris Coste is the epitome of the phrase 'never give up hope.' His dream was to be a major-league baseball player, and his determination and attitude finally paid off. At the age of thirty-three, Chris not only reached the majors but showed that he belonged."
—HARRY KALAS, Hall of Fame broadcaster for the Philadelphia Phillies

"Having been through my own baseball odyssey, I can relate to Chris's journey. And I thought I had it tough! Way to go, Chris!"
—JIM "THE ROOKIE" MORRIS

"[Coste] tells a straightforward story, giving readers an opportunity to understand the obstacles and tough times minor leaguers and marginal players endure. . . . Inspirational."
—The Associated Press

"[An] uplifting memoir . . . Don't give up on a dream is the message Coste delivers in [*The 33-Year-Old Rookie*]."
—*The San Diego Union-Tribune*

"[Chris Coste] is the archetype of the underdog."
—*Booklist*

"[An] intriguing rags-to-not-quite-riches tale . . . highly recommended."
—*Library Journal*

THE
33-YEAR-OLD
ROOKIE

☆

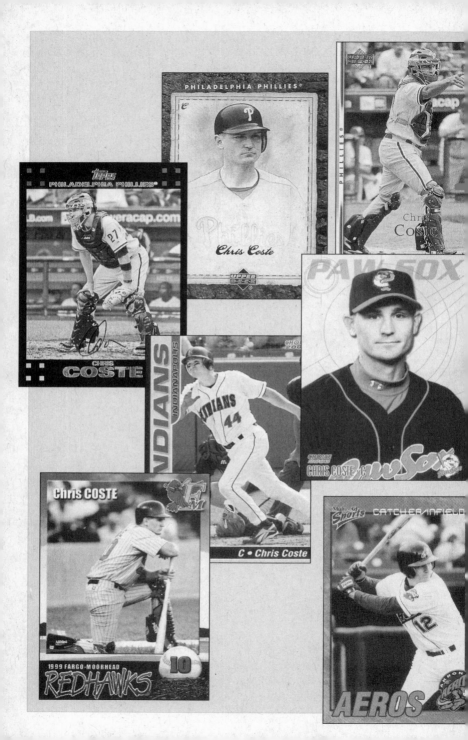

THE 33-YEAR-OLD ROOKIE

★

My 13-Year Journey from the
Minor Leagues to the
World Series

★

Chris Coste

Foreword by John Kruk

ESPN BOOKS

BALLANTINE BOOKS
NEW YORK

2009 Ballantine Books Trade Paperback Edition

Published in the United States by Ballantine Books,
an imprint of The Random House Publishing Group,
a division of Random House, Inc., New York.

BALLANTINE and colophon are registered trademarks
of Random House, Inc.

Originally published in hardcover in slightly different form in the United States
by Ballantine Books, an imprint of The Random House Publishing Group,
a division of Random House, Inc., in 2008.

Library of Congress Cataloging-in-Publication Data

Coste, Chris.
The 33-year-old rookie / Chris Coste.
p.   cm.
ISBN 978-0-345-50703-7
1. Coste, Chris.   2. Philadelphia Phillies (Baseball team)
3. Baseball players—Pennsylvania—Philadelphia—Biography.
4. Baseball players—United States—Biography.
I. Title.   II. Title: Thirty-three-year-old rookie.

GV865.C675A3 2008
796.357092—dc22
[B]   2007041368

Printed in the United States of America

www.ballantinebooks.com
www.chriscoste.com

24689753

Book design by Jo Anne Metsch

Like the families of so many minor leaguers, always waiting anxiously for the bus to roll back into town, my family was there for me through all the disappointing, exciting, and trying moments of my long minor-league career.

I would like to dedicate this book to the families of minor-league lifers like myself. No one knows better than me how important family is, and how much a good family can help a ballplayer catch his dream!

THE THROWBACK

John Kruk

I FIRST heard about Chris Coste in early March 2006. I was checking in on my old team the Phillies and came across an article about a guy who was tearing up spring training. He was hitting over .400 and had come up with clutch hits in something like four straight games. It seemed to me that the Phillies finally had that hot young prospect they'd been waiting for, so why hadn't I heard of him? I kept reading . . . thirty-three years old . . . eleven years in the minors. I knew I had to check this guy out.

I called the Phillies' hitting coach, Milt Thompson, my old teammate, to find out what the story was. I asked, "How long's this going to last? They surely don't have the nerve to keep a thirty-three-year-old guy." I knew there must be some reason why a guy like Coste, who had hit at every level, had been kicking around the minors for so long.

Milt just said, "He's making it awful tough to get rid of him."

It's hard to explain how high the odds were against Chris Coste making it to the major leagues at his age. I played for five years in the minor leagues, and I vowed to quit if I didn't make it to the big leagues after my fifth year. You don't make any money. You have nothing to support yourself with. Hell, I was single and I couldn't live on what I made. And even if you still love baseball, soon baseball no longer loves you. Every year that goes by makes it less and less likely that you'll make it, no matter how well you're playing. Baseball loves the hot young prospect. If a guy like me didn't make it after five years, the thinking goes, there had to be a reason.

A week before the end of my fifth season in the minor leagues, I was told I was going to be a September call-up for the Padres. (The minor-league season ends in August.) But after the last game, the manager, Bob Cluck, told me, "The fat man doesn't want you. Go home." He was talking about a certain Padres official whom I won't name. He told me they were going to put me on the forty-man roster for the next year and invite me to spring training, which they did, for the first time in my career. And I had the best spring of my life, leading the team in almost every category. But wouldn't you know, at the end of it they called me in and told me I was being sent back to triple-A. I said, "Screw that. I'm going home. I'm not going to play for twelve hundred dollars a month. I can go home and enjoy myself." I really was ready to quit. But shortly after that my team-mate Bobby Brown came over and congratulated me for making the team. He had decided to retire and told me I deserved to play. Without that, I probably never would have played a major-league game.

I began to tune in to games to watch Chris Coste play during that amazing spring training and the story kept getting better and better. Un-like a lot of the guys who come up today, Coste was not a mechanical bull with a textbook swing. In fact, he reminded me of myself somewhat with his tremendously unorthodox hitting style. He's got this hitch in his swing, and he dives at the ball, sometimes landing his front foot on home plate. I would watch him and think: This guy has got to be incredibly strong—farm strong—to hit the ball as hard as he does with that swing. And it wasn't always pretty. He would take a godawful swing, miss a pitch by a mile, and look foolish doing it. But then the pitcher, feeling confi-dent, would throw him the same pitch and he would hit it a country mile. You had the feeling he was just setting the guy up. Chris's catching style isn't textbook, either; when he throws the ball back to the pitcher, he'll lean to his left and throw sidearm. But the Phillies' pitchers told me they loved throwing to him. They told me he had a knack for knowing what hitters are looking for, and what's working for them that day.

Chris played *eleven* years in the minors, for twelve different teams. To hang around that long, after most people had given up on him—that tells you how special he is. Not to mention his wife, who must be even more special, given the level of sacrifice wives have to make to allow their husbands to chase their dream long after they have any decent shot of catching it. For everything I accomplished in baseball, I'd say that Chris Coste has accomplished more than I ever did because he had to work so damn hard to achieve it.

When I first met Chris at Citizens Bank Park last year, he was modest and unassuming, with no chip on his shoulder about how long it had taken him to get to the big leagues. By then he had become a hero to the demanding fans in Philly, who loved him instantly because he *is* them, making him just as popular as Chase Utley, Ryan Howard, and Jimmy Rollins—a different kind of player to be sure, but just as respected. He's true blue-collar: He's worked for everything he has, and he doesn't take the game for granted. I'm from West Virginia and Chris is from Fargo, North Dakota, but I could tell that he had that same "I know I'm lucky to be here and I'm grateful for the opportunity" feeling that I had when I first made it. He knows that, except for the birth of his daughter, this is the greatest thing that's ever happened to him. Not many guys feel that way. Guys get into baseball so they can make money; Chris plays because he loves baseball and that's his life.

For years now, the people who run baseball have been all about signing "the best athletes." What they tend to get are a lot of spoiled kids with great skills but nothing inside. There's something to be said about instincts, adaptability, and the mental aspect of the game, not to mention character.

Chris Coste's story inspires everyone, because in an era of spoiled, overcoached athletes, he's a throwback.

CONTENTS

THE DREAM

I FINALLY made it!

I'm still in shock as I arrive at Citizens Bank Park in Philadelphia. Walking up to the stadium, the most beautiful in all of baseball, the first thing I notice are the cars in the players' parking lot. Mercedes, Hummers, Escalades, and Bentleys in every direction. Incredible! Quite different from the usual array of Honda Accords, Ford Escapes, and Saturns in a typical minor-league parking lot—not to mention the Mitsubishi Endeavor that I'd just pulled up in.

I can get used to this, I think to myself.

Can it be true? Or is this all a dream? After eleven years in the minors and a lifetime of hard work and dedication, have I finally made it to the big leagues? I actually pinch the back of my arm just to make sure; I've had dreams like this in the past.

Yep, it's real. *I'm a major leaguer. It's not a dream. It's not a dream!*

Next I'm stepping through the door to the largest clubhouse I have ever seen and gazing at the perfectly pressed red-and-white home uniforms hanging in the players' lockers. The jerseys are emblazoned with *Phillies* across the chest in big red script, two blue stars dotting both *i*'s. I can't help but think of some of the legends who have worn these uni-

forms. Pete Rose, baseball's all-time hit leader, was a Phillie. Darren
Daulton. Tug McGraw. John Kruk. Steve Carlton, a 300-game winner.
Hall of Famer Mike Schmidt. Whoa! *Mike Schmidt* was a Philadelphia
Phillie!

  And look at some the names on the metal plates above the lockers.
First baseman Ryan Howard, the 2005 National League Rookie of the
Year. Chase Utley, his power-hitting partner on the right side of the in-
field. Suddenly first baseman Jim Thome—my new teammate!—hollers,
"Hey, Coaster!" How'd he know my nickname? "Great to see ya! Con-
gratulations, man!"

  "Um . . . thanks," I mumble back. Imagine that. My teammates know
how long it's taken me to get to the big leagues. Even superstars like
Thome and Howard can appreciate the path I've traveled.

  Gotta see the field! This is a moment I've envisioned my entire life,
and the one memory I want to hold on to until the day I die: to stroll onto
a major-league field as a major-league ballplayer. But it's more than that.
I want to take in the entire stadium.

  With the warm summer sun hitting me in the face, I want to squint up at
the furthest depths of the upper deck and imagine Citizens Bank Park
packed with forty thousand screaming fans. *Philadelphia* fans, possibly the
most intense and passionate fans anywhere. Then the smell of the grass:
that unmatchable aroma of the freshly mowed infield and perfectly
groomed outfield. *This* is the moment I've waited for, and I want to savor it.

  Just as I'm overcome with tears of joy, I'm startled by the sound of a little girl's voice.

  "Good morning, Daddy, it's time to get up!" piped up my six-year-old
daughter, Casey.

Talk to any minor-league baseball player, and he'll relate his own version
of "the dream." Maybe he's just smacked a walk-off home run in his first
game or notched an important save in relief. Or maybe he doesn't star on
the field at all; in his dream, he's just picked up the phone to hear a voice
tell him that he's being called up to the big leagues. Whatever the scene,
it always ends with the disappointing snap back to reality—in my case, a
cold, snowy January morning in Fargo, North Dakota.

While Casey dutifully reminded me that it was my turn to take her to school, I couldn't help but wonder if my playing days were nearing an end. In my eleven-year career, I'd spent five years in various independent leagues, one season in double-A minor-league ball, and parts of six years at the triple-A level for four organizations (Phillies, Cleveland Indians, Milwaukee Brewers, Boston Red Sox). I'd also played six seasons of winter ball in Mexico, Venezuela, and Panama. All told, I'd played on *twelve* teams, logging time at every position on the diamond except for center field. In my mind, I was probably the most experienced player to never have set foot on a major-league field as a major-league player.

Don't get me wrong: I loved playing baseball, and I was still good at it. But the yearly frustration and disappointment of not making it to the big leagues were becoming too much to bear. And with my thirty-third birthday just five days away, February 4, 2006, the odds that I would ever conquer my dream were not improving.

My family's needs also made me wonder how much longer I could pursue the dream. Casey had just started first grade and could no longer travel as much as she had in the past. At times I would go up to three months without seeing my wife and daughter, making it more of a grind than I had ever imagined. Combined with all the disappointments that I had endured over my career, I wondered if I could make it through another potentially heartbreaking season. How much longer could I possibly keep this up? I could only hope that it was my destiny to make the big leagues as a manager.

Stumbling out of bed, I made my way to the bathroom, and was painfully brought to life by the screaming aches and pains that came with being a five-days-shy-of-thirty-three-year-old athlete. As I looked at myself in the mirror, I was reminded of "Crash" Davis, the battered minor-league lifer played by Kevin Costner in the movie *Bull Durham*. A song began to play in my head: Garth Brooks's "Much Too Young (To Feel This Damn Old)."

Just then my wife, Marcia, walked past the open bathroom door. "Thirty-three going on eighty?" she joked.

"It's more like seventy," I protested. "And I'm not thirty-three for a few more days." Marcia, my high-school sweetheart, and I had joked for years about how she would be pushing me around in a wheelchair by the time

I was fifty. It wasn't just that my body was sore—hell, my body was always sore—but with the Phillies' 2006 spring training just two weeks away, I was less prepared than I had ever been in my minor-league career. I took pride in always being in perfect physical shape when I reported to camp, but having just returned from my fourth consecutive winter of baseball in Mexico, I was too worn out to work out like I had in the past. In any given year, between spring training, the regular season, and winter ball, I was playing up to two hundred games. The nagging injuries were adding up, and I was feeling a lot older than the age listed on my driver's license. Compounding my worries, I'd taken batting practice only once this month. "Unprepared" was an understatement. With that in mind, I drank my morning coffee, dropped off Casey at school, and headed for the gym.

Just as I pulled into the parking lot of the local YMCA, my cell phone rang.

"Chris? It's Pat." My agent.

Pat Arter has represented me since 2000, when I was a nobody in the Cleveland Indians farm system, and he's stuck with me the entire time. I think it's safe to say that it hasn't been for the money; if you totaled up the entire amount of money I've made for him in my career, you wouldn't be able to supersize your Happy Meal at McDonald's. Given Pat's loyalty and the amount of time we've worked together, I would say I trust him as much as a close relative.

Pat knew that I was exhausted from winter ball and had recently considered retirement, so he'd been calling on what seemed like a daily basis to talk me out of quitting and give me the usual pre–spring training pep talk. Besides Marcia, he was the only person who could always put things in perspective and cheer me up, consistently reminding me how close I was to the big leagues.

"It would be a disservice to all minor leaguers to give up now," Pat would typically say. "Just think how far you've come. How many independent-league players out there would kill to be where you are now?" He was right. Ten years earlier I had fought to get into the independent Northern League, a league full of undrafted college players, minor league cast-offs, and former big leaguers like Darryl Strawberry and Jack Morris. It was every independent player's goal to catch on with major-league organizations with the hopes of getting a shot at the big leagues. To get from independent ball to triple-A was considered a success, regardless of the fact that I might never sniff the big leagues, and every independent leaguer would gladly switch places with me.

And then I'd picture myself back in the late 1990s, and how I was lost in independent-league anonymity. With the number of times I had come so close to the big leagues since then, it was easy to forget just how far I was from the major leagues in those days. Brainerd, Minnesota (North Central League); Brandon, Manitoba (Prairie League); Fargo, North Dakota (Northern League)—I was a million miles away. Maybe even further than that; after all, I was so far from the big leagues in those days that the possibility of becoming a major leaguer had been totally erased from my mind. Now, I was going to attend major league spring training with the Phillies and share a clubhouse with the likes of Ryan Howard, Jimmy Rollins, and Chase Utley. He was always right—I had come a long way since then; too close to quit now.

This time, though, Pat was calling not just to offer encouragement but to pass on some intriguing news. A team from the Korean League was offering me $300,000 to play third base for them. Like many journeyman minor-league ballplayers, playing overseas was something I'd wanted to do for many years. I earned $60,000 as the Red Barons' starting third baseman and occasional catcher in 2005, a season in which I batted .292 with 20 home runs and 89 runs batted in for the Phillies' triple-A affiliate.

Before Pat had even finished sketching out the details for me, I replied, "Where do I sign?" Three hundred thou? It was a no-brainer, and I wanted to seal the deal before the Korean execs changed their minds.

Although I was slightly ashamed of my extreme and hasty desire to agree to the contract for financial reasons, my motivation had changed over the past few seasons. My motivation had always been to conquer the dream that began at the age of seven, to wear a major-league uniform in a beautiful major-league stadium and live the life I thought I was destined for. Money was never the primary factor. That's not to say that the money wasn't an issue—after all, financial security is a desire for any normal person—but the idea of making the major leagues was the culmination of a lifetime of hard work and dedication. Now, with no light at the end of the minor-league tunnel, I had to think about how I was going to support my family. Also, even though going to Korea meant that I would be leaving the big-league chase in my rearview mirror, I was still going to wear a uniform and play in front of thousands of passionate and crazy fans. I was still going to be a baseball player, and I was still going to be able to do the one thing that always gave me joy—I was still going to play baseball.

When I walked into our condo that night, I breathlessly told Marcia the news.

"Korea? You're actually considering it?" she asked, noticeably less than enthusiastic.

"Absolutely," I said. "Three hundred thousand dollars. I've never made that kind of money, and I'll never make that kind of money in triple-A. Just think, Marcia, we could pay off all of our credit cards, student loans—maybe even pay off the house. For the first time in our lives, we'd be debt free. I *have* to do this.

"And even more importantly," I continued, "if I have a good year in Korea, maybe I'll get a chance to sign with a team in Japan." Marcia and I had talked many times about the kind of financial security playing in Japan could bring; for six years running, I had tried to get to Japan, only to be turned down each time. But I knew one American minor leaguer who'd had a good season playing in Korea, then signed with a Japanese team. Three years later he was raking in $4 million a year. And he'd never even made it as far as triple-A.

"If everything went well, we could be set for life," I reminded my wife. Still, she remained unmoved; disappointed, even, probably thinking about life with a small daughter and a husband halfway across the globe.

"Honestly, Chris, that sounds great; it really does." The two of us sat down at the kitchen table. "But I don't care about the money, and I know deep down that you don't, either. It's never been about money. It's about making it to the big leagues—about catching your dream.

"You've played too long and have so much invested in this life," she said tenderly, "there's no way you can throw in the towel now. All those frustrating close calls and disappointments will make it mean that much more when you do make it to the big leagues. And you will make it. I know it." Whenever I got caught up momentarily in imagining what our life would be like if I could make the big money, Marcia would deliver variations of this little sermon to keep me from veering off-course. Yet her words always hit me as though I were hearing them for the first time.

"If you want to go to Korea," she added, "I'll understand. You do what you have to do."

As you can tell, I have always had an unbelievably supportive wife. We've been together since high school, and it is safe to say that Marcia lived and died that same dream as much as I did, if not more.

You would think that after hearing those incredibly prophetic words from my wife I would have totally agreed with her and given up on Korea, but that wasn't the case. I'm usually an open-minded guy, but when it came to playing baseball overseas I was usually a little hardheaded. I guess after I had been soured by the idea that I would never make the big leagues, the notion of playing baseball in Japan became more of a desire with each passing season. It wasn't that it was becoming a dream like the big leagues had always been, but it had become a lot more realistic, and it paid just as much, if not more. So if I could get to Korea, Japan was definitely within the realm of possibility.

Interestingly enough, I was never given the chance to sign the contract. Five days later, Pat called me back to inform me that the Koreans had changed their mind. Apparently, they had ultimately decided I wasn't quite what they were looking for and wanted to go in another direction—they had chosen a different player instead. Although I was once again disappointed and frustrated, I did have to laugh a little. This was the same thing I had experienced so many times in triple-A when I was bypassed by other players on their way to the big leagues—my teams had always chosen other players instead of me. Why would Korea be any different?

The next day, though, my agent called back with a tiny piece of good news. He assumed (correctly) that I was a little bummed by the Korean situation and wanted to cheer me up.

"Hey, Coaster!" Pat said excitedly, "I just got off the phone with the Phillies, and Charlie Manuel himself had asked if you were back with the team. He also said that the Phillies needed guys like you in triple-A because you can hit and play multiple positions, and could be called upon to hit off the bench if needed."

This was good news. I had known the Phillies manager from our days in the Cleveland organization. During the 2000, 2001, and 2002 seasons, Charlie managed the big club, while I divided my time between the Indians' double-A affiliate in Akron and their triple-A farm team in Buffalo. He'd told me candidly that he knew I could hit, but he wasn't sure what my best position was. Well, I had just caught fifty games in Mexico for the fourth season in a row, and it was obvious to me and the entire Mexican League that I was more than capable of catching in the big leagues. If I could impress the Mexican winter-league players and coaches, then maybe I could convince Charlie to give me a shot behind the plate. I knew I would never make the big-league club out of spring training, but maybe I could at least put myself on Charlie Manuel's radar and earn a call-up sometime during the 2006 season.

All I needed was a chance.

THE
33-YEAR-OLD
ROOKIE

☆

CHAPTER 1

Spring Training
2006

★ I ★

Spring training did not get off to a promising start. And this was even before I so much as strapped on my shin guards.

I arrived in Clearwater, Florida, in February 2006 with the rest of the pitchers and catchers for my second spring with the Phillies. My only hope to put myself on the club's radar, as in each of the other four spring camps I'd attended, was to prove that I could catch at the major-league level. Going in, I knew that Philadelphia had its two catchers in Mike Lieberthal and Sal Fasano, and there was nothing I could do to take either one's spot on the twenty-five-man roster for opening day. The most that a player in my position could hope for was to make enough of a positive impression that if someone went down during the season, I might get called up.

After pulling into the parking lot of the Hampton Inn in our rental car, Marcia, Casey, and I got out and began unpacking the car. I went straight to the trunk for the heavy bags and was dubiously greeted by one of the small Florida birds. I felt something soft and wet hit my head and couldn't believe what had just happened.

"Mommy!" yelled Casey with exhilarating laughter in her voice. "Did you see that? A birdie just flew by and pooped on Daddy's head!" My six-year-old daughter could barely contain her laughter at seeing her big and strong daddy getting pooped on the head by a tiny bird. Marcia didn't know whether to laugh or not because she was unsure how I would react. I normally have a good sense of humor, but to have a bird poop on your head certainly is not a pleasant experience. Fortunately, seeing the joy and laughter on Casey's face made me instantly realize that it was funny.

You have got to be kidding me, I thought to myself. My first instinct was that a bird pooping on my head was not a good way to begin spring training.

No sooner had we settled into our hotel room than I received a phone call from Steve Noworyta, the Phillies' director of minor-league operations. Simply put, he's like the general manager of the organization's minor-league teams and oversees all of its minor-league players.

"Hi, Chris," he said in a concerned tone. "Are you in Clearwater already?"

"Yes." *Why wouldn't I be?* I thought.

"Oh . . ." He sighed an ominous sigh. "Well, I guess we had a bit of a miscommunication. We didn't want you to show up with the pitchers and catchers, we wanted you to show up next week with the position players. As of right now, it looks like you will play mostly first or third base in triple-A. But since you are already here, I guess you can show up tomorrow and help catch some bullpens and stuff like that."

To put it mildly, I was pissed off. I had hoped to prove to anyone who would pay attention that I was a good catcher. I knew it, my teammates knew it, and virtually every pitcher who'd ever thrown to me always had great comments regarding my catching ability. By no means was I another Johnny Bench, but they always praised my game calling, my soft hands, my ability to catch the low pitch for a strike, and how I always gave a great target. Over the years, many pitchers had remarked, "Chris, I stare in at your glove, and it's like I can't help but throw a perfect strike into it!"

In fact, many of my batterymates had gone to the manager and requested that I catch them in their next start. All catching instructors preach the importance of earning the pitchers' confidence. "A catcher may be able to hit great, block every ball, and throw every guy out trying to steal, but the only thing that matters is if the pitching staff likes throwing to him," they'll stress. "If a pitcher insists that you catch him, that is the best compliment you can receive. And it is that kind of catcher that will not only get to the big leagues but stay there."

Well, *I* was that kind of catcher. So why hadn't I made it?

One reason, I'm pretty sure, was that my ability to play other positions actually undermined my career, in a way. What was my best position? Catcher? First base? Third base? It was always a mystery to them. I always considered myself a catcher who could play elsewhere if needed. However, the decision makers inevitably mistook me for a utility man who could play multiple positions—with catching being just one of them. It seems similar, right? But in the world of professional baseball, there's a huge difference between the two perceptions. The term *utility player* tends to refer to guys who play shortstop and second base, maybe third base, too. No team will put its trust in a catcher who is not primarily a catcher.

So to hear that the Phillies had no plans for me to catch during spring training made no sense to me. And they wanted me at *first base*, of all positions? They had to be kidding. Ryan Howard, the reigning NL Rookie of the Year, played there. All he did in 2005 was hit .288 with 22 homers and 63 RBIs in just half a season.

I hung up the phone in disgust.

"What did you expect?" my wife asked. "Did you really think things were ever going to be easy for you? This is totally par for the course."

"I really hoped the Phillies would be different," I replied. "And I'm thirty-three, Marcia. Time is more than running out. If they won't give me the chance to prove I can catch, I will never make it. Catching is my only hope. They will never call me up as an infielder, especially not at first base."

No one understood what I had gone through more than Marcia. As many times as I had received great comments from pitchers over the years, oddly enough, she also received the same kind of comments from pitchers' wives. "Is your husband catching tomorrow?" a wife would ask. "My husband is pitching tomorrow and he loves it when Chris catches." She heard things like that on a regular basis.

Her response was usually the same as my response to the pitcher. "He loves to catch, but your husband needs to tell that to the manager or the pitching coach—they are the only ones who will listen," Marcia would say. I had almost taught her word for word what to say when a wife would say these things to her. The typical response from the wife was that her husband had gone into the manager's office on several occasions and told him that I should be catching.

★   II   ★

HERE'S how you know you're a long shot to crack the opening day roster: When I reported to training camp, I was handed a uniform with a big red 67 on the back. Generally, the higher your number, the lower your status. I also took note that my locker was on the "hopeless" side of the locker room with all the other players destined for the minors. Or oblivion.

I decided to use my frustration as motivation. It may have been only spring training, but I approached every catching drill as though I were preparing for the World Series. Just as important, each and every day I was in Charlie Manuel's ear, reminding him that catching was my best position. He knew I could hit: In 2002, when he was managing the Indians, I batted .318, 8 HR, 67 RBI for the triple-A Buffalo Bisons and was named team MVP; the previous spring, Charlie's first as Phillies skipper, I hit at a .313 clip. Now I had to prove to him that I was good defensively. "Just keep your eyes open," I'd say before morning workouts. "I promise I will surprise you." He wouldn't reply, just smile and nod, as if to say, "Okay, go prove it."

One other factor would make this spring training difficult: It was the first spring that I would be mostly on my own, as Marcia and Casey had to leave the following week. In previous years, they had accompanied me throughout the entire baseball season. But with Casey now in first grade, she could no longer miss so much school. We would all have to try to get used to seeing each other for short stints up until school let out in June.

Through the first weeks of spring training, I knew I was making a bit of a statement. Three days before our first official spring training game, against the New York Yankees, the team's main catching instructor, Mick Billmeyer, approached me with some positive words. "Coastey," he said, "after watching you catch bullpens, seeing you in our catching drills, and going by what the pitchers are saying about you, I have been telling Charlie every day that I think you can catch in the big leagues. He also asks about you every day and tells me to keep an eye on you because he wants to know how good of a catcher you really are. He knows you can hit, and he definitely wants to give you a shot at catching in some spring training games. So be ready, you might actually get a chance to impress him." Mick, a former catcher, seemed empathetic, perhaps because he'd languished in the minors for eight seasons before turning to coaching in the 1990s.

"Also," he continued, "Carlos Ruiz will be gone for a while to catch for Panama in the World Baseball Classic, so that should also allow you to slip in and catch some innings." Ruiz had a lock on the starting catcher's job at Scranton/Wilkes-Barre and figured to put in a lot of time behind the plate during the spring. With him away to participate in the first-ever international baseball tournament, I'd get a few extra innings to show what I could do.

That brief exchange with Mick Billmeyer improved my outlook dramatically. Whether it was a coincidence or not, later that day I really put myself on the map as far as the Phillies were concerned. I got a chance to take live batting practice off Scott Mathieson, a hard-throwing right-hander from Vancouver whose fastball had been clocked as high as ninety-nine miles an hour in double-A the previous season. He'd just turned twenty-two and was viewed by many as a can't-miss prospect. Scott had been tossing bullpen sessions in preparation for the World Baseball Classic, slated to begin the first week of March; I was selected as one of the hitters to face him in his final practice before leaving to join his Canadian teammates. (Several other members of the Phillies would be going to the games, held in the U.S., Japan, and Puerto Rico, including Chase Utley, Philadelphia's representative on the American team.)

Excited at the opportunity to face live pitching, I was also a little nervous—especially after I glanced behind the batting cage and saw Charlie

Manuel standing next to most of the Phillies' brain trust. There was new general manager Pat Gillick; Ruben Amaro Jr., the assistant GM; and Gillick's special advisor, Dallas Green, the man who'd managed Philadelphia to its only World Championship, back in 1980. If I was going to open some eyes, this would definitely be an opportune moment to shine. Maybe my only moment.

As I stepped into the batter's box, catcher Dusty Wathan lifted up his mask and said with a sigh, "Don't you just hate these live batting practice sessions? Especially against a guy with a fastball like Mathieson's?"

"Not really," I said. "I kind of like this stuff." Most hitters dreaded taking live batting practice off their teammates, for a couple of reasons. One, they don't like to compete against one of their own, and, two, suddenly the ball is coming in much faster at a time when their reflexes and bat speed aren't ready for gamelike activity. Me, I'd always enjoyed it, in part because I was good at it. Batting practice is the only time when the pitcher tells the hitter what pitches are coming. Also, there's really nothing to lose. Either you hit the ball hard, impressing everyone; or you don't hit the ball hard, and people think you're not really trying because you don't like to hit off your team's own pitchers.

Scott's first pitch blew by me at around ninety-five miles per hour, according to the radar gun, but high and out of the zone. As it snapped into the catcher's mitt, I heard Charlie Manuel's distinctive West Virginia drawl: "How 'bout that Scott Mathieson? He's throwin' some heat today. Be careful, Coste!"

I looked back at Charlie, and in my best southern accent, said, "Gotta hit, Charlie," one of his pet phrases. He'd spent several years as the Cleveland Indians' hitting coach, and he loves guys who can hit. He'll walk through the clubhouse, saying to all the hitters, "Gotta hit, son! Gotta hit!"

"All right, then," he replied, a wide grin on his face. "Go hit him, son! Gotta hit!"

I have always prided myself on being able to hit any fastball. If I know it's coming, I'll catch up to it, regardless of its speed. As Mathieson released the next pitch, I gripped the bat tight and let it fly, rocketing the ball at least fifty feet over the fence in left-center field. "How about that

Chris Coste!" Charlie exclaimed with a small laugh under his breath. "Be careful out there, Mathieson!"

Next Scott hummed a fastball middle-in, and once again I brought the bat around and sent it over the left-field wall, this time by some seventy-five feet. Dallas Green, once a Phillies pitcher himself, yelled out, "Wow, Charlie, it looks like Coste brought his quick hands with him this year!"

"Well, he did hit twenty bombs last year in Scranton," the manager responded. I whipped around and looked at Charlie, pleasantly surprised that he knew my stats. The twenty home runs in 2005 was a career high for me. He gave me a quick wink, and I stepped back into the batter's box. Before I was finished, I'd cracked several more solid hits, including a few that disappeared over the fence. The Grapefruit League games, set to start in a few days, were the real tryouts, of course. Still, I drove back to the Hampton Inn that afternoon satisfied that I'd forced the team's decision-makers to notice me.

Two days later we held an intrasquad game so that some of the pitchers could get in an inning of work against hitters in a gamelike setting, and the rest of us could get acclimated to game-speed situations. We were all looking forward to the games, which would put an end to days spent practicing the same drills over and over: blocking balls in the dirt, throwing to bases, fielding bunts and pop flies. Five minutes before the intrasquad contest, I stood in the dugout, expecting to watch it from the bench. Gary Varsho, the bench coach, came up to me and asked, "Hey, Coastey, do you have your first baseman's mitt out here?" On my own time at the end of each day, I'd been taking infield practice with some of the minor-league coaches in camp.

"I've got all my gloves, Varsh," trying to remind him how versatile I was.

"Well, go get it. You're playing first base."

"Um . . . right now?" I assumed he meant that I would fill in at first toward the end of the game.

"Yes, right now!" he answered.

To be honest, I felt a bit startled and unprepared. Ryan Howard was scheduled to play first base. Ordinarily, he would have gotten two or three at-bats, then *maybe* I or someone else would take over in the sixth or seventh inning. I unloaded a mouthful of sunflower seeds—the ball-player's chewing tobacco of the twenty-first century—scrambled to find my hat, and yanked out my dusty old first baseman's mitt from the bottom of my catcher's bag. I searched around for some sunglasses, then out to first base I trotted, excited not to be sitting on the bench for three hours like the other minor leaguers from my side of the clubhouse.

My first at-bat, against Phillies ace right-hander Brett Myers, 13–8 the year before, brought a harsh reminder of the difference between facing a hot phenom and an established major-league pitcher. Unfortunately, I was a bit tentative and got around late on a slider, flying out weakly to short right field. While running back to the dugout, I chastised myself for not being my normally aggressive self. The second time up, however, I attacked the ball and doubled off the wall in left-center. Just like that, my confidence surged. Today was going to be a good day; I could feel it.

In the fifth inning, I came up with a runner on second and nobody out. Aaron Myette, another hard-throwing Canadian, stood on the mound. He'd signed with the Phillies after spending the previous season in Japan. Like me, the tall right-hander was fighting to make an impression and full of the same intensity.

I looked down to third-base coach Bill Dancy for the sign. He didn't flash any—just yelled at the top of his lungs, "Okay, Coastey, do your job!" With a runner on second and no one out, "do your job" meant to hit the ball to the right side or deep to the outfield so I could at least move him to third. This can be a very difficult situation for a right-handed hitter, especially against a pitcher with a good fastball like Myette.

Knowing where I was trying to hit the ball, he threw his best fastball inside for a ball. I looked down at Dusty Wathan and said, "I am really not a big fan of the 'get the runner over' situation." He just looked up at me and smiled.

I dug back into the batter's box and waited for the next pitch, knowing that another inside fastball was coming. This time the ball wandered over the plate, and I windmilled it. *Crack!* Off it sailed, high and deep over the wall in left. As I trotted around the bases, a voice from the dugout yelled, "Somebody on that!" a common expression after someone hits a home run in *minor-league* camp. It means "Retrieve that ball!" During a typical *minor-league* spring training, players who are not part of the game will be assigned to either home run or foul ball duty. Remember, there aren't any fans in the stands to toss it back. But since this was *major-league* spring training, "Somebody on that" was a joke used by minor-league lifers like me to lighten the mood.

Rounding third, I slapped a high-five with Bill Dancy. "Attaway to get the runner over!" he said jokingly.

I whacked another double in my fourth at-bat. So when I stepped up in the ninth inning, my day looked like this: 3-for-4, two doubles, one home run, four runs batted in. *I need to finish strong,* I thought to myself. On the second pitch I nailed an opposite-field single to right, driving in another run, solidifying me as the unofficial player of the game.

A bevy of Philadelphia reporters, down south for spring training, mobbed me as I entered the clubhouse, making for an odd scene. Ordinarily they would be found on the *other* side of the room, huddled around the locker of a Phillies star like Howard or Utley, but they were thrilled to have an interesting story emerge so early in camp. My mind raced as I answered their questions.

I wondered if any Japanese scouts had been in the stands. Damn, if they'd seen me, I probably would have been offered a contract for a half million dollars. *Well,* I consoled myself, *at least Charlie Manuel was paying attention, and Pat Gillick, too. I* hope *Pat was watching.*

I came to find out later that day that Ryan Howard had been sickened by food poisoning. Although I certainly would never wish illness or injury on anyone, his absence had opened the door for me, putting me on a path to an eventual unforgettable and amazing spring.

The next day we traveled to nearby Tampa to face the New York Yankees for our first official game. Replacing Howard at first base in the sixth inning, I flied out to right off the sidearming veteran lefty reliever Mike Myers. I got one more chance to make a statement in the top of the eighth, this time with twenty-one-year-old J. B. Cox on the mound. The highly regarded Texan boasted a wicked two-seam fastball that dropped off the table and, like a good two-seamer, induced countless ground balls. I took the first pitch, a two-seamer, for a ball. Normally I would have swung, but I wanted to get a good look at it first. Cox didn't want to fall further behind in the count, so he laid the next pitch right down the middle of the plate. Big mistake. My first memory after making contact with the ball was almost missing first base as I watched the left fielder run out of room while the ball sailed over his head for a home run. My next memory was thinking that Yankees skipper Joe Torre, one of the winningest managers in baseball history, was watching me, Chris Coste, round the bases. And my childhood hero, Reggie Jackson—Mr. October!—was at Legends Field in his capacity as spring training consultant. Maybe he saw it, too. Then I reminded myself that I needed to be more concerned about making an impression on Charlie Manuel than on Joe Torre.

We went on to win the game 6–3, and as I entered the clubhouse afterward, pitcher Ryan Madson gave me a high five. "That was awesome!" he said. "Keep it up, man, stay hot!"

The next day we faced the Yankees again, only this time at Bright House Networks Field, our home stadium in Clearwater. Once again I took over for Ryan Howard at first base in the sixth inning. With the score tied at ten apiece in the bottom of the ninth, I came to the plate amid a mix of cheers and disappointed jeers. We had two men out and runners on first and second, and it's safe to say that the remaining Phillies fans in attendance would much rather have seen Ryan Howard come to the plate with the game on the line.

"Hey, Charlie, put Howard back in the game!" yelled an angry fan. "This *Cawstee* guy has no shot! Besides, we didn't pay to see guys that have number sixty-seven on their back!" This pissed me off! Not because this fan had no faith in me but because he'd mispronounced my name, calling me "Cawstee" instead of "Coast." Silent *e*. Presumably, Ryan Howard has never encountered this problem. But it's something that has motivated me my entire baseball life. I can remember how embarrassed I felt the first time I heard my name mangled over a loudspeaker when I was fourteen. Back then I promised myself I would become the best baseball player who ever lived so that everyone in the world would know how to pronounce Chris Coste.

On the flip side, I could somewhat understand where the fan was coming from. I had replaced Howard earlier in the game after he had gone 4-

for-4 with two long home runs and five RBIs. If I were a fan, I too would have had a lot more confidence in Howard than a nobody with 67 on his back. Fortunately, after swinging and missing at the first pitch, I drilled the next pitch into the left-field corner for a game-ending RBI single.

The first person to greet me back in the clubhouse was center fielder Aaron Rowand. "Dude, you are unbelievable!" he exclaimed. "I was telling everyone that the game was over as you walked to the plate. If there was one guy that was guaranteed to get a hit and end the game, it was you!"

"Why is that?" I asked.

"Because you are locked in, and other than Howard, you are our hottest hitter." For a guy like Aaron Rowand to have that much confidence in me was incredibly uplifting. He was the center fielder for the 2005 World Champion Chicago White Sox before coming to Philadelphia in a big winter trade for popular slugger Jim Thome. Maybe the biggest off-season acquisition for the 2006 season, Phillies fans would put a lot of pressure on him.

Once again, I was besieged by reporters at my locker. They knew I had little or no chance of making the team, but they were going to ride this feel-good story as far as it would take them. That day's headline on the team website read "Coste's Single Lifts Phils over Yanks." Quite a compliment considering Ryan Howard's five-RBI day and Rowand's first homer in a Phillies uniform. Best of all, the manager was starting to take notice, with Charlie telling the papers, "He's got it going. You can tell he loves to play baseball."

Two days later, we faced the National League champion Houston Astros in Clearwater. After I sat on the bench for most of the game, Charlie told me before the ninth inning to be ready to pinch hit in the event we could get a runner into scoring position. I was excited to hear this because it meant he had confidence in me to come up big in a clutch situation. Well, we were down by two runs going into the inning, so clutch is what he was looking for. After scoring a run early in the frame, I came to the plate with two outs and a runner on second base. *This is a golden moment,* I told myself as I walked to the plate. *If I can get a hit here, who knows what could happen.* I was having a good spring to that point, and already had one walk-off base hit. Now I had to show everyone, especially Charlie, that it wasn't just a fluke, that I was indeed a clutch hitter.

Not wasting any time, I stroked the first pitch I saw up the middle to tie the game at three. We went on to win it in the bottom of the tenth, bringing our spring record to 4–0. My average stood at .700. Make that a *gaudy* .700, as sportswriters are fond of saying.

After the game my new friends from the press paid yet another visit to my locker. We joked about how they'd never spent so much time on the minor-league side of the clubhouse. Then one of them said, "You've been having a great spring so far. With David Bell suffering from a bad back and unlikely to be ready for the season opener in April, how do you like your chances of making the team?" Bell was the Phillies' thirty-three-year-old starting third baseman. I had no idea that he was out of action. Not that you ever want to see a teammate get hurt, but if he wasn't going to be ready for the start of the season, my chances of making the team definitely went up, still a long shot, but seemingly rising by the day.

☆   III   ☆

A FEW days later I was sitting at my locker when Charlie Manuel told me I was finally going to catch against the Tampa Bay Devil Rays. Better still, I'd be giving the signs to veteran right-hander Jon Lieber, a seventeen-game winner who carried a lot of clout with the coaches. He approached me right before the game.

"Hey, bro, I was hoping you were going to catch me today. Let's have a good day." I'd caught him in a few bullpen sessions earlier in the spring, and he went on to tell me that he liked the way I caught the ball and my big setup. "It feels like I can't help but throw it to the middle of your mitt," he said. I actually had to suppress a giggle, because I'd heard that same line, almost word for word, from many other pitchers in the past.

"Well, feel free to tell that to Charlie and Dubee!" I replied. Dubee referred to Rich Dubee, the Phillies' pitching coach.

"Believe me, I have," said Lieber. "Several of us have told both of 'em the same thing."

"That's awesome. I have fought my whole career to prove I am a catcher, and the pitchers have always said those kinds of things. Unfortunately, nobody has ever listened."

"Well, Charlie will listen."

Although Tampa Bay edged us out 4–3, scoring two in the ninth to take the lead, I had a good day. I went 1-for-2 against young fireballing lefty Scott Kazmir, but more important, Lieber threw great and I had a great day catching, even throwing out Ty Wigginton trying to steal second base in the first inning. I would have also thrown out another guy in the third inning, but the umpire, having clearly missed the play, called the runner safe at second.

Charlie Manuel lifted me at the start of the sixth. "Damn, Coastey, you can catch, son!" he exclaimed.

"Damn right! I've been telling you that all spring!" I had a big smile on my face, and Charlie flashed me his patented wink.

Still, several days would pass before I received a second opportunity behind the plate, and then only in a minor-league spring training game. Ordinarily, I wouldn't have been too excited to see action against the Toronto Blue Jays' triple-A team, except that I'd be handling another one of the Phillies' top starters, Cory Lidle, who needed to get in some work. He'd posted a 13–11 record in 2005. If I could impress him with my catching ability, I'd open some more eyes among the decision-makers.

Following Lidle's five shutout innings, the right-hander pulled me aside and had some great comments. "You know, Coastey, I had no idea you were such a good catcher. I really thought of you as an infielder. I am amazed! With the way you hit, how are you not in the big leagues somewhere—at least as a back-up catcher? Not only that, but we were on the same page all day long; I shook you off maybe only twice. You can catch me anytime!" That was the best comment of all. Cory had a repertoire of five pitches, which made it incredibly difficult at times to figure out which one he wanted to throw. I must have developed a psychic ability that day, because he seemed to throw every pitch I called.

"Well, if you are serious, feel free to tell that to Charlie," I said. "For him to believe in me as a catcher, he has to hear that kind of stuff from his pitchers."

"Absolutely, I will tell both Charlie and Dubee."

I knew this was the start of something good. Cory was not the kind of guy to keep his mouth shut; on the contrary, he always spoke his mind. Sometimes, in fact, his candor got him into trouble. The next morning, he called me over to a table in the clubhouse, where he was polishing off his usual breakfast from Chick-fil-A.

"Hey, Coastey, I just talked to both Charlie and Dubee, and I told them exactly what I told you yesterday."

"How did they take it?"

"They joked about how they're getting tired of all the pitchers saying the same thing. Apparently they have been hearing the same thing about your catching ability from a lot of the pitchers. It's not just me and Lieber."

It had been quite a spring so far. With several of the pitchers wearing out Charlie's and Dubee's ears, I knew I would earn more opportunities to impress. And with David Bell's back still acting up, there was likely to be an open roster spot. I had gone from an anonymous number 67 suiting up on the minor-league side of the clubhouse to a guy with a legitimate shot at making the opening day roster for the Philadelphia Phillies. But the best was yet to come a day later against the Pittsburgh Pirates.

✦ IV ✦

AFTER sitting in the hot sun out in the bullpen for the first six innings, I took over at catcher for Mike Lieberthal in the seventh. Earlier in the day I had come across some bats left behind by a former Phillies outfielder, Jason Michaels, who'd been traded to Cleveland shortly before the start of spring training. Normally I was fanatical about using only my model from Louisville Slugger, but I took Jason's bats in my hands and just *knew* they had hits in them. Knew it! They felt great—even looked great, with a dark-flamed finish that gave them a cool and unique look.

Now, like many ballplayers, I can be superstitious. Maybe it's because we play a sport where failing to get a hit seven times out of ten is good enough to land you in the Hall of Fame, so we figure we can use all the help we can get.

For example, I'll often smell my bat after I hit a foul ball. Why? I suppose it's because I used to go to the lake a lot while growing up in Minnesota. And I just *love* the smell of wood burning, like from a campfire; I associate it with my childhood. Sometimes if you foul off a baseball that's hurtling toward you at ninety, ninety-five miles per hour, the friction produces that same burnt-wood aroma. Or maybe it's the smell of the leather. Or both. Anyway, one time early in my career, I just got a piece of a fastball, then held the bat up to my nose. For a moment, there I was, a kid again, back at West McDonald Lake in Minnesota. I proceeded to send the next pitch into the bleachers for a grand slam. Ever since then, I will often sniff my bat, partly out of superstition and partly because I just plain like the smell.

Back to Jason Michaels's leftover lumber. In the bottom of the seventh inning against the Pirates, I stepped up to the batter's box with one of his bats. We trailed by four runs and had a runner on first. On a 1–0 count, I sent the next pitch deep over the wall in left center, cutting the deficit to 8–6.

If you've ever listened to a Phillies game on the radio, you're probably familiar with the resonant voice of Harry Kalas, the team's play-by-play announcer since 1971. From the day I signed with the organization in January, one of my goals was to hear the Hall of Fame broadcaster call one of my home runs. With the crack of the bat, here's how he called it: "Ooooh, watch that baby . . . deep to left field . . . and that ball is *outta* here! Chris Coste, a two-run home run, and it is now an eight-to-six game as the Phillies come fighting back."

If the game had ended right there, I would have been thrilled. But in the bottom of the ninth, with our team still trailing by two, I was due up fourth. We had the tying run on first and one out as Ryan Howard, get-

ting a day of rest, was announced as the pinch hitter. The reigning NL
Rookie of the Year had already launched seven home runs that spring.
Unfortunately, he lofted a high fly ball that just missed going out and
tying the game. As soon as the ball parachuted into the outfielder's glove,
the capacity crowd of eight thousand started making its way for the exits.

Wait a minute, I thought to myself. *I hit a two-run homer just two innings ago! We still have one out left. How can all these fans leave?*

Meanwhile, out in the bullpen, catching instructor Mick Billmeyer and
minor-league catcher Dusty Wathan were prognosticating my future. As
they told me after the game, Dusty remarked, "Another home run by
Coastey would be nice right now."

"If he hits another homer here, he can almost guarantee himself a spot
to go north with the team," replied Mick.

"Well, if he hits another home run here, not only will he guarantee
himself a spot on the team, he can probably pilot the team plane to
Philly."

"Giddyup with that!"

As the count made its way to 3–1, I called time out to gather my
thoughts and to clear my eyes. I'd noticed that the wind, which had
blown out to center field for most of the game, was now coming in from
left field. It would be difficult to pull the ball over the left-field wall
against the wind; I'd be better off trying to drive the pitch into the right-
field gap. Maybe get a double, which would put the tying run in scoring
position. I can also remember telling myself not to chase ball four—after
all, I was the tying run and if I could at least get on base it would bring
the winning run to the plate. My final thought was how much I despised
being the guy who made the last out of the game. In my mind, having to
walk off the field as the batter who made the last out was one of the most
humiliating situations a ballplayer can be in.

In dramatic fashion, I nailed the ball on a line to deep left field and over
the left fielder's head. To my surprise, it sliced through the wind and
cleared the left-field wall by the slimmest of margins, landing safely in the
Pirates' bullpen. Once again, here is how Harry Kalas called the action:

"There's a long drive, and this game is gonna be tied . . . I believe . . .
yes! Into the bullpen! How about Chris Coste! A two-run home run in

the ninth inning with two outs. Coste has had two at-bats, two homers, four runs batted in! Amazing!"

As I touched home plate and trotted toward the dugout, I thought happily, *There is no way they can keep me off the team now*! A barrage of high fives from my teammates greeted me. They all knew the kind of spring I was having and the significance of the situation. If there was any doubt that I was the front runner for David Bell's open roster spot, they had all been erased after that game.

For the first time in a week, my friends from the Philly media were back around my locker. "I didn't think you guys were ever going to come back here again," I joked. After they got their quotes and drifted off, reliever Clay Condrey planted himself in front of me with an angry expression on his face. Like me, he was a journeyman ballplayer; in fact, he'd signed with Philadelphia the same day that I did. Clay was also one of my spring training roommates.

We both broke up laughing. Without his saying a word, I knew what was on his mind: We'd planned to go golfing with our other roommate, pitcher Brian Sanches, later that afternoon; my two home runs sent the game into extra innings, causing us to miss our scheduled tee time.

"I'm *so* sorry," I said sarcastically, "I forgot all about our tee time. If I'd remembered, I never would have hit both those home runs today! I would have only hit one and then maybe only a triple in my other at-bat."

"A triple? You haven't hit a triple since the Clinton administration," Clay retorted.

"Okay, maybe a double, and then I would have gotten thrown out trying to stretch it into a triple."

"That sounds better. Seriously," he added, "you'd better be careful, because if you keep messing around like this and continue to get all these big hits, you might actually make this team. And guys with number sixty-seven don't make big-league teams."

I was still on a high the next day when Charlie Manuel put me in at first base in the eighth inning against the Cincinnati Reds. I'd have just one at-bat, against the well-traveled forty-year-old lefty Chris Hammond, to keep my springtime momentum going. This was his fifth major-league team in the last five seasons, and his ninth major-league stop overall. Why he pinballed around baseball is a bit of a mystery; in the previous four seasons, pitching for the Braves, Yankees, A's, and Padres, he posted a 19–6 record including an amazing 0.95 ERA with the Braves in 2002. I knew Chris well, having caught him for the triple-A Buffalo Bisons club in 2001. Not blessed with an overpowering fastball, he featured a devastatingly slow changeup—so slow that even if you were waiting for it, you were likely to be way out in front. And when he did fire his version of a fastball, the contrast in speeds made it hard to catch up to it. You never quite found your balance against him.

Facing Chris, now in a Reds uniform, I pretended that I was playing slow-pitch softball. Sure enough, on the second pitch, his changeup came floating toward me, and I hammered it into the left-center gap for a stand-up double. As Hammond got the ball back from the shortstop, he looked at me with a grin as if to say that he knew I'd been sitting on his changeup. If he'd thrown me three straight eighty-five-mile-per-hour fastballs over the heart of the plate, I would have stared at each one dumbfounded.

By the way, with less than two weeks left in spring training, my batting average now stood at .478.

☆ **V** ☆

AS good a spring as I was having, Ryan Howard's was even better. Against the Tigers, in Lakeland, Florida, he had two hits and three RBI, including his tenth home run of the preseason. The two-time minor-league Most Valuable Player was on a mission to prove that his rookie season had been no fluke and that the Phillies had not made a mistake by trading Jim Thome to clear the way for him. Thome, injured throughout much of the 2005 season, had *averaged* 48 home runs and 119 runs batted in the four seasons before that. So Ryan was facing his own kind of pressure, to be sure, but not quite the same as fearing that your future hinged on every at-bat. The difference between Howard and me was that we had different things to prove. I didn't have to prove that I was a star, I just had to prove I was capable of playing in the big leagues. And although I was incredibly motivated at all times that spring, each time I replaced Howard at first base the fans let me know their displeasure, increasing my desire to shut their mouths.

In the top of the eighth against Detroit, I took Howard's place in the on-deck circle while Chase Utley (.291, 28 HR, 105 RBI in 2005) stood in the batter's box. We were behind by one run, with speedy Jimmy Rollins on second. Not surprisingly, the Tigers opted to walk Utley and pitch to me. Some of the fans made their displeasure known to Charlie that he'd given Ryan the rest of the afternoon off.

"Attaway, Charlie! Good job of taking out Howard with the game on the line! You're a genius! Number *sixty-seven*?!? Who is he? You gotta be kidding me!"

Who is he? I thought to myself as I stepped in against right-hander Mark Woodyard. *Hey, I'm the guy with the .478 batting average!* I really felt that it was my destiny to come up with yet another clutch hit. Woodyard was a hard thrower with a good two-seam fastball and a nasty split-finger fastball. The split-finger starts out looking like a fastball, but then acts like it had been hijacked and drops out of the zone. Since the split-finger has no discernible spin, unlike, say, a curveball or slider, hitters usually have a hell of a time picking it up. My one perceived "weakness" as a hitter is that I don't always have the best strike-zone judgment, so I'll hack at pitches I shouldn't. But like Kirby Puckett before me, a notorious bad-ball hitter, I usually make contact when it counts.

True to form, I waved at the first pitch, a ninety-three-mile-an-hour fastball just off the plate. On the second pitch, I expanded the strike zone again with my most feeble swing of the spring. No balls, two strikes. I stepped out of the box, furious at myself for having dug such a deep hole. Now I had Woodyard's unhittable split-finger fastball to look forward to.

Just don't swing. He's going to throw a split-finger in the dirt and hope that I chase it.

To my surprise, instead of throwing the split-finger, he made a mistake and threw a straight fastball right down the middle of the plate. Readjusting my sights, I lined the ball up the middle, scoring Jimmy Rollins from second base for the tying run. I had done it again! I thought I had no chance with the count 0–2, but only seconds later I was standing at first base, having come up with yet another clutch hit. It was almost too good to be true.

The game got even more interesting. The tenth inning brought a virtual replay of the eighth: runner on second, one out, and Utley coming to bat. Again Detroit had to decide: Walk Utley and pitch to me? Or take their chances with him? From the on-deck circle, I glanced at the Tigers' dugout and saw manager Jim Leyland tugging at his mustache while talking with his third-base coach, Gene Lamont. Gene had been my skipper at Scranton the previous season. I couldn't hear their conversation, naturally, but based on what happened next, I assume that Gene told him I was actually a pretty good hitter, not just some lowly minor leaguer.

Instead of holding up four fingers, indicating an intentional walk, Leyland simply pointed at Utley. *Pitch to him,* he was instructing his catcher. It's hard to describe what a moment like that meant to me. Had it been a regular-season game, Detroit probably would have walked Utley. Still, what a confidence booster!

Utley eventually popped up for the second out, leaving me to try to come up with another clutch hit. This time, however, it would be against Fernando Rodney, a hard-throwing right-hander with a ninety-seven-mile-per-hour fastball and one of the best changeups in all of baseball. He had recently solidified his reputation as a top-shelf major-league relief pitcher by having a strong 2005 season, with nearly a strikeout per inning to go with his 2.86 ERA.

Most pitchers will start you off with a fastball in order to gain an advantage by getting ahead in the count. I wasn't about to give Rodney an opportunity to hypnotize me with that changeup. I jumped on the first pitch—a fastball, as predicted—and lashed it into left field. In fact, I hit it so hard that third-base coach Bill Dancy had to hold our runner at third. We never did get him across home plate and went on to lose the game. Though it was a tough defeat, my two at-bats provided more proof that I could hit when it counted.

My teammates had taken note of this and began joking that we needed to keep each game close so I could manufacture some late-inning heroics. After the extra-inning loss, Ryan Howard coined a nickname for me.

"You know, Coastey," he said with his huge smile, "after playing with you last year in triple-A, none of this surprises me at all. You have always been a clutch player.

"Yes, that's it: 'Chris Clutch.' That's your new nickname." It really made me feel like I was finally one of the guys; on a par with the likes of Howard, Utley, and Rollins. For the first time in my entire baseball career, I felt like I'd earned the right to wear a major-league uniform.

When I got home that night, I sat down with my two roommates, Brian Sanches and Clay Condrey. We tried to think of any reasons why I wouldn't make the team. It appeared as if I was a lock, but I wanted to be sure I wasn't overlooking anything. Feeling a little obsessive-compulsive, I whipped out a notebook that had belonged to my daughter and wrote down the potential twenty-five-man roster. If you included the usual twelve pitchers and eight starting-position players, there was room on the bench for five bench players. David Bell was sidelined, of course, leaving newcomer Abraham Nunez, a free-agent signing over the winter, as the main candidate for third base. The four bench players were going to be catcher Sal Fasano, outfielder Shane Victorino, and infielders Alex Gonzalez and Tomás Peréz. I was a perfect fit for that last bench spot because of my hitting and ability to play multiple positions, especially since I'd proved I could catch. Charlie had told the media on many occasions that he would like to carry a third catcher to give him some flexibility to make more moves late in the game. This was great news for me.

The only potential problem was that the team had only four true outfielders, and reports surfaced that the Phillies were talking to other teams about trading for a fifth outfielder. Dustan Mohr of the Red Sox was a candidate, as was Lew Ford of the Minnesota Twins. The most prominent rumor had the Phillies trying to acquire thirty-two-year-old David Dellucci from the Texas Rangers; however, the buzz had died down a bit because he was coming off his best season (.251, 29 HR, 65 RBI) and seemed to fit the profile of an everyday outfielder rather than a fifth outfielder or pinch hitter. For the time being, I was in good shape—on paper, anyway.

The next day we were back home in Clearwater to face the Pirates. Just before the game started, I heard someone yelling at me from the other side of the field. It was Pittsburgh shortstop Jack Wilson. "Hey, Coastey! Take it easy on us today, will ya!"

I hollered back, "I'm not in the starting lineup, but if you want to win the game, you'd better be ahead by more than four runs this time!"

Wow, even guys on the other teams were starting to take notice of what I'd been doing!

With destiny still on my side, I came to the plate in the seventh inning with Pittsburgh up by a score of 4–3. We were threatening, though: two runners on base and two outs. It was almost getting ridiculous! I couldn't remember being involved in so many key situations in a whole season, much less one spring training. *This is no simple coincidence! This is meant to be!* I thought while digging in at the plate.

As if on cue, I came up big yet again, this time ripping a hanging curveball down the left-field line for a two-run double. We held on to win, 5–4. I'd raised my average to an even .500, with three home runs and eleven runs batted in.

After the game Charlie took questions from the media. When asked about me, he said, "As far as a guy coming up with big hits, that may be the best spring I've seen a guy have. That's very impressive." Charlie Manuel had been in professional baseball for more than forty years, since signing with the Minnesota Twins as an outfielder. He told me later that night that he was almost getting sick of all the questions regarding me and the spring I was having. He was joking, of course. He simply wanted to make sure I knew he was paying attention.

A couple days later I received another chance to shine, this time starting behind the plate against the Boston Red Sox and Josh Beckett. This was my biggest opportunity to date to show what I could do. Admittedly, most of my really big hits had come late in games against pitchers who were bound for the minors. But Beckett, 15–8, 3.38 ERA with the Florida Marlins in 2005, was one of the best young pitchers in baseball.

Cory Lidle, scheduled to pitch for us, had some good news to tell me as we made our way to the bullpen.

"Hey, don't assume that the fact you are catching today is coincidence," he said.

"What do you mean?"

"I requested that you catch today. Who knows, you may have been catching anyways—we all know you deserve it—but I wanted to make sure, so I requested that you catch me today."

"How did they respond when you told them that?" I asked him.

"The way I read it was that Charlie was already considering it," Lidle replied. "I got the idea that he wanted you to get a start in a big game to see how you would do. He seems to really want to give you every opportunity to be on this team."

I didn't have a great game, but I did lead off the second inning with a double and came around to score. I finished 1-for-3. Plus, I received some welcome encouragement from Red Sox catcher Jason Varitek, the Boston team captain, during the game. When I came up for my second at-bat, he said, "Hey, Chris, you're having a great spring, man! Keep it up!" I had gotten to know Varitek during the spring of 2003 when I was in the Red Sox organization. I was the last position player sent down that spring, and although I was never going to make the team over him and fellow receiver Doug Mirabelli, he knew a little of my story and knew I was a capable major-league catcher. His kind words made for another proud moment. Between that and getting the start against Beckett, I again felt like an equal, a true major-leaguer, a somebody.

Two days later Charlie penciled me in against another major-league superstar, Toronto Blue Jays ace Roy Halladay. Over the past few seasons, Halladay was the pitcher I most wanted to hit against. Having seen him only on television, combined with his obvious success as well as his nasty repertoire of pitches—namely his explosive fastball and big curve—I viewed him as the toughest pitcher in all of baseball. In 2005 the big right-hander looked as if he was on his way to twenty-five wins, maybe more. Just before the All-Star Game, Halladay was 12–4 with a 2.41 in 19 starts. In his final game of the season's first half, a line drive back to the mound fractured his left leg, sending him to the disabled list for the rest of the year.

I had a lot to gain by opposing him, but a lot to lose, too. A bad showing could possibly wipe out my incredible spring, making people question my ability to hit first-rate major-league pitching. To me, the one thing I had to fight constantly was my minor-league label. I could have been hitting .777 with twenty home runs, and you would still find skeptics to say things like "There's a reason he spent so many years in the minor leagues" and "Anyone can get hot in a few spring training games." But if I could produce against the likes of a perennial All-Star and Cy Young Award winner like Halladay, it would help to shake some of that doubt. The trick against Halladay is to avoid falling behind. He has so many quality pitches to choose from that you can never sit on one, because he'll ambush you with something else.

During my first at-bat, my only hope was to get a hit early in the count and avoid having to see his devastating curveball with two strikes. Things didn't go quite as planned: Roy quickly had me in the hole, 1–2. He tried to blow a fastball by me—and would have, except that I was looking mainly for the curve. Luckily for me, the pitch was too high. Count even.

I didn't know what Halladay would throw next. Maybe that was just as well, because I ended up lining a fastball into the gap in right-center field for a leadoff double, my fifth two-bagger of the spring.

Here's one baseball memory that I will never forget: Roy Halladay blurting out an angry "Dangit!" as the ball sailed past his outfielders. He was upset at himself for giving up a hit to a guy he'd never even heard of. I came around to score our first run of the afternoon on a Mike Lieberthal single.

Second at-bat: Having not seen a curveball my first time up, I assumed it'd be coming. No way would Halladay serve up another fastball to a guy with number 67 on his back. It didn't even matter if a batter anticipated the curveball—that's how unhittable it was. In fact, most times, a hitter would be better off not looking for the curve. Then maybe he had a slim chance of being fooled and taking the pitch for a ball.

Once again, the Blue Jays star got ahead of me, 1–2. Here came his curveball. As soon as I recognized it, I started my swing and hoped for the best. You can imagine my surprise when I heard a solid *thwack!* I lowered my head and ran hard to first. Unfortunately, the line drive carried straight into the left fielder's glove. Normally I would have been disappointed at having made an out, but not this time. Not only had I made contact with a Roy Halladay curveball, but I'd squared it up and hit one of my hardest line drives of the spring. When I got back to the dugout, the first person to greet me was right fielder Bobby Abreu.

"*Cómo lo haces?*" he asked. Bobby, from Venezuela, spoke perfect English. But he usually chose to talk to me in his native language. Apparently, he found it somewhat amusing that an American from North Dakota could speak Spanish. Six years of winter ball in Mexico, Central America, and South America will do that. Simply put, *Cómo lo haces* means "How do you do it?"—a phrase he'd said to me quite frequently since the intrasquad game three weeks earlier. It was his way of expressing appreciation for the spring I was having. Considering that Bobby was generally a man of few words, I accepted his compliment proudly.

I got one more chance to face Roy Halladay in the sixth. It would most likely be his last inning of the day, so I figured that he would want to finish on a strong note and go with his best stuff. I'd be prepared. Yet *again*, the count went to one ball and two strikes. I guessed curveball, just like last time, and I was right. In a near repeat of the previous at-bat, I drove the pitch to left, only this time it fell in front of the left fielder for a hit. I came around to score again on a single by Tomás Peréz, giving me the only runs Philadelphia managed all day. The fact that both my hits came off one of the best pitchers in the game proved once and for all that my impressive spring was no fluke.

I was on top of the world. We had only one exhibition game left in Florida before we were to head north for two final spring training games against the Red Sox at Citizens Bank Park. The Phillies would then open the 2006 baseball season the following day, April 3, at home against the defending National League Central Division champion St. Louis Cardinals, last year's winningest team in all of baseball.

If I could have changed the schedule, I would have ended spring training following the final out against Toronto and Roy Halladay, because at that moment, I was a lock to make the club. Third baseman David Bell had miraculously come back from his back injury ahead of schedule, which made me nervous at first, but my worries had all but faded after hearing the last few days' sports reports. Supposedly Philadelphia was putting its search for a fifth outfielder on hold for a while; what's more, I kept hearing that I was going to be kept and Tomás Peréz released. This kind of came as a shock because he had been a Phillie for several years and had established himself as a fine defensive player at nearly every position. However, the team already had two other super utility guys in Abraham Nunez and Alex Gonzalez.

Although many people, including teammates and reporters, were constantly reassuring me that I was about to make my first major-league roster, barring any unforeseen circumstances, I still found it too hard to believe and too good to be true. I'd been victimized by unforeseen circumstances several times before. Until Charlie Manuel or someone else from management sat me down and told me "Chris, you made the team," I wouldn't—couldn't—believe it.

No matter how things panned out, though, I felt incredibly proud of the spring I'd had, with one big hit after another, and even prouder that I was finally able to convince baseball people that I was capable of catching at the major-league level.

★ VI ★

A GOOD sign: Just before going to bed that night, I happened to be channel surfing and on came *The Rookie,* the Disney movie starring Dennis Quaid as Tampa Bay Devil Rays pitcher Jim Morris. It had come out a few years before. Morris's story resembled mine on many fronts: His promising pitching career is derailed by a shoulder injury while he is in the minors. Retiring from baseball, he teaches physical science and coaches baseball at a high school in his native Texas. To motivate his underachieving players, Morris agrees to their demand that if they win the district championship, the first in the school's history, he'll try out for the big leagues again. Incredibly, the Reagan County Owls do go all the way, and Morris makes good on his promise. Despite age and injury, he can still throw ninety-eight miles per hour. The Tampa Bay Devil Rays take a chance on him, and in 1999, at the age of thirty-six, Jim Morris makes his major-league debut, striking out his very first batter. The film's tagline? "It's never too late to believe in your dreams."

I'd tuned in right at the climactic moment where Morris gets the call to the big leagues. For me, this was the final sign that the stars had aligned for me.

After the next day's game in Clearwater, we boarded our charter flight for Philadelphia. Because it was still technically spring training, this wasn't an "official" major-league flight. But it was sure close enough for me! Arriving at the airport, I was surprised when the team bus pulled right up to the plane, enabling us to avoid the long lines of passengers going through airport security. *I can get used to this!* I thought to myself.

To my even greater surprise, as we took off I looked around and saw nearly all the players either playing video games, watching movies on DVD, messing around on their computers, standing in the aisles, or chatting on their cell phones. Weren't we supposed to stay seated, with our seat belts fastened, tray tables and seat backs in the upright position, and all cell phones and other electronic devices turned off until reaching cruising altitude? Guess not.

If I harbored any doubts about the big-league life, they were erased when the flight attendant asked me what I wanted for dinner. The choices? Grilled chicken Caesar salad, bison burger, chicken primavera, and steak and lobster.

Did she just say steak and lobster? No way!

"Wait," I asked, a bit confused, "is that steak *and* lobster, or steak *or* lobster?"

"Steak *and* lobster," she replied with a wide smile.

"I'll have that!" I said excitedly. I'm really not much of a steak-and-lobster kind of guy, but this was too good of an opportunity to pass up. It was my first taste (no pun intended) of what the big-league life was all about. Triple-A was cheeseburgers and middle seats on a commercial jet, while the big leagues were first-class seats with steak *and* lobster on a chartered plane. *Yep, I can definitely get used to this!* I thought to myself.

After finishing what I considered the best meal of my life, I sat back in my seat and fought back the tears as I reflected back on how far I had come during this incredible spring training, and how things had all come together . . .

For someone like me to get this close to making a major-league roster out of spring training, an almost impossible sequence of events had to go my way. For instance, if Charlie Manuel and GM Pat Gillick hadn't been watching pitcher Scott Mathieson's simulated outing, Charlie probably wouldn't have thought to play me at first base when Ryan Howard got sick. Likewise, if the World Baseball Classic hadn't hijacked a Phillies catcher and an infielder, I probably wouldn't have received so much playing time. Not to mention all of those opportunities to hit in clutch situations against some of the game's top pitchers.

So there I was, on a plane bound for Philadelphia and Citizens Bank Park. I'd never seen the stadium before, except on TV. Arriving at the ballpark that night was a moment I will never forget. I got off the bus, looked up, and felt like I had ascended to heaven. *Could I actually be here, playing as a Phillie?*

As I reached to grab my jersey out of my locker, I was approached by the Phillies' director of team travel and clubhouse services, Frank Coppenbarger. Frank was the man in charge of everything that went on inside the clubhouse as well as all equipment and team travel.

"Hey, Coastey, not that it's official," he said with a wink, "but on Monday for opening day against the Cardinals, we are going to change your number from sixty-seven to twenty-seven. Twenty-seven is just a better major-league number, don't you think?" That it was, one worn by two Hall of Fame pitchers, Jim "Catfish" Hunter and Juan Marichal in the 1960s and 1970s, and by catcher Carlton Fisk, another Hall of Famer. No Hall of Famer has ever worn 67. To be given a "respectable" major-league number put a huge smile on my face.

Then Frank turned serious. "You know, Coastey, I have been in Philly for a lot of years, and I can never remember a time when the entire clubhouse staff was pulling for a guy to make the team like we have been for you. We have to deal with so many players that after a while we try not to get emotional about players' situations, but you are definitely a guy we have all been rooting for since the beginning of spring training. You deserve it, man."

Later that night a few of us were eating at a downtown restaurant when a man and his twelve-year-old son appeared at our table. "Excuse me," the stranger said politely. "This may sound stupid, but are you Chris Coste?"

"Yes," I said. "Do I know you?" I assumed we'd met before; I actually felt kind of bad that I couldn't place him.

"No," replied the man, "but I am a big Phillies fan, and I, like a lot of Phillies fans, have been following your spring. My son and I were even at the game in Clearwater when you hit those two home runs against the Pirates. That was amazing! You are a great story, and I hope you stay with the big team for a long time!"

To be recognized in Philadelphia by a Phillies fan just blew me away. Dusty Wathan, sitting next to me, was equally impressed. "Now you've officially made it," he said. "To be recognized by fans is a sure sign that you've officially made your mark."

The next morning we returned to Citizens Bank Park for the first of two exhibition games against the Red Sox. I got to walk around the inside of the stadium and through the incredible new clubhouse, just like in the dream I'd had over the winter. But not even my dreams could compare with the reality of how well appointed the facilities were: plasma screen TVs everywhere, the weight room, trainer's room, indoor batting cage. Plus, compared to what I was used to, the place was *huge*.

As we took the field for pregame batting practice, we were introduced one by one by the Phillies' Hall of Fame broadcaster, Harry Kalas. Normally the gates open an hour and a half before game time, but on this occasion fans were allowed in well ahead of schedule to give them a close-up look at the 2006 Phillies. I waited patiently in the dugout until it came time for Harry to announce my name.

" . . . And next for the Phillies, this guy has played a lot of years in the minor leagues. With an incredible spring and an impressive .463 batting average, it looks like he has opened the door and will make his major-league debut with the Phils at the age of thirty-three. Number sixty-seven, Chris Coste!"

The crowd erupted in cheers, and as I jogged out to the first-base line to line up with the rest of my teammates. I was overcome with emotion like never before in my baseball career. In fact, I was very lucky that I had been wearing sunglasses, because a small tear had formed in my left eye. I'm not one of those stoic kind of guys, but on the other hand, you try not to make a habit of shedding tears on the ball field. When I pulled up next to Dusty Wathan, he observed, in a shocked tone of voice, "That was amazing, Coastey!"

"What do you mean?"

"Didn't you hear that applause?" he said. "That was the biggest applause of the day. Seriously, it was bigger than the applause for Rollins, Utley, and Howard. You got a bigger applause than even Ryan Howard!"

I could barely utter a word, for fear that I might lose it. The Phillies' fans are notoriously tough, but they loved an underdog. And by anybody's definition, that was me. *What a city,* I thought. *I was made to play in Philly.*

Just then Dusty nudged me in the ribs. "Dude," he instructed, "tip your cap!"

"What?"

"Tip your cap!" The crowd was still cheering. "They are not going to stop until you tip your cap!" he yelled over the buzz of the crowd. Trying to appear as if this were an everyday occurrence, I whipped off my cap and waved to the crowd, making their ovation even louder.

Next was batting practice. Here was the moment I'd anticipated my entire life: to step onto the infield and take my position in the batter's box in a major-league ballpark.

Afterward we retired to the clubhouse. I didn't expect to play that day, so I headed to the weight room for a quick pregame workout. When I went to take a shower, there, sitting next to the many soaps and shampoos was a bottle of Coast liquid soap. I didn't even know they still made the stuff. Another sign that things were meant to be? By this time, I was beginning to overanalyze the meaning of every little thing, starting with the Florida bird that took a big ol' crap on my head at the start of spring training.

Just before I left the ballpark, left fielder Pat Burrell came up to me. "Hey, bro," he asked, "have you heard anything yet?" Now, Pat's career could have been the mirror image of mine. Baseball's number one draft choice in 1998, he came up to the big leagues just two years later and established himself as a top-line player immediately. The 2005 season had been his best season to date: .281, 32 HR, 117 RBI. Nevertheless Pat was one of my biggest supporters on the team.

"Nope," I replied, "nothing yet."

"Well, I don't think I have to tell you, but the whole team is pulling for you on this one." I'm sure you can guess how good that made me feel.

Later that night I settled into my hotel room, brushed my teeth, and called Marcia before heading to bed.

"So, what do you think? What have you heard?" she asked calmly. We had been together for a long time, and if there was one person in the universe who could understand the emotion of the situation, it was my wife.

"Well, as of right now it looks like there is a ninety percent chance that I'll be a Phillie. It's ten-thirty right now, so as long as they don't do something crazy like make a last-second trade before midnight, I will be a major leaguer in the morning. And as far as all of the reports go, for now it looks like they have given up on trying to trade for a fifth outfielder. My hope is that they will start the season with the team they have right now, and after a few weeks they will realize that they don't really need a fifth outfielder." I was having a hard time containing my emotions, and Marcia knew it. Like me, she was flooded with excitement, but since she'd endured the disappointments of my career alongside me, she knew not to take anything for granted. Also, being a baseball player's wife, she didn't want to jinx things.

As we wrapped up our conversation, I received a text message from Shane Victorino. "Hey, are we gonna be teammates again or what?" We'd played together at Scranton/Wilkes-Barre the previous season and had become pretty good friends.

"Nothing new," I texted back. "I guess we will find out in the morning."

I'd thought I'd be sitting up wide-eyed all night, too excited to sleep, but I was out for the night the moment my head hit the pillow. In fact, I enjoyed one of the best night's sleeps I'd had in a long time. When I awoke the next morning, I looked over at Dusty Wathan, who was still sleeping. I turned on the television to ESPN to wake him up and went to take a shower. *This is the day! This is the day I will remember for the rest of my life!* No matter what happened, I knew it would possibly be the most emotional day of my baseball life. Either I would be on the team and I would cry tears of joy, or I would be sent to triple-A and cry the most disappointing tears of my career.

Coming out of the bathroom, my eye was drawn to the sports-news ticker rolling across the bottom of the TV screen: "Philadelphia Phillies acquire outfielder David Dellucci from the Texas Rangers."

✮ VII ✮

BY the time Dusty Wathan and I pulled into the players parking lot, I felt like Cinderella at the stroke of midnight. Only instead of wearing glass slippers, this Cinderella had on a pair of cleats. (And needed a shave.) The moment I'd seen the news flash about Dellucci, I understood that I was going back to the minors. That's not the same thing as saying I'd accepted how my future had been shaken upside down. My main concern was that I not break down and cry or yell and scream when management told me the news. But this was going to be tough; with the range of emotions I'd experienced in just the last day and a half, I really couldn't say how I would react.

Pat Burrell was the first person to greet me in the clubhouse. "Man, this is unbelievable, isn't it?" he said, his voice tinged with disappointment. "I'm sorry, bro. This is partly my fault because of my foot problem. If my foot was one hundred percent, they probably wouldn't have gotten Dellucci. But since they are unsure if I will make it through a full season, they felt they needed to get him as insurance." I definitely gained a lot of respect for Pat that day. He'd encouraged me since the beginning of spring training, and for a guy like him to be that concerned with my situation showed a lot of heart and true character.

Next to approach me was Sal Fasano. Having gone through daily catching drills with Sal, and also having played against him earlier in our careers, we had become good friends. He also felt horrible when news about the trade spread throughout the clubhouse. Sal gave me a hug and, unable to speak, looked at me with a tear in his eye. Then he had to walk away.

One by one, most of the players slowly made their way over to me to convey their condolences, which raised my spirits slightly. More often than not, when a player gets demoted, the other guys avoid him as if he's got a communicable disease. I don't know if it triggers fears of their own baseball mortality—"There but for the grace of God go I"; but to Scranton, not the Great Beyond—or if they simply don't know what to say to the dearly departed. Most kept their words to a minimum; they could see the emotion building up in my eyes. It was brutal, and I would have given anything to get out of there and hide in a corner somewhere.

Oddly enough, management still hadn't told me anything. So I had to suit up and go through the agony of the pregame workout with the rest of the guys—guys whom I would soon be leaving. What were they waiting for? Following batting practice, I parked myself right in the middle of the clubhouse, so I could readily be found for the inevitable call into the manager's office. It was embarrassing, like having to tie your own noose before being hung.

It only got worse thirty minutes later when the media descended upon the clubhouse. They knew. Everybody knew. All you had to do was the math, and it was obvious who would be playing eighty miles away in Scranton instead of in the City of Brotherly Love. Before I could escape, Marcus Hayes of the *Philadelphia Daily News* came over. He always seemed like a good guy and a big supporter, so I didn't mind talking to him. But the next thing I knew, I was surrounded by about twenty reporters from the papers, radio, and TV. Ten microphones were thrust in my direction, and the bright lights from a half dozen television cameras stung my eyes.

Ordinarily, I enjoyed talking to the media. For the first time in my entire baseball life, I was speechless. For one thing, I couldn't really think straight. But also, I didn't want to burn any bridges and blurt out something that would offend Phillies management. All they got out of me that day was some dazed yes and no answers. I couldn't even tell you what the questions were, except for one.

"Do you think you received a fair shot at making the team?" someone asked.

My stuttering response was: "Well . . . I , uh, got to play a lot, but . . ." That's when my eyes started filling up with tears.

"Can we do this some other time?" I asked, although it wasn't a question at all.

I stormed past them and out of the clubhouse. "Sure, no problem," I heard Marcus Hayes say. I hid in one of the bathroom stalls and sat down on one of the toilets, with my hands covering my face, not in tears, just in utter shock and disappointment. I couldn't believe how things had transpired. To get that close and come up short was almost unbearable. And *still* management kept me hanging! How much longer could the misery last?

Finally I gathered my emotions and walked into the kitchen area. I sat down by myself at a table. Before long I was joined by Tomás Peréz. Like me, the thirty-two-year-old Venezuelan was also awaiting bad news. He'd known for a while that he was probably going to be released at the end of spring training. Still, the finality of it all hit him hard. He'd spent a fun and productive six years in Philly, had built up a local fan base, and was popular in the clubhouse. After so much time in Philadelphia, Peréz considered it home. Now he would have to move somewhere else. However, there was one crucial difference between the two of us: Tomás, an established major leaguer, would most certainly get another job in the big leagues by the end of the day. And he did, with Tampa Bay. Furthermore, he had a guaranteed contract, so the Phillies were obligated to pay him more than $700,000 for the 2006 season whether he played or not. That certainly helps to ease the hurt and disappointment somewhat.

Finally, after sitting in the kitchen for over twenty minutes, I was summoned by bench coach Gary Varsho. All spring, he'd had the dubious honor of tracking down players and accompanying them to Charlie's office for the delivery of the bad news.

"So where are we going?" I tried joking as we made the dreadful walk down the corridor. I knew that Varsho had been pulling for me to make the team, so this was not pleasant for him, either.

"Believe me, Coastey," he said sadly, "this is a walk I never thought I would have to make."

When we reached the manager's office, I promised myself that I would say as little as possible. Keep my feelings in check. But the moment I sat down on the sofa and saw Charlie, Pat Gillick, and Ruben Amaro Jr. there, I could feel my disappointment and frustration starting to brew.

"Hi, Coastey," Charlie said sympathetically. "I saw you over there talking to the reporters, and I figured we had better get on with this and not make you go through this anymore." He continued talking for a few more minutes, but I honestly had no idea what he said. I knew Charlie wanted me on his team and didn't want to be telling me I'd be going back to Scranton. Then Pat Gillick started talking. I tuned him out, too. It was the usual GM rhetoric: " . . . Go down there and play your hardest, and, who knows? It's a long season, and anything can happen . . ." In fairness, what could you possibly say to a player you've just demoted that would make him feel better? Nothing really.

At long last, somebody asked me if I had anything to say. I numbly shook my head no, stood up, and respectfully walked out of the room while holding back a barrage of tears.

I had been to several major-league spring trainings in the past, and each time I had been sent down, I always had plenty of positive things to say to the manager and general manager. The difference this time, however, was that I'd finally been given a chance to prove myself. Yet still I was dealt the ax. Those other springs I mostly rode the bench, caught bullpens on occasion, and was eventually sent down without ever getting a real opportunity to show them I was a big leaguer. Sure, that was frustrating. But to finally receive a fair shot, have an amazing spring, and then still not make the big club somehow made it worse than all the disappointments of the past put together.

As I pictured it, going back to triple-A almost guaranteed that I would get lost in the shuffle because I would not be the first person called up in the event of an injury. If they ever needed a catcher, they would call up Carlos Ruiz, the main catcher slated for triple-A. If they ever needed an infielder, they would call up Danny Sandoval, the triple-A shortstop. Finally, if they ever needed an outfielder, they would call up the speedy center fielder Chris Roberson. I would only get to play first base in triple-A, so, in my mind, it was probably now or never.

Outside the manager's office, Gary Varsho tried giving me a pep talk. "Hey, keep your head up! You more than proved you belong on this team," he said, "and we were all hoping for you to be on this team! I don't know what else to say."

All I could manage was a weak "Well, that's the way it goes."

He corrected me. "Not *this* time! That's *not* the way it should have gone *this* time."

I was incredibly happy to hear Varsho's words. Although I was distraught at the time, to have this kind of support from the coaching staff was amazing.

The next thing I remember, I was throwing my bags into the back of my SUV. Although I was parked in the players parking garage, I thought to myself how appropriate it would be if a Philadelphia bird came along to take a crap on my head. That would have really topped off what had been, despite everything, an incredible spring.

Just as I slipped into the driver's seat, I received a text message from Marcia: "How R U doing?"

I messaged back, "Well, back to the minors. Again!"

CHAPTER 2

No Ordinary
Fourteen-Year-Old

★ I ★

I GREW up an only child of a very young single mother in Fargo, North Dakota. I never met my father, who was only fifteen when I was born; my mom, Donna, was sixteen. She worked as a waitress at a local Mexican restaurant, and since she was on her own, and we had little money, she decided it would be a good idea to have her two younger sisters, Gloria and Patty, move into our apartment in a government-assisted housing project. So there I was, five years old and living with my mother and two aunts—all of them strong, independent women—who ranged in age from eighteen to twenty-one. As a result, you can imagine what kind of respect I developed for girls. In fact, I grew up with the notion that women were much smarter, mentally stronger, and better at everything than men, and basically ruled the world. *God* was a woman, as far as I knew!

While growing up, I realized that our household was a bit unorthodox. But most of the people who lived in the Community Homes projects were fairly poor; that was true of many of the kids who attended my elementary school, too. The whole area was very diverse ethnically and racially. In that regard, living there helped prepare me for a life in professional baseball, because in sports you encounter people from many different cultures. Anyway, single-parent families were very common. So aside from the fact that my mom was younger than most of my friends' mothers, my situation wasn't all that unusual.

Until I was five, we'd lived with my maternal grandfather, Bob Coste, who took me under his wing and has been a father figure to me my whole life. Gramps, a postal worker and a pretty good athlete (he's in the Minnesota Bowling Hall of Fame), is the main reason I wanted to play baseball as a kid. He used to play amateur softball, and on weekends Mom would take me to his games. Now, I worshipped Gramps. Watching him on the diamond week after week sparked a flame of interest for playing the sport that will burn in me for as long as I live. I thought he was the best player in the world, and I wanted to be just like him—both on and off the field. In an age when it sometimes seemed like the only role models for kids were actors, rock musicians, or athletes, I was lucky to find one so close to home.

Once I'd seen my grandfather play, I was always doing something involving baseball. For instance, if I was at West McDonald Lake, about an hour away in Minnesota, I would find a stick that was straight enough and sturdy enough to pass for a makeshift bat, and swat rocks into the woods for hours. To make it even more fun for myself, I would devise a game out of it. Even though I devoutly followed the Minnesota Twins, the team closest to Fargo, I was a huge fan of Reggie Jackson, then a star for the New York Yankees. So naturally I would pretend to be Mr. October, belting one home run after another into the bleachers at Yankee Stadium.

For fielding practice, I would throw a tennis ball against the steps of our three-story gray-brick apartment building, catching the rebounds with the worn mitt my mom had picked up for ten cents at a garage sale. She always offered to buy me a better glove, but the floppy old mitt was already broken in and caught everything that came my way. Most important of all, to me, was that it looked just like the glove that my gramps wore for his softball games, so an expensive, newer model just wouldn't have cut it.

The manager of the apartment complex complained that my throwing the ball against those three steps disturbed the other tenants, and so anytime he caught me taking "infield practice," he'd chase me away. No problem. The moment he left, I'd go right back to doing it. A number of times, the man confronted my mother about her son's lack of discipline. She would nod her head as if in full agreement, but not once did she tell me to stop. In fact, she encouraged me, because she knew how much I loved it. Mom also knew that the only person disturbed by my playing ball was the manager. Seemed to me that the man should have been more concerned with fixing the broken mailboxes and the building's faded-orange front door, which was always coming off its hinges.

Looking back, these seemingly innocent games (innocent to everyone but the building manager) really helped to sharpen my hitting and fielding, so that by the age of six, I'd already become a good ballplayer. The fungo sessions with a stick and stones developed my hand-eye coordination, while firing a tennis ball against the steps increased my arm strength and accuracy.

When I wasn't practicing on my own, I was usually playing some sort of sandlot baseball with friends from the neighborhood. From the start, it was clear that I was better than all the other kids in my age group—partly because I was at least a half foot bigger and twenty pounds heavier than most of them, but mainly because of all that practice. Whenever we chose up teams, I always got picked first. At six, I joined a T-ball league. Of course, smacking a stationary ball off a rubber tee isn't the same thing as hitting live pitching, but I used to hit a home run almost every time up. My ability in the field was also beyond that of most of the other kids. I don't want to sound conceited, but I was convinced that I was going to grow up to become the best player in the history of the national pastime. It became my childhood fantasy, to the extent that I'd actually wonder if people around me realized that they were in the presence of a future baseball great. Little did I know that there was a big, wide world outside of Fargo, North Dakota.

★ II ★

AS I got older, better, and stronger, my passion for baseball grew and grew. My friends and I played hockey, basketball, and football, too, but my heart was always in baseball. It was the sport that I had the most fun playing, and after a while, being a baseball player—like Gramps—became my identity. Sometimes people would refer to me as "that kid who's way too good for his age." However, on several occasions, my obsession with baseball, coupled with my throwing ability, got me into trouble.

Once, when I was about five years old, a few of my friends got into a heated argument with some little girls, and things quickly escalated into a rock fight. I still had a hard time telling right from wrong from time to time, and with no adults in sight, I let a rock fly. It struck a girl named Crystal in the head, drawing blood. She ran home crying, and I knew I was in big trouble. Crystal's mom called my mother, who exacted the worst punishment she could think of: taking away my glove and ball for a week. I was crushed! Fortunately, Crystal's injury required only a few stitches, and the glove and ball were eventually returned.

Three years later, at age eight, I got into another rock fight. Don't ask me why. Once again, several of my buddies were engaged in a heated battle with some other kids from the neighborhood. This one more resembled trench warfare, with the targets a good distance away. No one was getting hurt because no one, frankly, could throw that far. So who do you think my friends enlisted? Me and my strong right arm. I was dumb enough to give in and join the fray. Luckily, I didn't hit anybody. However, I did send a rock crashing through the living room window of a nearby house. As you can imagine, with finances so tight, my mother wasn't too pleased to have to pay for a replacement window.

Still another time—in fifth grade, I think—the combination of a strong arm and a weak will got me into trouble yet again. I was home reading a book, probably about baseball, when a group of friends turned up at my door.

"We're gonna go egg some cars!" they announced. It wasn't even Halloween. By this time I was old enough to know the score: *I'd* be the one doing most of the throwing, which meant that I'd be the one to probably get into trouble. But, once again, I succumbed to peer pressure and went off with them to the grocery store for a carton of eggs. You'd think that the cashier would have been suspicious of a bunch of ten-year-olds buying eggs—at night, yet—and figured out that they weren't merely hungry.

Heavily armed, we took to the streets looking for potential victims. Suddenly someone spotted a large house with an open window on the second floor. Too tempting. And guess who was elected to show off his throwing accuracy? Yep, me. I grabbed an egg, sized up the target like a pitcher staring at his catcher for the sign, wound up, and let it fly. If I say so myself, the throw was a thing of beauty. My buddies were suitably impressed, oohing and ahhing as they watched its trajectory. The egg sailed silently through the open window, and, judging by the plainly audible *splat!* it made, terminated its flight against the nearest wall.

We all scattered as if a bomb had gone off. From a ten-year-old's perspective, it was a hilarious moment, and I felt like the coolest guy in the world. Ah, but the night was young—and we still had eleven eggs in the carton.

Our next victim was a parked car with its driver-side window rolled down, and, like before, I got the call. This toss would be made from about forty-five feet away while riding my bike, not unlike a second baseman snagging a hot grounder deep in the hole, then getting off the throw to first in the same motion. The egg found the window frame, so that egg guts oozed onto the seat. More hysterical laughter.

By now I was feeling *really* cocky. Looking for greater adventures, we headed toward Main Avenue, the busiest street in Fargo. This time, from point-blank range, I nailed a passing car going twenty-five miles per hour, and the chase was on. We all took off as the vehicle circled around the block looking for us, but little did the driver know that he would never find us. Not only was it dark, but we were in a perfect hiding spot: camouflaged by thick bushes and obscured by a big old tree on one side and an abandoned car on the other. No streetlights, either. We could have stayed there undetected for hours, but when I saw his car on the other side of the block, I tried to make a break for it. I thought I was safe because there was no way he could see me from that distance.

To my shock, I didn't get more than twenty yards away before the angry man leaped out of nowhere. He'd cleverly had his wife circle around the block while he walked around from the other side. He grabbed me by the neck, and before I knew it, I was flat on my back and about to wet my pants. He then lifted me off the ground and ordered me to lead him to where I lived, so he could have a word with my mother. His hand gripped my collar tightly the entire way. Luckily for me, he was able to wash the egg off his car before it damaged the finish, but, more important, no one got hurt—Main Avenue was an extremely busy road. That night provided me with one of the biggest life lessons I have ever learned, and for a long time the mere thought of an egg made me sick to my stomach. In retrospect, I am very fortunate that the driver caught me. Who knows what kind of more serious trouble I might have gotten into if I'd continued doing things like egging cars.

I don't want you to get the idea that I was some juvenile delinquent. Aside from these few incidents, I had a pretty wholesome upbringing, with baseball always at its center. Once, when I was fourteen, I went with Gramps to watch him play in the regional postal workers softball tournament in neighboring Minnesota. (Fargo straddled the border between the two states.) Only eight members of his team showed up, and the tournament board threatened to declare a forfeit if they couldn't field a full nine-man squad. My grandfather called his players together. "Let's have Chris here play shortstop," he suggested. Not surprisingly, his fellow postal workers were pretty skeptical. Let a fourteen-year-old play with a bunch of men? Not only did it seem like a recipe for defeat, what if I got hurt? Especially playing shortstop, where I might have to face a base runner coming in hard at second. But Gramps could be mighty persuasive. "Trust me," he told them. "My grandson is better'n half of *you* guys!" He didn't have nearly as hard a time convincing the opposing team to let me play. I'm sure they took one look at me and could practically taste victory.

We edged them by one run. As for me, I pounded out four hits, including the winning run in the top of the seventh. I also roved all over the left side of the infield to take away several sure hits. After the final out, the other team was livid and threatened to protest the game. One of them whined, "It's not fair! He's too young and shouldn't be playing in this tournament. He—he's not even a mailman!"

Gramps hollered back, "He's only fourteen. Besides, you agreed to let him play in the first place."

The other fellow countered with a sheepish, "Yeah, well, he's no *ordinary* fourteen-year-old!" Although the tournament officials allowed the victory to stand, they decreed that I couldn't play in any more games. I was disappointed—that was the most fun ballgame I'd ever played—but at the same time I felt incredibly proud. So did Gramps.

As I got older, it was clear to me that baseball was my path to follow. Even in the middle of the freezing Fargo winters, I thought about baseball every day. In junior high school, I messed around with hockey and basketball, but it was apparent to me and everyone else that I was a baseball player through and through. Although I couldn't put it into perspective in those days, later in life I realized how lucky I was to have had baseball be such an integral part of my life. It helped build my self-esteem at a young age and made me feel like I could conquer the world. It also kept me out of trouble—for the most part—because it gave me a sense of direction and purpose. I wasn't about to let anything stop me from realizing my goal to play the game professionally, be it drugs, alcohol, or any of the other vices that all too often dash young people's dreams.

★ III ★

ONE day when I was sixteen, Gramps sat me down for a talk. No, not the one about the birds and the bees. He explained that my natural abilities had helped me develop a love for the game, and that was great. But if I wanted to make a life out of baseball, he emphasized, I would have to work a lot harder in the future. "Before long, the other kids will catch up, too, and you won't always be the best. If you don't prepare yourself, it'll be a real slap in the face."

As much as I admired my grandfather, I thought he was basically full of crap on this score. What else would you expect from a teenage boy who believed that he had the world by the tail? Gramps had one other piece of advice for me: "Chris, I know you are a good pitcher, but I guarantee that if you become a catcher, you will make the major leagues someday." He went on to say that the sport was full of pitching, and although I was a good hitter, I didn't run well enough to play shortstop or the outfield.

"There was, is, and will always be a shortage of good catchers in the world," he observed, "and with your natural abilities and strong arm, you would make a very solid catcher."

I understood a lot of what he was saying. But I'd always been the best pitcher on my team, so why would I switch? Especially to catcher. No one in his right mind wanted to play that position, the most difficult in all of baseball. To be honest, I'd always thought that catching was only for short and stocky kids who couldn't play anywhere else.

Catch? Ugh. You have to wear heavy, bulky equipment, including a strange-looking mitt that resembles a seat cushion; your face is hidden by a metal mask that blocks your view; you spend hours per game squatting awkwardly; and your job is to catch a small, round object that comes hurtling toward you at anywhere up to one hundred miles per hour. Also, the ball is always doing different things—sometimes it curves, other times it is straight or in the dirt. Or it nicks the hitter's bat and ricochets painfully into your face mask, your chest protector, or sensitive regions below. No thanks.

I soon discovered that my grandfather had been half correct. I still had no interest in becoming a catcher but just as he'd predicted, other kids did in fact catch up to me in size and talent. Fargo South High School didn't field a baseball team—which was true of most North Dakota secondary schools—so at sixteen I played for the Fargo Bombers, our city's version of a junior varsity team to the Fargo American Legion Baseball team.

American Legion ball, founded in the days of Babe Ruth, is like Little League for older kids, ages eighteen and younger, while a "senior" league accepts players nineteen or older. To a kid like me, American Legion ball seemed almost on a par with the pros. I'd attended several games at beautiful Jack Williams Stadium, where the stands were always packed, especially anytime Fargo played its archrival, the Moorhead Blues. (Bear in mind that the nearest big-league city was Minneapolis, a good four hours away.) Fargo and Moorhead are close enough to be Siamese twins. Whenever the two teams squared off against each other, both cities practically shut down.

I hit .468 for the Bombers, a class-B team, and didn't strike out once the entire season. But at seventeen I moved up to class-A ball, which featured a higher caliber of player. I whiffed several times in just the first few games, and although I finished with decent numbers, it was clear that I was no longer the best.

For the first time in my life I was average, simply average, and I hated it! Understanding the wisdom of Gramps's words, I realized that having a natural ability and a love for the game would take me only so far—certainly not all the way to the big leagues. I started working out with weights at the local YMCA and practiced as much as I could in preparation for my final season of Legion ball.

This would be my ticket to a college baseball scholarship. I was a good pitcher, but my offensive numbers were too low, especially for a kid from the frozen tundra of Fargo, North Dakota. When the season started, it looked like all my hard work was paying off, as I propelled myself back into the upper echelon. Batting third, I jumped out to a record-setting pace in many offensive categories.

I was convinced that I would receive several scholarship offers. Who knew, maybe there was even a chance of being drafted by a major-league organization. Although big-league scouts rarely visited Fargo, it wasn't beyond the realm of possibility. In fact, at several of our games, scouts came out to see one of my teammates, third baseman Mike Wieser. The best athlete in North Dakota, Mike excelled in four sports and was the only kid in Fargo who was as good a ballplayer as I was all the way through Little League and junior high school. His one edge over me was greater speed.

In June 1991, at the age of eighteen, Mike was drafted by the Atlanta Braves. I remember him climbing aboard the bus the day of the amateur draft wearing a Braves cap and a smile as big as the Grand Canyon. Mike had been a good friend of mine since childhood, and while I was extremely happy for him, I have to admit to pangs of jealousy. Man, I would have given anything to be in his shoes. It didn't matter that he wasn't a high pick and didn't receive a lot of money; just the accomplishment of being drafted out of Fargo was huge. Although Mike never made it to the big leagues, two other American Legion players from our area did. In 1990 the New York Mets drafted pitcher Rick Helling, who went on to win twenty games for Texas in 1998; and in 1992 they picked outfielder-infielder Darin Erstad, a future star for the California Angels and the Chicago White Sox.

For me, the 1991 draft came and went, and all I could hope for was to finish my senior season on a high note and earn a college scholarship. However, thirty games into the season, I woke up one morning with a dull, gnawing pain in my lower right side. An MRI scan eventually revealed the problem: a bulging disc in my spine. It sidelined me for seven weeks. Just before the playoffs, the coaches put me on the mound to see if I could pitch. After just ten throws, I stumbled off the mound in agony. I was so depressed, thinking that my baseball career was over at the age of eighteen. But, miraculously, the pain vanished overnight. I mean, it was completely gone. I was able to pick up where I'd left off pitching-wise, but my timing at the plate suffered from the long layoff. I knew I was a much better hitter than a pitcher, but you wouldn't have known it to look at my final stats.

After the season ended, Rick Helling contacted me. "I think you've got a bright future as a pitcher," he told me. The graduate of Fargo's Shanley High School was now pitching at Stanford University. The reason for his call was that he wanted to recommend me to his former coach at Kish-waukee College in Malta, Illinois. According to Rick, the junior college had a great baseball program. Over the past five seasons, every one of its sophomores had signed either to play professional baseball or to play at a respectable four-year college. "I never would have gotten into Stanford if I hadn't gone to Kishwaukee first," he said. It sounded like an ideal situation for me, so I told Rick that I would look forward to hearing from Coach Smith.°

Which I did, not long after. It took only a five-minute phone conversation before the coach offered me a scholarship. There was just one catch: If I accepted, it would be strictly as a pitcher. Since college ball observed the designated-hitter rule, I wouldn't even be allowed to so much as

---

°I've changed the coach's name for reasons that will become clear very soon.

touch a bat. I wasn't happy about it, but the sad truth was that I didn't have any choice. No other college had called, not even North Dakota State University, or the University of North Dakota, or any of the dozens of division II and division III schools in my area.

It was the first of many times in my baseball career that I would fall through the cracks, so to speak. I gratefully accepted Coach Smith's offer, and off to junior college I went.

CHAPTER 3

My Kishwaukee Nightmare

* I *

IT took some time for me to come to grips with the fact that my hitting days were now in my rearview mirror. And with the bat having been taken out of my hands for good, there went my hopes of playing baseball professionally. From the time I was little, I'd always been one of the best pitchers in Fargo, but I knew that I didn't quite have what major-league scouts looked for in a right-handed pitcher. Although I possessed a good curveball and a decent changeup, in order for a pitcher in junior college to get noticed, he'd better light up the radar gun with a ninety-five-mile-per-hour fastball. Given that reality, I assumed that college baseball was the highest level I would ever reach.

Nevertheless, I was content knowing that I'd be attending a top-notch baseball program. Just to be offered a baseball scholarship was an accomplishment in itself, especially for someone from North Dakota. There was also a touch of excitement to be going away to college. In an odd way, it was as though people from Fargo earned more respect by leaving to chase their dreams than by staying there.

I looked at it this way: Baseball was all I ever wanted to do, and just a few months earlier I had worried that I was never going to get the opportunity to move on to the next level. Now I was in a positive frame of mind and looked forward to a productive, fun year at Kishwaukee.

Boy, was I wrong.

★ II ★

THE hardest part was leaving behind my girlfriend, Marcia, who I'd been with since the two of us were sixteen. We had attended the same junior high school but never met until the beginning of eleventh grade. Apparently she'd seen me play with the Bombers over the summer. One of her best friends, a girl named Tammy, was in three of my classes. "That Chris Coste is kinda cute," Marcia shyly admitted to Tammy, who promptly took it upon herself to set us up on a date. Not long afterward, Marcia herself invited me to the Sadie Hawkins Day dance at school. (As you can see, I didn't have to do much to set the ball rolling; it was all done for me.) From that moment on, we've been a couple.

It's funny: I suppose you could say that my early life was less stable than many kids have it. But while still just a teenager, two crucial life decisions were already settled in my mind: I was going to become a baseball player, and Marcia and I were going to get married one day. She was athletic-minded, plus our backgrounds were similar in that both of us were unusually independent for sixteen. My mom had recently met her current husband, Tony, and moved in with him. She felt I was mature enough to stay in our old apartment, which I did for about a year. Then I went to live with Marcia and her mother, who became like a second mom to me. Given how close the two of us were, it was hard to imagine being separated for so long.

Driving my 1986 Ford Escort, with only AM radio to stave off the boredom of a ten-hour trip, I traveled through Minnesota and Wisconsin and into northern Illinois, where Kishwaukee was located, near DeKalb, just west of Chicago. But this was my first time away from home, and it took me a while to get acclimated to my new surroundings.

My first look at the campus was comforting, though. I'd never been to a junior college before and had no idea what to expect. With its small classrooms and only a handful of buildings, Kishwaukee felt more like a glorified high school than an actual college. And the fact that it was surrounded by farm country made for a tranquil setting.

I was exploring the campus with a sophomore who knew his way around, when he pointed and said, "Hey, look, it's Coach Smith. I'll introduce you." The baseball coach was much younger than I expected, about thirty-five years old, and looked like a cross between Al Pacino and Robert De Niro. My immediate impression was that he seemed very energetic and personable; the type of coach who forged close bonds with his players. We talked for about an hour, and he emphasized how happy he was that I'd chosen Kishwaukee and how much he thought I could help the team. I walked away feeling pumped up and looked forward to the next day's team meeting.

I arrived at the gym to find approximately twenty-five guys hanging around. *Big* guys. By the time I graduated high school, I stood six-foot-one and weighed two hundred pounds, which made me one of the largest players on my American Legion team. Not here. And from talking to my new teammates, I discovered that most of them had been drafted out of high school by major-league organizations. They'd decided to attend Kishwaukee only because either they hadn't been offered enough money to sign with a team or their grades weren't good enough to get them into a major division I school.

What had I gotten myself into? For the first time in my life, self-doubt started to creep in. *I'm out of my league coming here. There's no way I'm good enough to compete at this level.* My anxious thoughts were interrupted by Coach Smith's instructions to take the field for our first practice. I'd always been a team leader; now I was just some lowly freshman pitcher on a roster full of draft picks. It was the first time I can ever remember feeling nervous on a baseball diamond.

After we warmed up, the first activity called for the position players to take batting practice while the pitchers shagged fly balls in the outfield. Already I was getting a little depressed at not being able to swing the bat. At one point during the practice, I picked up a bat and casually swung it back and forth, just to loosen up my back and shoulder muscles. From fifty yards away, a voice yelled, *"Don't even think about it, Chris!"* Coach. I never picked up a bat again the whole year.

We pitchers assumed our position along the outfield fence as the first group of hitters began their round of batting practice. Man, was it impressive! Line drives were screaming all over the field—standing there you were tempted to hit the dirt like an infantryman who'd just landed on a hostile beachhead—and towering fly balls disappearing over the fence, one after the other. I thought I'd get whiplash from twisting around to watch balls rocket all over the field. No wonder so many of these guys had attracted major-league scouts.

When the first group of hitters finished their impressive display, the second group stepped in for more of the same. Then the third. It was like a three-ring circus where the action just doesn't stop. There was one guy in particular that I really wanted to see hit: Charles, a big first baseman from Indiana. From talking to him during the team meeting, I learned that he'd been drafted in the twentieth round and had been offered several football and basketball scholarships as well. Ultimately he chose Kishwaukee because of its baseball program's reputation and also because he didn't have the grades to qualify for a four-year college. Charles explained that his plan was to improve his grades and, hopefully, earn a scholarship to a major division I school. Better yet, maybe he'd get drafted in a higher round and sign for around a half million dollars.

Standing six-foot-five and tipping the scales at 245 pounds, Charles had muscles on top of muscles; his physique reminded me of a young, more chiseled Frank Thomas. There was no doubt in my mind that he was going to put on a batting display that would humble all the hitters before him. Charles strode up to the plate, adjusted his cap, tightened his batting gloves, and prepared to take the single biggest cut I had ever seen. I felt sorry for the terrified baseball as it traveled reluctantly toward Charles's mighty swing.

Whoosh! The big man missed the ball completely, stirring up a breeze that could have been felt in the Windy City. He looked utterly ridiculous in doing so, too. It might have been the worst swing I had seen in my life. I had to suppress a giggle. Maybe he was just fooling around. However,

Charles connected with nothing but air for the next eight tosses. When he finally did make contact, he barely nudged the ball out of the infield. I'd seen ten-year-olds hit balls harder and farther than that. And this was a twentieth-round draft pick? I came to realize that sometimes pro scouts get too excited by a player's appearance and overlook whether or not he has the skills to play the game. Obviously scouting is an imperfect science, but this was ridiculous. To use an old baseball expression, Charles couldn't hit the wind with a two-by-four. In a hurricane.

After the big man exhausted himself and sat down, the guys who followed him continued the earlier pattern of knocking the cover off the ball. It wasn't long before everyone forgot Charles's name, and by the spring semester you no longer saw his gargantuan frame around campus.

Once batting practice ended, we moved on to work on our pregame infield and outfield routine. This was where things got ugly for the first time. Coach Smith started hitting hard grounders into left field, and the outfielders were supposed to scoop up the ball and fire a strike to second base. After taking just three swings, he abruptly called in the whole team. We all trotted toward him, somewhat confused. It was only the first day, and we were trying to figure out what kind of coach he was. We were about to find out.

Coach Smith waited for everyone to gather in a tight circle. Then, without warning, he exploded with a verbal assault that no one could have expected. Talk about transforming from Dr. Jekyll to Mr. Hyde. His face turned tomato red, and he was as scary as Freddy Krueger on a bad hair day. To make matters even more interesting, the verbal abuse quickly became physical, as he plowed both his fists into the nearest player's chest, knocking him back into three other players. They all tumbled to the ground like dominoes. But Coach wasn't finished yet. He shoved a few more players to the turf, where they lay dazed and angry. What was going on here?

All the while he was filling the air with a stream of expletives. I've drained them of some of their . . . color, but they were on the order of *"What the hell do you guys think you're doing out there?! I can't believe the shit I'm seeing out here!!"* We still had no idea what had provoked this irrational outburst.

Finally Coach calmed down enough to let us know in a harsh, angry tone that we weren't cheering loudly enough. He wanted a rah-rah attitude not only during the game but during pregame infield and outfield practice as well. I remember thinking, *You just knocked the crap out of a bunch of your players all because there wasn't enough infield chatter?* I hoped, as I'm sure everybody else did, that he was just trying to send us a message on the first day, and we wouldn't see any more fireworks, at least not of that magnitude. No such luck.

Every practice that fall was pure hell. Coach Smith constantly searched for trivial infractions—or invented them—so that he could launch into one of his tirades. If an infielder missed a ground ball during practice, he would accuse him of staying up too late the night before watching TV. Take a few bad swings at the plate, and Coach would be in your face insisting that you break up with your girlfriend. According to him, women were as detrimental to the national pastime as corked bats. Why? Because they distracted his players. And if Coach ever saw a player talking to a girl in the hallway during school hours, watch out. That poor guy had better not mess up, because if he did, he could count on hearing, in a shrill voice, "Get your mind off that goddamn girl and back on baseball!"

Marcia and I missed each other so much that just two weeks into the school year, she came down to Illinois and enrolled in Kishwaukee. Once Coach got wind of that, he came down on me even harder than before, blaming my failures, whether real or invented, on her presence. After a month of this, Marcia and I concluded that Kishwaukee wasn't the right school for her, for several reasons, and she reluctantly moved back to Fargo.

I began to feel that I had made a serious mistake by coming to Kishwaukee College. Practice was so stressful that for the first time in my life, baseball was no longer fun. Baseball? Not fun? How was that even possible? I wasn't the only one to feel that way, not by a long shot. I'd hear teammates joke that they woke up every morning praying for rain so that practice would get canceled. The only thing that kept my head on straight was that I was proud to be on such a good team full of future professional ballplayers. It was a special group of guys, and we all felt that we were destined for the Junior College World Series. That is, unless Coach Smith's marine boot-camp tactics didn't drive people to quit.

Admittedly, he did calm down a bit by October, although we were still subjected to random flare-ups. Then came Scout Day, an annual tradition at Kishwaukee. One practice would be set aside for scouts from well-regarded division I colleges to come out to Kishwaukee to evaluate players. Pro baseball scouts, too. One thing you had to say in Coach's favor: He had some great connections, particularly with the Pittsburgh Pirates organization. That's why he was able to attract so many quality players from all over the Midwest.

Scout Day was Coach Smith's proudest day of the year, and he stressed over and over that it could be a life-changing opportunity, not that we needed to be reminded. Rick Helling had explained to me that it was a dazzling bullpen session at last year's Scout Day that led Stanford University to offer him a scholarship.

A class of mine had run over, so I arrived at the field a few minutes late. It was hard not to marvel at all of the scouts milling about waiting to appraise our talents. Of the sixty that I counted, half worked for major-league organizations, while the other half came from assorted four-year schools, including perennial national powerhouses such as Stanford, Louisiana State, and Oklahoma State. I'd seen a few scouts in the stands at American Legion games now and then, but this was absolutely amazing. It was clear to one and all that this "practice session" amounted to a tryout. What an opportunity.

The afternoon began with the position players running the sixty-yard dash while dozens of stopwatches tracked their times. A few rounds of batting practice followed, then the position players finished up by making throws from their respective positions. Last on the day's agenda, all eight pitchers had to throw forty pitches in front of the scouts. The showcase was especially nerve-racking for me. First of all, as one of the only freshman pitchers on the squad, I was slated to pitch last; not only would all the scouts be watching but my teammates, too. The tension from waiting for my turn was unbearable.

Finally I took my place on the mound. I looked up to see about twenty radar guns pointing at me from behind the backstop. It looked like a mega speed trap on Route 90. As I began throwing, Coach stood behind me, giving me pointers and telling me which pitches to throw. Six of the previous seven hurlers had topped ninety miles per hour. Since I didn't have that kind of velocity, Coach Smith had recently tried to alter my mechanics, to add more movement to my fastball. It was the right idea, except that with Scout Day only a few days away, the timing wasn't the best. I hadn't perfected any of these modifications yet, and it showed. By the fifth pitch, the scouts lowered their radar guns. Clearly I wasn't what they were looking for. I gave it my best, naturally, but I couldn't help feeling dejected as I trudged off the mound.

That would be nothing compared to the following day's individual evaluations with Coach. This, too, was a Kishwaukee tradition. We all sat in a classroom next to the gym. For the next hour, he went around the room and gave his opinion on how each of us had performed. For the most part, he was very encouraging. Many of the scouts, he reported happily, expressed high interest in several players. Then he spotted me.

"And now for *you*, Chris Coste," he began. From the glare in his eyes, I could tell this was not going to be pretty. "That was absolutely horrible yesterday! What the hell happened to you out there? I couldn't goddamn *believe* what I saw! You were complete *horseshit*! You were a complete *embarrassment* to this team! If Rick Helling had seen you yesterday, he would have been embarrassed to say you were from Fargo, *and* he would have apologized to me for recommending you! You don't deserve to be on this team!" He went on to inform me at the top of his lungs that I didn't have the heart and physical makeup of a good ballplayer and that I should get in my car and drive back to Fargo that night. Thanks, Coach.

You can probably imagine how humiliated I felt getting scolded in front of the whole team like a juvenile delinquent. I *didn't* put on a brilliant exhibition of pitching for the scouts, that was true. But, I thought to myself, seething, *Never question my effort*. Just when I thought it couldn't get any worse, he started in again.

"And another thing, you are soft and out of shape—you have a flabby ass!" Flabby ass? I was in better physical condition than 90 percent of the team. More than that, even. If I looked out of shape to him, it was because by the time I got to the clubhouse for Scout Day, the equipment guy had run out of size 38 pants. All he had left was a size 30, which I had no choice but to shoehorn myself into. (Looking back, maybe I lost a mile or two off my fastball from the circulation being cut off at the waist.)

When I got back to my apartment that night, I was a complete mess. Who wouldn't be? I felt sad, disappointed, but mostly just mad as hell. No one deserved such harsh treatment. Go ahead and tell me I pitched lousy, but don't do it in such a demeaning, brutal manner in front of my teammates. I made up my mind to do just as Coach told me and return to Fargo. He convinced me that I wasn't good enough to play for his team, shattering my confidence, a feeling I'd never experienced before coming to Kishwaukee. I'd always been under the impression that it was a coach's job—especially at the college level—to instill confidence in his players, not crush their spirit.

One thing about a team that's saddled with an abusive, oppressive coach: They develop a real camaraderie. I guess that's true of any group, whether it's an army battalion at the mercy of an excessively harsh drill sergeant or cell block prisoners under the thumb of a particularly bad-tempered warden. The second example probably best describes us.

Fortunately, with the help of some teammates and the assistant coach, I changed my mind and decided to stick it out. I knew I would never be a potential major-league player like some of the other guys on the team, but I knew I could at least become a good college pitcher. I wanted only one thing—to prove I belonged. Not only did I want to prove it to Coach, but I wanted to prove it to my teammates as well. If I was going to look them in the eyes every day, then I needed to gain their respect and prove I was good enough to stand alongside them. Even more important than that, I needed to prove it to myself. I had doubted my abilities from the moment I arrived in Kishwaukee. Not anymore. I made a promise to my-self to never again doubt my abilities, and I made it my goal to be the best pitcher on the team by the end of the season.

✷ III ✷

THE schedule worked to my advantage. We were at the end of the fall baseball season anyway, which allowed things to simmer down somewhat.

Coach actually gave us a few weeks off before starting our daily workout and weight-lifting program. It was the best three weeks of the year for the entire team, and for the first time I could actually concentrate on life and school. Coach Smith had us so brainwashed to think of nothing but baseball that it was odd to go through a whole day without him yelling in our faces or slamming his fists into our chests.

When workouts resumed in mid-November, so did Coach's outbursts. He put us through the most grueling sessions you could imagine: push-ups, sit-ups, bench presses, bar dips, biceps curls, and pull-ups—and that only scratched the surface. It was especially tough for me because my years in the YMCA gym had been spent using mainly the cardio equip-ment and Nautilus machines, not free weights. Once again, Coach kept up a steady stream of verbal abuse, calling me weak. I was determined not to let him get to me, but let me tell you, there were plenty of times when I entertained thoughts of breaking his kneecaps with a lead pipe.

Over time, though, a funny thing happened: We all became desensi-tized to his eruptions, to the point where nothing he said bothered us too much—even me, the object of much of his rage. The strenuous workouts continued throughout the bitter Midwestern winter until it was time for the spring season to start. As much as I hated Coach's approach, I couldn't wait to play ball again.

The Kishwaukee Kougars opened on the road in Mississippi, then Louisiana. It was a long van ride from Illinois, especially for me, because I wound up sitting in the passenger seat next to Coach. I braced myself for approximately nine hundred miles' worth of wrath, but instead Coach Smith chatted away amiably. He even looked me in the eye and told me that he was happy I'd come to Kishwaukee. "I think you can really help this team, Chris," he said. I'm not exaggerating when I say that this was the first nice thing he'd said to me since the first day of practice, so I had no idea how to read it. Maybe he had changed.

We began our spring trip as hot as could be, beating several nationally ranked teams to start out 4–0. I was proud to be on such a good team. However, I had yet to pitch and still felt like I had something to prove to Coach and my teammates. On the ride back to the hotel, he informed me offhandedly, "You're starting tomorrow." Just like that. I was excited, but nervous, too, because I'd be facing Mississippi Delta Community College, the seventh-ranked junior college in the country. For motivation, I replayed his cutting words in my head: *"You don't belong here. You don't deserve to be on this team!"* As much as I wanted to succeed for myself and for the other guys, I was determined to prove him wrong.

Fortunately, I seized the moment by throwing a four-hit 4–0 shutout, in what had to be the best game I'd ever pitched. When the Trojans grounded into a game-ending double play, I pumped my fist and immediately stole a glance at Coach Smith. He was rocking back and forth on his heels, nodding his approval. For the first time, I truly felt like a Kougar. Not only did my performance earn me respect, but I had demonstrated to myself that I belonged here. When we got back to the hotel in Moorhead, Mississippi, that night, Coach Smith was waiting for me outside my door. He ran up to me, wrapped me in a hug, and with a tear in his eye told me how proud he was of me and the pitcher I had become. I was shocked. Maybe there actually was a heart buried in that cold chest after all.

★ IV ★

WITH the Kougars off to a blistering 6–1 start, Coach was about as happy as he could be. We'd gone down South as an unranked team and had beaten several nationally ranked teams convincingly. There was no doubt in our minds that we had a good chance to make it to the Junior College World Series. As a reward, in New Orleans, Coach allowed the team to spend its one off-day exploring Bourbon Street unsupervised. We were given explicit instructions to meet back at the vans by nine-thirty that night. If we were just one minute late, he warned, there would be serious consequences.

One of the guys I was rooming with, Phil, took it upon himself to round up some of the less-sober players just before deadline, and as a result, he arrived huffing and puffing at the designated meeting place at nine-forty. He hadn't touched a drop of alcohol, no small feat when you're with a bunch of wide-eyed twenty-year-olds prowling the city's French Quarter.

After we'd driven back to our hotel, I was hanging out with him and our other roommate, Aaron. Suddenly we heard the door slam, and there stood Coach. His face wore a livid expression, as if the devil himself had taken over his body. He went right for poor Phil, slamming his hands into my roommate's shirtless chest. Then came the screaming, accompanied by more hard shoves. Phil, showing remarkable restraint, tried to explain why he was ten minutes late, but I don't think our furious coach heard a word he said. I felt like I was watching a performance. I also felt like Coach secretly enjoyed all this. He hadn't had a chance to vent in weeks, so he was going to put on one hell of a show.

As abruptly as he'd stormed into the room, Coach then turned on his heel and stalked out. Phil, whose chest bore bright red handprints, might have taken off after him, except that Aaron and I managed to calm him down. The whole display was absolutely disgusting. I suppose that we could have complained to the college administration, but we decided that the team was on the verge of something big and didn't need what would certainly be an uncomfortable distraction. So we didn't tell anyone about the incident.

As the road trip neared its conclusion, the Kougars started to tire, losing a few games to teams that weren't nearly as talented as us. Outwardly, Coach seemed to handle the losses with relative calm. Inwardly, it must have been eating him up. The long drive back to Illinois brought out his ugliest tirade to date. And that's saying something.

This time the target of his outburst was our best pitcher, Greg Something-or-Other, a right-hander from Indiana. Greg had been drafted by the Cleveland Indians, and Coach Smith regarded him as the guy who would carry us to the Junior College World Series. Greg pitched well, although not quite up to Coach's expectations. The night before we left, Greg's parents had dinner with Coach in the hotel restaurant, and they made the *big* mistake of offering a few unsolicited suggestions.

They told Coach that he wasn't handling Greg the right way and that he shouldn't treat their son as harshly as the other players because he was more mature and didn't need the added pressure. They also felt that Greg wasn't being used in the right situations. None of this sat well with Coach, as it probably wouldn't with any collegiate coach. However, he didn't reply to Greg's parents directly. He saved his resentment for Greg the next day.

From the moment we got into the van and headed north, Coach started in. He began by asking us how we could have lost some of the games we did. Gradually he became more and more agitated. Then he turned on Greg, expressing his disappointment in his best pitcher and how he had let down the team.

It started out as a typical Coach rant, but we could tell that we were in store for a Lou Piniella–caliber blowup, but without any need for an umpire's missed call to set him off.

In a nasty, sarcastic voice, Coach reenacted the dinner conversation with Greg's parents. "How dare they tell me how to run my team!" he roared. Then he really crossed the line, calling Greg's mom and dad stupid, how they needed to mind their own goddamned business, and so forth. He fixed Greg with a glare and yelled, "Your parents are two of the most screwed-up people I have ever met! Those no-good pieces of shit! I hope they never come to a game again! In fact, they're not allowed to! I'm banning them from the ballpark!" Once again, I'm cleaning up his language for you, with an industrial-strength mop. Barely pausing for breath, Coach plunged on.

"And one last thing: Your parents are alcoholics! I'll bet they had over ten drinks apiece during dinner!" Two glasses of wine was more like it. To prove that nothing was off limits, our coach turned his rage onto Greg's innocent girlfriend, calling her every nasty name in the book and banning her from the ballpark, too.

This went on for well over an hour. (If nothing else, you had to admire the man's lung power.) Meanwhile, he's driving the van down these dark, winding Mississippi roads in the middle of the night, turning around to Greg as he's delivering his tongue-lashing. Sitting in back, we were all terrified, not to mention appalled by his demeaning Greg's family like that.

The trip set the tone for the rest of the spring season. Once again we all dreaded going to the ballpark. Coach had turned a game that we all loved into a chore. Plus, the fear of incurring his wrath began to impair our play in the field. Scared to death to make a mistake, everyone started playing defensively. And when you do that—with infielders playing back on ground balls instead of charging them, hitters guarding the plate instead of taking their hacks—you're in trouble.

Oddly enough, amid this toxic environment, I thrived on the mound. At first Coach was complimentary toward me, a welcome change of pace. But before long, it seemed my success came to annoy him. After all, he'd repeatedly put me down and told me I didn't belong here, and I'd proved him wrong. The final week of the regular season, I was on my way to another win. In the fifth inning, with a sizable lead, I wheeled around to try picking a runner off at second and threw the ball low and toward the second-base side of the bag, allowing him to dive back safely just before the tag. Then, with an 0–2 count, I tried pounding a high fastball past the hitter. It was a textbook 0–2 pitch. But he managed to tomahawk a line drive down the third-base line. Luckily, our third baseman snared it to end the inning. No harm done.

Back in the dugout, I could feel the storm brewing. Sure enough, our fuming coach came barreling up to me and laid both fists into my chest. *That* I wasn't expecting, and the force of it knocked me back into the hard dugout wall.

"What the hell do you think you are doing out there, Coste?!?" he screamed. "First you throw a ball in the goddamned dirt! Then you throw an oh-and-two pitch that the guy smashes! What the hell is the problem?!? Now bear down and show me something, you piece of shit!"

Curiously, once the playoffs were upon us, Coach more or less held his tongue. I hurled a complete game against South Suburban Community College to advance us in the playoffs. We got to within one round of the Junior College World Series but were eliminated by a team from Southern Illinois. For a season that had held so much promise, it was a bitterly disappointing end.

We thought for sure that Coach Smith was going to lace into us afterward, but much to our surprise, the man broke down in tears and went around the team, dispensing hugs. "I'm really proud of you guys," he blurted, and it was clear that he meant it. He went on to explain that he'd been so hard on us because he wanted to toughen us up and prepare us for a life in baseball beyond Kishwaukee College.

I didn't totally buy it, and I don't think many of my teammates did, either. That kind of cutting criticism from a coach, especially at the college level, doesn't build people up, it breaks them down. Certainly our play suffered as the year wore on. Ordinarily I would have felt bummed out now that baseball season was over. Not with Coach Smith at the helm. I was *thrilled* to drive back to Fargo. I knew it wouldn't be just for the summer, either, but for good. Kishwaukee held nothing but bad memories for me. Free tuition or not, there was no way I'd be coming back.

CHAPTER 4

Back in the Batter's Box

★ I ★

WHILE I was twisting myself in knots trying to come up with an excuse for Coach as to why I wouldn't be returning to Kishwaukee, I received a phone call from assistant coach Nathan Durst. Ironically, Coach Smith had left the college to take a position with a major-league organization's farm system. According to Nathan, most of the team's other freshmen were transferring to Triton College, a two-year school outside Chicago, for their sophomore years. He would be going there, too, and he strongly suggested that I do the same. What a relief! I'd never have to face my old coach again, even if only over the phone.

Given that the baseball program at Triton was even more respected than the one at Kishwaukee, enrolling there seemed like a no-brainer. A few days later, a guy named Bill Ibach called to ask if I'd be interested in joining an amateur baseball team that he pitched for in Glyndon, Minnesota, just a few miles away, for the summer. Bill was an older guy; in fact, he'd coached me when I was fourteen. I thought, *What a great idea.* I'd get to keep my arm in shape until school started.

On the first day of practice, the manager asked me to take some swings. At first I was a little hesitant to try—I mean, I hadn't taken any cuts in nine months—but eventually I hopped into the batting cage. Al-

though I handled the bat only okay, I was able to get around on a high inside fastball, and I didn't get fooled by any curves. Besides, it sure was
fun!

A week later the Braves were in Detroit Lakes, Minnesota, for our first
game. I showed up ready to pitch a few innings and coach some first base.
However, we were shorthanded that day. "Hey, Chris!" the manager called
to me. "How about playing third? I'll bat you ninth." Now, I'd played third
base before and had developed a reputation for being very quick, with
sharp reflexes. But I could feel my anxiety rise. I'd been so brainwashed
during my year at Kishwaukee College that just picking up a baseball bat
felt like a criminal act. I acquitted myself just fine, as it turned out, nailing
two of my team's five hits. I even made some decent plays at third.

As the summer progressed, I started to enjoy swinging the bat more
and more, and my hitting improved dramatically. I still considered myself
strictly a pitcher, but maybe I could become known as one of the rare
good-hitting pitchers, like Steve Carlton or Orel Hershiser. Or how about
Babe Ruth?

By midsummer I'd become our team's top hitter. One day a teammate
of mine, outfielder Wade Beavers, suggested that I transfer to his alma
mater, Concordia College, a division III four-year liberal arts school one
town over from Fargo. "Why go to Triton and just get to pitch?" he asked.
"At Concordia, you could pitch and play third. I'm telling you, Chris, go
there, and you'll be conference MVP because you can pitch and hit."

Initially I dismissed the idea. For one thing, from what I remembered
about Concordia's baseball program, it paled in comparison to the one at
Triton. But also, after a year away from hitting, I didn't believe anymore
that I could make it at the college level, much less the pros, with my offense alone. Except that I kept hitting and hitting for Glyndon, until the
manager moved me up to the number three hole. When I saw my name
on the lineup card, I had a bit of an epiphany. *Wait a minute! I'm batting
third. I didn't even hit third in American Legion ball.*

Wade was right. Why limit myself to just pitching? He put me in touch
with Donald "Bucky" Burgau, head coach of the Concordia Cobbers (this
is corn country) since 1979. When I met Bucky, a Minnesota native in his
early forties, I sensed right away from his good-humored, easygoing man-

ner that he'd be a pleasure to play for—not to mention a refreshing anti-
dote to what I'd endured my freshman year. And once I researched the
school, I discovered that not only had Concordia's baseball program improved markedly, but academically it had an awesome reputation, pro-
ducing socially conscious citizens with bright futures in the real world. It
was an ideal fit, on several levels.

There was just one complication: At the same time, North Dakota
State University had jumped into the mix with a scholarship offer. The
school's baseball program had never been much to brag about, but now it
had a new coach in Mitch McLeod. He was young, motivated, and energetic; the kind of guy who could transform NDSU into a successful baseball program for many years to come. Mitch had seen me play over the
summer, when his amateur team played the Glyndon Braves.

Choosing between Concordia and North Dakota State was incredibly
tough. I kept seesawing back and forth, so one day I wrote down all the
positives for why I should attend each school. I guess I needed to see
them on paper. Although it was a virtual coin toss, Concordia came out
on top. Even though NDSU had offered me a scholarship, there were
reasons other than money to go to Concordia. It had a stable program
with the same coach for more than ten years, the team had recently been
to the postseason, and one of its players, Brad Keenan, had been drafted
by the Cincinnati Reds the previous year. But the most appealing factor
for me was that I knew a number of people already enrolled there, making Concordia feel more like home.

☆ II ☆

IT took only the first day of fall baseball practice to know that I'd made
the right decision. Throughout the opening exercises, I kept looking over
my shoulder, waiting for a coach to scream and yell for no apparent reason. It never happened, that day or any other day in the three years I
spent at Concordia College. Bucky Burgau was the exact opposite of
Coach Smith, always positive and composed, even when one of his players made a mistake.

Ever the skeptic, it took me at least two weeks before I became totally convinced that Bucky could actually be a role model and a nice guy, and nothing like my previous coach. With his short stature, professorial glasses, and reserved manner, Bucky wasn't the type of man who could lead through intimidation. He commanded respect because of the type of person he was. After I got to know him, I could see that he was a terrific father to his two daughters, an aspect of his personality that was very appealing to me, for obvious reasons. He became almost a surrogate father to me.

Best of all, Bucky put the fun back in college baseball. In contrast to the year before, I looked forward to practice. I felt as if playing for the Cobbers was my karmic reward for having been an unhappy Kishwaukee Kougar. Another thing, though, that improved my attitude immeasurably was my status on this team. I wasn't some lowly freshman who "didn't belong" but an integral part of the lineup, at third base and on the mound. I proved Wade Beavers prophetic by earning the 1993 MIAC (Minnesota Intercollegiate Athletic Conference) Most Valuable Player award, in addition to being named a third-team All-American. Concordia tied for the conference championship and ascended to the regional playoffs for only the third time in its history. Fantasies of a future in professional baseball, while still a long shot, started to percolate once again.

The 1994 season surpassed my sophomore year, as I won a second straight conference MVP award and this time moved up to a second-team All-American. The team's performance was a disappointment, however. As talented as we were, a rocky start prevented the Cobbers from making the postseason. But there was a lesson to be learned in this from Coach Burgau, who modeled how to handle adversity with dignity.

Soon after the end of my junior year, a number of major-league teams came a-courting with letters and phone calls. Nothing concrete, though. I resolved to have an even better senior season, the kind that would prove to any organization that I could cut it at the major-league level. Over the summer, my motivation to succeed changed in a much healthier direction. During my first two years at Concordia, I'd been on a mission to show Coach Smith—wherever he was—that he'd been wrong about me.

While it may have been an effective motivator, I no longer needed his approval. From then on I focused on my future, and, specifically, becoming a professional ballplayer. At long last the nightmare of Kishwaukee was truly behind me.

With so much riding on the upcoming season, I started working out more than ever before, two or three times a day. My major weakness as an athlete had always been my speed. That is to say, I had none. I was determined to improve that aspect of my game. In the summer of 1994 I entered the treadmill acceleration program at Red River Valley Sports Medicine Institute in Fargo. Simply put, I needed to make myself faster or risk getting overlooked by scouts because of that one glaring drawback.

And that's exactly what I did. By the start of the season I was considerably faster, stronger, bigger—in the best shape of my life. The treadmill acceleration program cut my time in the sixty-yard dash from 7.5 seconds to 7.0 seconds. Perhaps I still wasn't a Rickey Henderson, by any means, but it was a significant improvement. Physically and mentally, I was prepared for the season of my life.

It all paid off, as I had the best of my four college seasons: a .488 average coupled with a 1.28 ERA, and a third consecutive conference MVP award. And, for the first time, I was named a first-team All-American. I would graduate from Concordia holding fourteen school batting and pitching records.

Just as important, our team jumped out to a fast start and took the conference title outright for the first time in school history. It was a tremendous achievement for the Cobbers and important for me on a personal level, because winning the conference title put us on the postseason stage, where I'd get to showcase my talents for major-league scouts. As in high school, I seemed to have slipped between the cracks again. Despite putting up three MVP years in a row, I'd attracted relatively little attention from big-league teams. Hopefully the 1995 regional tournament in Oshkosh, Wisconsin, would change that.

The first game paired us against our conference rivals, Minnesota's University of St. Thomas. Besides turning in a complete-game victory, I chipped in a few hits, too. Great, right? Yes and no. The scouts didn't get to see me play third base, which created some confusion. Is this guy Coste a pitcher? Or is he a third baseman? Which is it?

In the end, Concordia went down to defeat at the hands of the defending national champs from the University of Wisconsin-Oshkosh. But I finished the tournament 10-for-16, with three home runs and eight runs batted in. All I could do now was sit back and hope that I'd caught some scout's eye. With the 1995 amateur draft only two weeks away, the future of my baseball life would apparently hinge on the opinions of the dozen or so scouts in attendance at the tournament.

CHAPTER 5

A First Shot at Pro Ball

★ I ★

WITH college behind me and the June 1995 amateur draft looming, I felt that I had done everything in my power to get drafted. In addition to having had a great senior season, I excelled in the postseason. Tons of scouts had come out for the regional tournament—not to see me but to watch the University of Wisconsin-Oshkosh's Jarrod Washburn. Upon graduation, he would be drafted by the California Angels and go on to become an eighteen-game winner. In Oshkosh, the talented lefty stifled the Concordia Cobbers' bats. Our only two hits, a double and a home run, belonged to me. On the bus ride home, I felt confident that *somebody* was bound to select me.

But as draft day drew closer, panic began to set in. Was it possible that I'd get overlooked yet again? The Dodgers, who'd come to check me out back in high school and college, had scouts in the stands at Oshkosh. Certainly they'd seen what I'd done—not just the pair of hits off Washburn but my .625 average overall. The Reds, Pirates, and Atlanta Braves were well represented, too. *What am I going to do,* I worried, *if I don't get drafted?*

Probably go into accounting, not that I wanted to. In high school, where I had been a decent if unspectacular student, I was always good at math and had taken accounting courses both there and in college. Oddly enough, most of the men in the Coste family are incredibly mechanical; if something goes wrong in your house, they can fix it like *that*. Me? I can barely check the oil in my car. My mother would always say to me, "If you don't make it as a baseball player, you're going to work with your brain, not your hands," and stressed the importance of doing well in school. I always felt that my grades didn't reflect how smart I really was, and, looking back, I know that if it weren't for baseball, I would have been a much better student. Not just because playing sports demands so much of a teenager's time, but because I never truly thought that one day I would have to pursue a different path. So I really didn't have a backup plan in case a pro baseball career didn't pan out.

By the time draft day finally arrived, I was a nervous wreck. Every time the phone rang, I sprung up excitedly to answer it, wondering which team might be on the other end. I even bought an answering machine so that I wouldn't miss any calls. But day one came and went. Darin Erstad of the University of Nebraska was the first player to be snatched up, by the California Angels. Round one included several soon-to-be bona fide major-league stars: The Blue Jays chose pitcher Roy Halladay right out of West High School in Arvada, Colorado, while first baseman Todd Helton, from the University of Tennessee, wound up in the Colorado Rockies' shopping cart. Round two delivered outfielder Carlos Beltran to the Kansas City Royals; in round three the Chicago White Sox bid on hurler J. J. Putz.

Maybe day two would be my day? The following evening, I came home with Marcia from having dinner out to find my message light blinking seductively. Could this be it? I pushed the Play button:

"Hi, Chris, this is Tom Jenkins with the Los Angeles Dodgers . . ." My heart nearly burst out of my chest.

" . . . I just wanted to let you know—just kidding, Chris. This is your Uncle Steve. I was just checking in to see if you'd heard any news yet." Steve, my mom's stepbrother, has been in the family my entire life and has always been like a blood relative to me. He was just joking around as usual, but at the time it felt like a balloon deflating. The rest of the evening followed the same pattern: no calls, no messages. I couldn't believe it. I mean, not *one* team was interested in me? In all, 1,664 players were auctioned off in the 1995 amateur draft. It wasn't as if every one was major-league caliber. Sure, of the thirty players taken in round one, two-thirds would go on to careers in the big leagues. But by round forty, only three would make it that far. (Although one of them was Aaron Rowand, then a shortstop for Glendora High School in California—proof that scouts are not infallible judges of talent.)

I felt sad, confused—hollow inside—but most of all frustrated and angry. You mean to tell me, a three-time conference MVP and three-time All-American, that I wasn't better than the guy who came in at number 1,664? No way. In that moment, the finality of it all set in, and I could almost visualize the baseball career I'd longed for my whole life crashing to the ground in flames like the *Hindenburg*.

★ II ★

I COULDN'T have known it at the time, of course, but my getting bypassed in the draft was probably the best thing that could have happened to me. How's that? Well, it allowed me to follow an incredible, if protracted, path to the major leagues, against all sorts of crazy odds.

A week after the draft, I received a call from Mitch McLeod, the North Dakota State baseball coach who'd offered me a scholarship three years before. According to Mitch, he could help me get into the independent North Central League, which had teams in Minnesota, Indiana, and Illinois. He had a connection with the franchise in Brainerd, Minnesota, and set up a tryout for me. The two-year-old North Central League, headquartered in Mora, Minnesota, wasn't affiliated with professional baseball, but it was a pro league nonetheless; a successful season there could certainly enhance my chances of getting signed by a major-league organization. In fact, several Brainerd players from the previous year had moved up to affiliated ball, with some now playing as high up the ladder as triple-A.

My only other option was to try to get into the better-established six-team Northern League. However, that league, founded in 1993 and based in Chicago, would be much harder to crack. It boasted probably the highest talent level of any independent league in the country. Numerous ex–major leaguers hooked on with the Northern League in the hopes of playing themselves back into the game's good graces, including longtime superstars like outfielder Darryl Strawberry and pitcher Jack Morris. At the other end of the spectrum, you had unproven young players like Jason Varitek and Kevin Millar, who viewed it much like I did, as a stepping stone.

Figuring what the hell, I called Mike Veeck, the colorful owner of the league's most successful franchise, the St. Paul Saints, to see if I could get a shot. His late father, Bill Veeck Jr., was the equally eccentric, innovative owner of several major-league clubs; he's best remembered for signing a midget to play for his St. Louis Browns, allowing fans to manage from the stands by holding up placards, and igniting fireworks every time one of his Chicago White Sox hit one out of Comiskey Park. Mike, not knowing who I was, gave me the same runaround he would have given any other nobody seeking a job: The Saints didn't have any openings, he said. I made calls to several other independent teams around the country and received the same discouraging responses each time, falling through the cracks once again. So it appeared that trying out for the Brainerd Bears was my only option.

I was quite impressed when I arrived at the Bears' stadium and complex. I was also impressed with their players, who'd won the 1994 North Central League pennant. Luckily for me, the team needed a third baseman. My tryout consisted of taking a few ground balls and batting against a few of the team's pitchers. Extremely motivated, and realizing this was my last chance at salvaging a career in professional baseball, I had the tryout of my life. My arm felt great, and I did well in the field. But my hitting is what really stood out.

The first pitcher I faced was the Bears' closer, a fireballing righthander who had pitched in triple-A the previous season. He reared back and rifled the first pitch right down the middle at about ninety-four miles per hour, grinning at me as if to say "You got no shot, kid." I readjusted the bat in my hands and prepared for the next pitch, another hard fastball. With the crack of the bat, everyone stopped what they were doing as the ball flew hard and loud into the metal scoreboard in left-center field. *Clang!* The closer's facial expression hardened. He pumped in another strike, only to whip his neck around as I laced the ball into right center for what would have been an easy double. Now he acted personally offended. I say that because the next pitch flew by the back of my head at about ninety-five miles per hour. *Relax, buddy,* I wanted to say, *we're gonna be teammates soon; no reason to get mad.*

Switching tactics, he came in with a slider, only to see it sent bouncing off the top of the left-field wall. At that moment, I knew I was going to make the team. Brainerd needed a good-hitting third baseman, and I fit the bill. The temperamental closer, however, still wasn't accepting me as an ally yet; his next pitch, the best fastball he threw all day, drilled me right between the shoulder blades. Ouch! I hobbled out of the cage feeling proud of what I'd done. Quite a lot of pain, too. The coaches gave the reliever the rest of the afternoon off and took over throwing batting practice. I continued to spray line drives and powder home runs all over the field. When I finished, the team's manager, Bryan Clutterbuck, a onetime Milwaukee Brewers pitcher, hustled toward me and immediately offered me a contract for $700 a month with another $200 in potential performance incentive bonuses.

"Let me have my agent look over the terms, and we'll get back to you in a couple of—"

Nah, I didn't say that. Are you kidding me? Sure, it wasn't much money, but the thought of being paid any salary to play baseball was still beyond my comprehension. How could life get better than that? I accepted the offer.

I drove home from the tryout as content and happy as I had been in a long time. Proud, too. The frustration of not being drafted had all but subsided. Although I had no idea what the future held, right now the only thing that mattered was that—for the summer, at least—I could say to the world that I was a professional ballplayer.

One week later Brainerd was scheduled to play its 1995 season opener against the Minnesota Skeeters, from Hibbing. Now, in college we got to use aluminum bats. But this was a professional league; as in the minor leagues and major leagues, only the traditional wooden bats were allowed. I'd practiced with wooden bats throughout my college career; still, this would be the first time that I had used them under actual game conditions. It's always a concern for college players to go from aluminum to wood, and I'd heard many grim stories about great college hitters who saw their power deteriorate without the extra pop you get from the metal.

Over two thousand fans poured into the stadium. I couldn't believe it! Nervous but excited, I was the team's starting third baseman and batted fifth in the order. It was apparent that the job was mine as long as I didn't stink up the place. In my second at-bat, I drove a hanging curve ball up the middle for a single and finished 2-for-4, in addition to making some good plays at the hot corner. Although we lost the game, and losing is never fun, it was a memorable night.

As the season progressed, everything kept getting better and better. We started winning, and after fifteen games I was second on the team with a .340 batting average. The Bears continued to draw near-sellout crowds in the neighborhood of two thousand a night—amazing for a small resort town of just thirteen thousand. Then stories began to surface about other teams in the league, and how they weren't selling tickets and losing tons of money; by July 1 some clubs weren't able to pay their players. One owner, deciding to bail, actually backed a trailer up to the club-house and stadium offices in the middle of the night, loaded up every asset he had left, and hightailed it out of town. With one franchise having officially bitten the dust, panic spread throughout the league. We were left to wonder how the North Central League could possibly survive.

It couldn't. Two days later Bryan summoned the team together and informed us that the league was folding after just one year and one month due to insufficient finances; we'd be handed our unconditional releases. I was sad and upset, as were most of the other guys. The season had been going so well—we were getting paid to play baseball in a great little city, and I was having the time of my life—but after just twenty-two games, it appeared as though my pro career had come to an abrupt end. My mood certainly didn't improve when I discovered that the two paychecks I'd received had bounced, along with my incentive bonuses, meaning that I was out $900.

With nothing to do all of a sudden, I sat around Fargo thinking about what kind of job I could get and what I wanted to do with the rest of my life. I didn't have time to arrive at a decision. My former manager Bryan Clutterbuck called to tell me that he had just been offered the top job for the Brandon, Manitoba, Grey Owls of the Prairie League, and he wanted me to be his third baseman. This was a brand-new independent league consisting of a four-team Canadian division and four U.S. teams, covering the Dakotas and Minnesota. The Grey Owls, losers of forty-five of their first fifty-three games (that's no typo), were the worst team in the league, if not the world, and with a month left in the 1995 season, new ownership had hired Bryan to turn things around.

You might think that I'd have been skeptical—was this another fly-by-night league?—but I was a twenty-two-year-old who just wanted to play ball. Without even knowing where Brandon was, I told Bryan that I'd be thrilled to join him. I really didn't have much to lose. I packed my bags, and off I went. Strangely enough, although I grew up just one hundred miles from the Canadian border, I'd never been there before. Brandon was six hours away by car, west of Winnipeg.

I didn't know what to expect when I arrived at the stadium in Brandon. The word *chaos* springs to mind. For one thing, the proud new owners of the Grey Owls had somehow neglected to inform the current manager that his résumé was about to become outdated. They showed the same consideration to a number of players who were also being shown the door. In fact, these poor guys didn't learn of their fate until after they'd already loaded their bags on the team bus for a road trip. What a scene: me and the other new recruits watching our predecessors having to retrieve their stuff from the bottom of the bus in order to make room for us. It was not a good feeling, I'll tell you that much. It was probably the first time I realized how coldhearted professional baseball can be.

Our first road trip took us to Moose Jaw, Saskatchewan, to face the second-best team in the league, the Moose Jaw Diamond Dogs. (Named after the song and album by David Bowie? We'll never know.) The name Grey Owls was something of a misnomer; Baby Hoot Owls was more like it. Our roster consisted mostly of younger players like me who had little or no professional experience. Moose Jaw, on the other hand, was made up primarily of older athletes with several years' professional experience. Although we jumped out to an early 3–0 lead, the contest was an utter mismatch, and we wound up losing 15–5 in embarrassing fashion. We were pathetic, almost of the *Bad News Bears* variety. Here's an example:

In the third inning, our pitcher had the runner on first picked off but threw wildly past the first baseman. He, in turn, tried to cut down the runner at second, even though the second baseman was practically taking a nap on the bag. *His* throw sailed over the shortstop's head into left field. As the runner giddily scampered to third base, our left fielder inexplicably returned the ball to the *second baseman,* who by this time had apparently lost interest in the play. He never even saw the relay, which ricocheted off his leg and rolled into right field, while the runner scored with ease. How he managed to complete his 270-foot jaunt without falling down laughing at our ineptitude is beyond me. To this day, it stands as the worst play I have ever seen on a baseball diamond, with the possible exception of Little League. The next two games were carbon copies, leaving us gasping for breath with an 8–51 record. I'll spare you the math: That's a .*136* winning percentage. It'd be more accurate, I suppose, to call it an .864 losing percentage.

Next it was back to the States to face South Dakota's Aberdeen Pheasants. In contrast to their nonthreatening name, they were the best team in the league, with a staggering 45–4 record. Again we were laughably outmatched, although somehow we did manage to steal one of the three games. Our road trip over, the revamped Brandon Grey Owls got on the bus for the eighteen-hour trek home. There we would get to play our first six games in front of the hometown fans.

A 1–5 road trip to Moose Jaw and Aberdeen isn't anyone's idea of fun, but I took comfort in the fact that at least the Prairie League appeared to be stable. The Diamond Dogs sold out all three of their games, and Aberdeen was equally impressive, attracting almost four thousand fans a night. I was also pleased by the caliber of talent: Most rosters included several players who'd made it as far as double-A or triple-A, plus two or three former major leaguers, such as catcher Greg Olson, late of the Atlanta Braves, and forty-year-old pitcher Juan Berenguer, who'd spent fifteen years with the Detroit Tigers, Minnesota Twins, and several other teams. Just as important, maybe more so, the front offices seemed to know how to promote and market their teams. They'd put on great shows between innings with promotions like the "bat spin" and the "mascot race" as well as timely music and funny announcers. I couldn't wait to see what Brandon would have.

Um . . . not much. Only 750 fans turned out for our return home, which, I was told, far exceeded the usual attendance. The game felt more like a Sunday church softball league than a professional baseball game. The few spectators who were there seemed to be more into hockey (referring to the umps as "refs" on occasion) and barely made any noise. But, then, did a team with a 9–53 record really have a right to expect more support?

★ III ★

AS the season came to a close, the Grey Owls rattled off a few wins but still lost far more games than we won. I wasn't helping much, batting in the neighborhood of .240 with not one home run in fifteen games. If we checked the standings at all, it wasn't to see how many games back we were but to make sure the league hadn't disowned us. One day Bryan decided to give the regular catcher a day off. "You interested in catching?" he asked me, catching me completely off-guard. I'd never been behind the plate in my life and didn't have any idea what to do. But I was happy to accept the opportunity, albeit nervous. *Just concentrate on catching the ball,* I told myself. *If you do that, everything else will take care of itself.*

Our opponent's leadoff hitter, Tom Williams, led the league in stolen bases, so I knew I would probably be tested at some point in the game. He did not disappoint. On the very first pitch of the game, Williams laid down a perfect bunt single. And on pitch number two, he took off for second. The only thought racing through my head was to catch the ball and get rid of it as fast as possible. Maybe I could at least make the play close enough not to embarrass myself. Luckily, the pitch came in just above the strike zone, making it easy to handle. I felt the ball strike the pocket of the mitt, transferred it to my throwing hand, and let it fly, just like hurling tennis balls against the steps as a kid. Before Williams even went into his slide, the shortstop was already waiting at second base with the ball tucked in his glove. He was out by five steps.

I couldn't believe what I'd just done. Back in the dugout, several of my teammates joked about the scene from the comedy *Major League* where "Willie Mays Hayes" doesn't even make it to second before being tagged out. It seemed so easy. Of course, we still had eight innings to go.

The next few innings went by without any challenges to speak of, with the exception of two painless foul balls off my chest protector. However, in the fourth, the other team's shortstop swung hard at a pitch, and his follow-through caught me directly on the left elbow. It felt as though the bone had been shattered into fifty pieces. Somehow I made it through the end of the frame and walked, wincing in pain, into the dugout. When the trainer rolled up my sleeves, we both looked at each other in astonishment: A lump the size of a tennis ball protruded from the joint. The trainer put my mind at ease by explaining that the blow had simply burst open a bursa sac in my elbow. "Nothing serious," he said as he applied ice. "Looks a lot worse than it is." Your joints are full of fluid-filled bursae, which allow the two bones to glide smoothly against each other.

How do you treat a ruptured bursa? Probably not the way this trainer did. From out of nowhere he grabbed a thick American history textbook—it had to be at least six hundred pages—and pressed it hard against my elbow. I tried not to scream from the pain while he explained that the pressure (and, oh, what pressure) would help to keep the swelling down. What he did not explain was why in the world the book happened to be sitting there in the dugout in the first place.

The sixth inning was a virtual replay of the fourth. Believe it or not, the same shortstop hit me with his bat on the same elbow again. More pain! What had I gotten myself into? And why would anyone be stupid enough to want to be a catcher? But wait, there's more.

In the seventh inning, with two runners on base, I went down on my knees to block a ball in the dirt. My inexperience showed when I instinctively raised my chin to protect my face from the ball. This was a big mistake, as catchers are taught to tuck their chins *down* and use the mask for protection. The ball bounced in the dirt, hit me square in the throat, and, just for good measure, somehow lodged between my Adam's apple and the chest protector, leaving me unable to breathe for about fifteen seconds. My throat felt sore for the next ten days. Adding insult to injury (literally), the umpire ruled that because the ball had gotten stuck in my chest protector, it was technically dead. Therefore both runners were awarded one base.

In the eighth inning, the shortstop's bat found my left elbow again. Had he come up another time that night, I would have caught from the box seats. As it was, during the same at-bat, he fouled another pitch directly into my groin. Down I went, lying in the dirt in the fetal position. Somehow I managed to finish the game, having suffered a season's worth of assault and battery in just nine innings.

If nothing else, I developed a newfound respect for catchers. I couldn't imagine what it must be like to be a starting catcher and play in 100, 120 games a year. That night I consoled myself with the thought *At least I'll never have to do that again!* Somewhere the ghosts of Gabby Hartnett, Bill Dickey, and Mickey Cochrane, in chest protectors and shin guards, must have been laughing themselves silly.

CHAPTER 6

Becoming a RedHawk

★ I ★

THREE weeks before the end of the season, it was announced that Fargo had been awarded its own team in the Northern League for 1996. I wanted nothing more than to play for my hometown. How cool would that be? Problem was, I'd batted only .255 in my twenty-two-game stint as a Brandon Grey Owl, with not one home run. And that was in a league far less talented than the Northern circuit. I knew I was a much better player than my lackluster stats showed, but it wasn't going to be easy convincing the Fargo management that I deserved a tryout, much less a spot on the team.

In the meantime, I went back to Concordia College, attending accounting classes during the day and working out at night. To help my cause come the spring, I knew that I would have to be in great physical shape and stronger, too. I pretty much lived in the weight room, focusing on upper-body and hand strength, with the hopes of increasing my power.

Staying motivated was easy: Every day, it seemed, the local radio stations and TV news reported excitedly on what would be the city's first baseball franchise in thirty-five years. Fargo had fielded three professional ballclubs, all of them in the Northern League, going back to 1902. First there was a team known unofficially as the Fargo Nines, which lasted until the league disbanded in 1908. When the league re-formed five years later, Fargo and neighboring Moorhead were represented by the Graingrowers. The name didn't quite have the same ring as, say, the Pittsburgh Steelers, but, hey, farming was what drove the local economy. World War I put an end to the Northern League on July 4, 1917, and the two cities remained without baseball until yet another Northern League formed in 1933. The third time was the charm, and the Fargo-Moorhead Twins franchise continued until it ceased operation following the 1960 season.

In October 1995 the new team's name and logo were unveiled in a celebration at a huge Fargo sports bar and nightclub called Playmakers Pavilion. To give you an idea of what a big deal this was for the city, more than two thousand citizens paid to crowd into the place. That's more people than many minor-league clubs pull to a typical ballgame. I was one of them.

Former Minnesota Twin Dan Gladden, the popular left fielder for the 1991 World Champions, modeled the team's uniform down a makeshift runway. It was perfect: bright white with black pinstripes and red trim. The jersey bore one of several logos: RedHawks. The Fargo-Moorhead RedHawks. I'm not kidding when I tell you that I got chills imagining myself wearing it. I *had* to be part of this organization! If I could just get a tryout, I knew that I would make an impression, especially being a local guy. Just before Christmas, I received a phone call from the RedHawks' recently appointed manager, Doug Simunic. A deep, nasal voice barked, "Chris Coste, Doug Simunic here, Fargo-Moorhead RedHawks. How ya doing?" He could have been an army recruiter.

I'd heard him interviewed on a local radio show recently, and came away with the impression that Doug was a bit of a hard-ass—a tell-it-like-it-is kind of guy. No opening pleasantries; right down to business. "I am calling to let you know that we would like to offer you a contract for the upcoming season. Are you interested?" Just like that.

"A-are you serious?" I stammered.

"Well, yes."

I couldn't believe it. I'd assumed I would have to audition for a spot on the team. Instead I was already a member. When I hung up the phone, I jumped up and down with joy. To me, playing for my hometown team for $750 a month was as good as making it to the major leagues.

The euphoria didn't last long. In the kind of 180-degree turnaround that has plagued my career on and off, Simunic called back a few days later. "Chris Coste, Doug Simunic here, Fargo-Moorhead RedHawks." This time his voice was different. Sharper. I could sense something was up.

"I gotta be honest with you," he said. "I got some bad news. I kind of misled you the last time we talked, and I thought I needed to clarify some things. First of all, I saw your stats from the Prairie League, and to put it mildly, you really have no chance to make this team. In fact, I never really wanted to offer you a contract in the first place, but the front office thought it would be a good idea to sign a local guy like yourself to help us promote the team. That's the only reason I am giving you a contract." Blunt? Yes, I'd say Doug was blunt.

I probably shouldn't have reacted defensively, but, frankly, I felt like I'd been sucker-punched by the unexpected change of heart. "Really?" I said sarcastically. "Who do you have on the team? Are the 1927 Yankees coming to the RedHawks? How can you be so sure I won't be good enough?"

His tone softened. Doug was a onetime catcher who languished in the minors before turning to coaching. He probably understood my disappointment. "Well," he explained, "I have several double-A and triple-A guys coming in. I am about to sign a former double-A third baseman and a former major-league first baseman in Brian Traxler. I am going to have a full roster, and there is just no place for you to play."

My way of handling adversity has always been to let it motivate me rather than discourage me. It's not always easy, but that's my personality, and I've always been the kind of guy who perseveres. Right after hanging up with the RedHawks' manager, I drove over to Concordia for some batting practice, then on to the YMCA to work out and lift weights. Not only was I going to make the team, I told myself, I was going to be a star.

When I got home, I felt compelled to call Simunic, just to let him know where I was coming from and the kind of player I was. "I know you think I'm just some local guy, from Fargo of all places," I said intently, "but I guarantee you: I will surprise you. I know you are bringing in some really good players, but the only thing I want is to be a RedHawk, and I will be more motivated and more prepared than anyone. Not only will I make your team, but one day I will be your biggest surprise. I can play third, first, second base, I can play the outfield if you need—heck, I can be a catcher if that's what it takes." I probably talked way too fast, trying to cram everything in before he cut me off, or even hung up on me, but he did neither.

"Hey, you'll get your shot," Doug responded appreciatively. "You'll come to training camp with the rest of the team, and I'll let you fight it out. But once again, I gotta warn you that you pretty much have no chance." Like before, I was put off by his negativity, but at the same time, I had to admire his honesty. Besides, I thrive on disproving people's misconceptions about me.

RedHawks training camp was still four months away. That gave me the whole winter to practice hitting indoors at Concordia College, then hit the gym. I did this two, three times a day. To further improve my odds of making the cut, I used a tactic not often employed by athletes. That was courting the media.

Simunic himself had said that the organization was predisposed to including a local boy on the roster, to help build excitement. Since word got out that I'd signed with the RedHawks, I was receiving two or three requests for interviews per day. Now, many ballplayers try to avoid reporters the way that vampires shun sunlight. Me? I was more than happy to answer their questions and, in the process, promote baseball in Fargo. The city had recently lost its pro basketball and hockey teams, and so there was some well-founded skepticism about whether or not the public would support the RedHawks.

Fortunately, the organization was building an incredible new baseball stadium and seemed determined to follow the template of the St. Paul franchise. For the past three seasons, the Saints had sold out every one of their games, averaging nearly 6,500. They'd also attracted national media attention with their entertaining, fan-friendly brand of ball. Remember, this came in the wake of the major-league players strike that scuttled the

1994 season and delayed the start of the 1995 campaign, leaving many baseball fans disillusioned. Over the next few years, a number of them began to regain their enthusiasm for the national pastime after attending independent-league games. There you got to see a competitive game, wolf down some hot dogs, and, in general, have a lot of fun, without breaking the bank. I'm convinced that the success of teams like the St. Paul Saints had a hand in reviving baseball's fortunes with the American public at a time when the game's future seemed in jeopardy.

☆ II ☆

BEGINNING in January, I started working out with my Jamestown, North Dakota, neighbor Darin Erstad, the number one pick in the 1995 amateur draft. He'd recently moved to Fargo and needed someone to practice with to prepare for his first spring training with the California Angels. Each morning we would go to Concordia and Bucky Burgau would throw batting practice to us. I would also hit grounders to him at first, the position for which the Angels were grooming him. Darin was an incredible outfielder, but the big club had Tim Salmon, Jim Edmonds, and Garret Anderson at the time, and if he wanted to make the team out of spring training, he'd have to learn to play solid defense at first. Adjusting from the outfield to first base in a matter of weeks is an extremely difficult transition to make. But Darin would eventually become a Gold Glover there, a true testament to the kind of athlete he was.

Working out with him was a priceless experience for me because I would try to keep up with Darin, which improved every aspect of my game. It didn't happen a lot, but I did have days when I out-hit him in the cage. When Darin left for spring training in February, I was proud to have had the opportunity to train with him, but I was also a little jealous; I would have given anything to be in his shoes. He was off to Arizona for major-league spring training and was going to play alongside the likes of Edmonds, Salmon, Chili Davis, and Troy Percival, *and* earn a major-league salary. The word *jealous* doesn't even begin to scratch the surface.

In February, the RedHawks commenced a weeklong winter caravan tour to start drumming up excitement for the team's inaugural season. The promotion included having manager Simunic and his pitching coach, Jeff "Bitt" Bittiger, make appearances around the area and speak to the media. I met him for the first time when the two of us were guests on an AM radio sports talk show being broadcast from a local bar and restaurant. Now, my image of Doug, based on his abrasive tone over the phone, plus his burly, rugged appearance in the photo you always saw of him in the papers, was that of a fortyish marine drill sergeant—kind of like Coach Smith at Kishwaukee. *That* was a scary thought. I quickly found out that my preconception couldn't have been farther off the mark.

When I walked into Lauerman's No. 2 Saloon, I had butterflies, like I was about to deliver a speech in front of my eighth-grade class. After all, Simunic and Bittiger would be deciding whether or not I was good enough to be on the team, so I wanted to make a good first impression. It was no different from going to a job interview in any field.

Doug surprised me immediately with his warmth and humor. He struck me as the kind of manager who genuinely cared about his players and wanted to see them move into organized professional baseball, the ultimate goal for any independent leaguer. He was quick with a comeback but also brutally honest. You know how some people have a filter that stops them from saying the first thought that comes into their head (because it's what they truly believe)? Not Doug.

Another thing I noticed right away was the unique relationship that Doug and Jeff had developed over their three previous seasons together in the Northern League. In 1993 Simunic managed the Rochester Aces, then moved with the franchise to Winnipeg. He spent two more years with the renamed Goldeyes. Bittiger, who'd logged parts of four seasons pitching in the big leagues, was his pitching coach in both places and now in Fargo. Bitt also doubled as one of the team's best pitchers despite being thirty-four years old. If I didn't know better, I would have guessed that they were brothers—not because of the great affection between them but because of the constant bickering. They spent three hours that night locked in debate about everything from inflated baseball salaries

and the baseball strike, to health food and junk food, name-brand underwear, and Northern League coverage in national sports magazines. It was
absolutely hilarious, and after watching and listening to those two all
night, I knew it was going to be an interesting season for the 1996 Fargo-
Moorhead RedHawks.

The day before Doug returned home to West Virginia, he gave me a
big lift when he told me I had a shot to make the team after all because
of my ability to play several positions, though nothing, of course, was
guaranteed. "Be sure to bring all of your gloves with you," he joked. "I'm
going to throw them all up in the air, and whichever one lands first is
where you'll play that day." However, he wanted me to work on my skills
at *second* base, a position I'd never played before; that might be the only
spot up for grabs. If that was the case, then I was more than happy to turn
myself into another Roberto Alomar, or at least try. Nothing was going to
stop me from becoming a RedHawk and playing in the team's beautiful
new ballpark.

I'd seen many architectural drawings of the stadium, which was still
under construction as spring arrived. To think that *Fargo, North Dakota,*
would be home to such a state-of-the-art facility was incomprehensible to
me. I considered the Fargo Legion Stadium, also known as Jack Williams
Stadium, the nicest ballpark I'd ever played in, but *this* was truly something.

The RedHawks' home opener was scheduled for June 17, 1996. From
March through May, Marcia and I used to drive past the new stadium at
least five times week. It became our ritual to go work out at the gym, then
pick up some sandwiches for lunch and sit eating in the car while watching the construction crew do its thing. They must have thought we were
nuts. It was so cool to watch this building evolve.

But what if it wasn't ready in time? I wanted to play here! Sometimes,
I swear, I would grow impatient with what seemed like, at least to me, the
slow progress. I had to fight the urge to jump out of the car and yell at the
workers to hurry up. In fact, I had a dream one night that I hollered at
the crew, "Hey, come on, let's go! Pick it up a little, pound some more
nails! We got a ball game to play!" Then I picked up a hammer and
started knocking in nails myself like I was pounding a hanging curveball.

Every time we left the construction site, I could practically hear my name echoing over the P.A. system as I strode up to bat before a capacity crowd of five thousand.

☆ III ☆

AFTER what seemed like an eternity, May finally rolled around: The first order of business for the new franchise was to hold an open tryout at Jack Williams Stadium. It was an opportunity for anybody and everybody to make an impression, thus earning an invitation to the RedHawks' two-week training camp set to begin on May 15. The day before the tryout, Doug Simunic called to ask if I would help him run the camp; I happily offered my services.

I showed up at Jack Williams Stadium the next morning expecting to hit some ground balls to the infielders; maybe throw some batting practice. Looking around at the group of hopefuls as they stretched and prepared to impress the manager, I marveled at the array of young men who'd come to try out. Six months before, I would have been one of them. You had some good players, some not-so-good players, and some guys who had no business being on a baseball field. Some even showed up wearing jeans and denim shirts.

The first leg of the tryout called for the position players to run the sixty-yard dash. To my surprise, Doug decided on the spur of the moment that I should take part in the tryout just like everyone else, despite already having a contract. My performance wouldn't determine my fate or anything; the manager wanted to see what he was getting. Still, if I did poorly, it wasn't going to help my chances of making the team. And although I'd worked hard over the years to improve my speed, I didn't exactly leave a cloud of dust behind me in the sixty. Or as Doug put it, in his typically poetic way: "Wow, Coste, you are slower than fog off dog crap!"

Next the outfielders were to show off their arms by gunning balls to third base and to home plate from center field, as if trying to nip a runner hell-bent on beating the throw. Most of the guys had the distance if not always the accuracy, but then there were a few who couldn't fire a ball ninety feet with a bazooka. It kind of made you wonder if they knew how out of their depth they were. But, then, the desire to play baseball can be so strong, a little self-delusion is understandable. I suppose it's no different from an audition for *American Idol* or any other talent show, where folks who should be legally banned from holding a microphone wail off-key for the judges without a hint of self-consciousness.

On the flip side, during batting practice I saw several candidates who had a legitimate shot of making it to RedHawks training camp. Moorhead native Tony Kunka was one such player. In fact, he was the only greenhorn to win an invitation to camp, on account of the show he put on in the batting cage and in simulated game action. Years later, Doug Simunic confessed to me and Tony that he'd had no intention of signing a single hopeful from the pubic tryout; essentially, the whole thing was a farce imposed on him by management, for public-relations purposes. Kunka's productivity, however, forced the manager's hand. Not only did he win a spot in training camp, he became a RedHawk for the next two seasons until an elbow injury ended his career.

I was a different story altogether. My performance was so average that had I actually been auditioning, there's no way I would have joined the others in camp. In one simulated game situation, I fanned against a pitcher who wasn't anywhere near the level of your average Northern Leaguer. In fact, this pitcher was a friend of mine who actually worked in the RedHawks' front office. As a result, I knew that I'd have to really be at my best the next two weeks, especially during the six exhibition games against other Northern League teams.

Over the next week, RedHawks players began filtering into town, starting with center fielder Chris Powell, from Southern California, and Texan Brian Traxler, our first baseman. I felt intimidated introducing myself to these guys; after all, I was just some lowly local guy signed for promotional purposes, whereas Chris and Brian both had impressive résumés to brag about. Powell, a standout at college powerhouse California State University, Fullerton, was the Northern League batting champion in 1994, when he hit .357 for the Sioux Falls Canaries. Brian, a career .300 minor-league hitter, had been promoted to the major leagues once, in 1990, for the proverbial cup of coffee. A Los Angeles Dodger for all of eleven at-bats, he stroked a double, giving him a lifetime batting average of .091. Maybe it doesn't sound like much, but just making it to "the show," meaning the big leagues, is still quite an accomplishment.

On May 12 I got to meet everyone when we had our first official team meeting at Moorhead's Madison Hotel. Most of the guys were older than me. My feelings of inadequacy only intensified, and even I had to ask myself if I truly belonged here. In an odd way, it was similar to the feeling I'd had during the first team meeting five years earlier at Kishwaukee. As with every other baseball situation I'd been in, I had something to prove, to the manager and to my "colleagues."

A few days later, Doug and I were driving together to a local hardware store to get some tools to fix the batting cage. (In what ways is independent ball different from major-league ball? This would be one example. It's safe to assume that Lou Piniella and Alfonso Soriano do not have to head to the nearest Home Depot because someone's torn the cage at Wrigley Field.) "Coaster," he said kindly, "just be patient. You never know when someone will get hurt. When that happens, you'll get your shot."

Being all of twenty-three, that didn't satisfy me. "What if I do well in the exhibition games in training camp? Is there a chance I can beat someone out for a starting job?"

Doug paused. "No, Chris," he answered, "there is one thing you have to understand. Like I said to you a few months ago, I have brought in a lot of double-A and triple-A ballplayers, and even a few that have played in the big leagues. You should feel lucky that you have a chance to be on the team at all. Just sit back and wait for your shot."

Naturally I had to get in the last word. Before we got out of the car, I said to Doug, "I know you think I am just some local-guy division-III ballplayer who hit .255 in the Prairie League, but just keep your eyes open, because I guarantee I will surprise you." It wasn't the first time he'd heard those words from me.

The RedHawks' first official team practice, on May 15, was preceded by a carnival-like media session. All over Jack Williams Stadium, players were having their photos taken and were talking to reporters. Professional baseball hadn't been played here in three and a half decades, so it seemed as if every media person within one hundred miles had descended on the stadium. Being a Fargo native, it was interesting to observe the other players' reactions to the media onslaught. Many of them hailed from larger towns, or they'd knocked around the minors and independent leagues for some time, so perhaps they didn't have high expectations of the city's enthusiasm for its new team. If so, they were pleasantly surprised.

The biggest excitement, however, was reserved for outfielder Darryl Motley, the RedHawks' biggest signing of the winter. The moment the thirty-six-year-old Oklahoman stepped on the field, he siphoned all the attention away from everyone else. Here you had a bona fide World Series hero. In 1985, as a member of the Kansas City Royals, number 24 hit .364 in the seven-game series and played a key role in enabling the Royals to overcome a 3–1 deficit and sweep the last three games. In the deciding game, Motley's two-run homer in the second inning set the Royals on the road to an 11–0 victory and the first world championship in team history.

He hadn't played in the big leagues since being released by the Atlanta Braves in 1987, but Motley was the Northern League's best player, a 1995 All-Star for the St. Paul Saints. The RedHawks wanted a name player, one they could build the franchise around. In many respects, Darryl was the face of the 1996 Fargo-Moorhead club. His presence also instilled a certain level of confidence in the clubhouse, sending a message to the players that the team ownership placed a high priority on winning.

The first few days of practice were very exciting. I was working out at every position, improving defensively at each one, and hitting the heck out of the ball like never before. The only problem was that Doug's preseason assessment had been accurate: He did indeed have a star at every position. The recent signing of Lance Migita, an All-American second baseman out of George Washington University, pretty much slammed the door shut on any chance I had of breaking the starting lineup. At most, I could expect to be a bench player and hope for the best. Other than that, my only option was to go back to the Prairie League, which I really didn't want to do. I'd grown so excited by the potential success of the RedHawks, not to mention the idea of playing in my hometown, that I had no interest in going anywhere else.

The first week of training camp only reinforced that feeling, as we were treated like celebrities around town. The RedHawks' front office had set up several p.r. functions for us, ranging from free dinners and drinks at some swank restaurants, to autograph sessions at shopping malls and car dealerships. We even taped television commercials and radio spots at various media outlets. Heady stuff!

One night we attended a dinner at the Treetop Restaurant in Moorhead, held by team president Bruce Thom, a local businessman in his mid-fifties. An incredibly passionate person in all aspects of his life, he was instrumental in bringing the RedHawks to Fargo. Thom started off by saying, "I'm probably more excited about the team than you are!" Judging by his enthusiasm, he may have been right. After a few minutes of pleasantries and introductions of his staff, Bruce completely switched gears.

"Now let's talk about winning. This is all very simple: You guys were brought here for one reason—to win!" With each word, his voice grew more thunderous. "We are not just building a team for the future, we want a winner right now. This is something I feel strongly about. Let me show you what I mean!" With that he walked out of the room.

The guys looked at one another, puzzled. Their expressions seemed to say, "What is up with this guy, and what have we gotten ourselves into?"

Thirty seconds later, Bruce marched back into the room wearing a World War II army helmet on his head. "You see, guys," he continued, "I live my life according to the same principles as General George S. Patton! And to show you what I mean, we are going to watch this tape about the general and how he lived his life. When you finish watching the general, you will see not only how I live my life but how we need to approach this season!" He then popped a videotape into a VCR, and we watched in silence as actor George C. Scott, portraying Patton, delivers the fiery general's inspirational speech to his troops that opens the 1970 Oscar-winning film *Patton*. A bit before our time, perhaps, but the guys were spellbound.

By the end, everyone in that room understood unequivocally how serious Bruce and his staff felt about the upcoming season. This was no hobby for them, and certainly not some tax write-off. Bruce had gotten involved with the Northern League to win, and anything less than a title would be a failure. Luckily, everyone in the room that night felt exactly the same.

As the meeting wound down, Darryl Motley asked Bruce a question that got everyone's attention. "Say, Bruce, if we win the championship, do we get rings?" Motley, of course, had his from the 1985 K.C. Royals as well as the 1995 St. Paul Saints. As if attached to one body, every head in the room swiveled as one toward Bruce with anticipation.

"Darryl, if you guys bring home the title, you can design any kind of rings you want!" Bruce replied. The man's energy made us want to win the title for him as much as for ourselves. From that point on, practice sessions crackled with energy, and the team seemed to improve in every aspect of the game.

Like Coach Smith at Kishwaukee, Doug Simunic—Simmy, we called him—had incredible connections and was always on the prowl to up-grade his team any way he could. One day, while he was throwing batting practice, we all heard an odd bleeping sound. No one could figure out what it was.

Doug reached into his back pocket and whipped out a cell phone, which weren't nearly as common as they are now—certainly not on a pitcher's mound. "I gotta take this," he grunted and turned the thing on. "Whaddaya got?" he shouted. We realized it must have been one of his baseball connections on the other end. After a short pause, he responded, "Well, can he hit? No? Then we don't want him!" Simmy slammed the phone shut, shoved it back in his pocket, and kept right on throwing as if he'd never stopped.

He knew that on-field strategy wasn't what won games in the Northern League so much as the quality of your players. During the season, Doug talked on that phone so much that his cellular phone company shut down his service on several occasions, assuming that the phone had been stolen.

★ IV ★

FOR the RedHawks' first exhibition game, we traveled to St. Paul, Minnesota, to face the defending champion Saints. I knew I wouldn't be starting, but this was really exciting, because the club had further improved itself over the winter by signing thirty-four-year-old Darryl Strawberry and St. Paul native Jack Morris. Strawberry, who at one point in his career had seemed destined for the Hall of Fame, was hoping to play his way back into the big leagues after years of troubles stemming from drug and alcohol abuse. Morris, author of 254 major-league wins, had won twenty games as recently as 1992, but at age forty-one was coming out of a short-lived retirement.

When we stepped off the bus in front of Midway Stadium, I experienced another level of RedHawks professionalism, the kind that you normally associated with the major leagues. I went to grab my equipment bag from the luggage bay. The bags were gone, having been unloaded earlier and already placed in our lockers. For someone who's played in the Prairie League and the late North Central League, now *this* was class. Our equipment manager had even unpacked the gear for us and arranged everyone's uniforms, mitts, spikes, batting gloves, and wristbands neatly in our lockers. If I'd had a camera with me, I would have taken a picture. By my standards, this was on a par with turn-down service at the Ritz-Carlton.

From the first pitch of the preseason, you could tell that the 1996 Fargo-Moorhead RedHawks possessed the kind of camaraderie and spirit that are often synonymous with winning, regardless of the sport. Our leadoff man, shortstop Chad Akers, watched the first pitch come in high for ball one. Chris Powell leaped off the bench and yelled in an agitated voice, "Hey, come on Akers! This guy hasn't thrown a strike all year!" The rest of the dugout exploded with laughter, and Akers had to call time-out in the batter's box to regain his composure. The RedHawks had finally taken flight.

The game was locked in a scoreless tie when the Saints brought in Jack Morris to start the fifth. Most of us had never faced major-league-caliber pitching before, and certainly not someone with the credentials of baseball's winningest pitcher in the 1980s and the Most Valuable Player of the 1991 World Series. Yet we managed to push across one run against Morris, which proved to be enough to squeeze by St. Paul 1–0. I got to see some action at second base in the eighth inning and made the most of the opportunity. With the bases loaded and one out, I started an inning-ending double play off the bat of former Minnesota Twin J. T. Bruett, to maintain our fragile one-run lead.

From St. Paul we traveled up to Winnipeg, Manitoba, to play two exhibitions against the Goldeyes. I'd hoped to start one of them, but no such luck. I can remember sitting in the cramped visitors' dugout after the first game, swallowed up in disappointment. Realistically, with the squad Simunic had assembled, it looked as though I would have to go somewhere else in order to get any playing time. But in game two Doug once again inserted me into the lineup for the last two innings. And this time I would get a chance to bat. It was just one at-bat, but whole careers have turned on a single plate appearance. If I got a hit, I'd live to see another day. If not . . .

I lined a hard single into right and eventually came around to score. The pitcher probably wasn't good enough to make it in the league, but I'd done what I needed to do. I'd bide my time until I was called upon again, whenever that might be. That was how I had to approach things, making the most of my limited opportunities at the plate and in the field.

We returned home for our last three exhibition games. The front office was seeking to introduce RedHawks baseball to the surrounding areas, too; consequently our first "home" appearance took place in Perham, Minnesota, a small city in the lakes region about seventy miles east of Fargo. I'd played a few amateur games there over the years. We arrived to find a lively sellout crowd—another promising sign for the future of base-ball in Fargo-Moorhead. The scorecard confirmed a favorable sign for me, too: Simunic had penciled me in as the starting designated hitter. Well, all right!

My first two at-bats produced a pair of hard-hit balls that died on the warning track. Then came the top of the ninth. Remember how Doug had counseled me that my big chance would probably come about when least expected, due to injury? Well, the guy pitching for us, a former minor-leaguer named Jamie Surratt, hurt his elbow badly enough that he had to exit the game with one out and trailing by three runs. With no one else on the staff scheduled to pitch, Jeff Bittiger looked at me and asked, "Can you finish this for us?"

"Yes sir, you bet I can!" Stunned but excited, I grabbed my glove and ran to the mound. It wasn't until I got there and looked in the direction of home plate that I became unnerved. Just as I'd once thought of myself as a pitcher, not a hitter, now the reverse was true. I hadn't thrown off the mound in a game situation since college.

Catcher Mike Crosby came out from behind the plate. "So," he asked, "can you pitch?"

With all the false bravado I could muster, I replied confidently, "Of course! I was an All-American pitcher in college, Jack!" He looked at me with a sort of dismissive expression and hurried back behind the plate without comment. I let out a nervous giggle as I awaited my first sign. (It was only a half-fib: I'd been a three-time All-American, but as a third baseman.) The first hitter popped the ball a mile in the air for out number two.

That brought up center fielder Gerald Young, a pretty good hitter and a prolific base stealer who'd logged eight seasons in the big leagues. After running the count to two balls and two strikes, both strikes coming on dangerously long foul balls, I reared back and threw the one pitch I could always rely on in college: the 12/6 curveball. The typical 12/6 goes straight up, then drops straight down. (The name well describes the pitch's motion: Imagine the hand on a clock going from the 12 to the 6.) Young took a mighty swing and missed the ball by about three feet. Strike three, inning over.

I hopped off the mound and proudly ran for the dugout. As much as I would have liked to enjoy the moment, the RedHawks hadn't signed me to pitch, and I was due to lead off the bottom of the ninth. Not wasting any time, I laced the first pitch I saw to left for a single. The hit sparked a rally that ultimately fell one run short, with the tying run stranded on third.

We walked off the field in disappointment, but to everyone's amazement, the Perham fans were on their feet in a standing ovation. It was awesome. Some of the players on the winning team stopped and looked around in wonderment, as if to say, *Wow, these are some fans!*

The bus drove us back to Jack Williams Stadium, where everyone's cars were parked. I heard the manager's voice calling me. "Coaster, step into my office, young man." Like before, I could sense from the playful tone in his voice that I didn't have anything to worry about, at least not tonight.

"Yes, sir."

He let out an exasperated sigh. "First of all, you don't have to call me 'sir.' You don't have to call me Doug, either. Only people that don't know me call me Doug. Call me Simmy."

"Okay . . . Simmy." That felt odd. "What's up?"

"Nice game tonight. Listen, Bitt and I have been doing a little talking, and we are both in agreement. Do you think you can play second base and hit second in the lineup for us? We need someone in the two spot who can drive the ball and create some extra-base hits on a regular basis. Do you think you can handle that?"

Now, what do you *think* I said?

CHAPTER 7

The 1996
Fargo-Moorhead RedHawks

★ I ★

I FLOATED out of Doug Simunic's—sorry, Simmy's—office as if I had just won the North Dakota State Lottery, and for the first time I truly felt like a member of the Fargo-Moorhead RedHawks, not some local promotional tool. But if there's one thing I learned early on in baseball, it's that you can't take your current status for granted.

Our next "home" exhibition game took place in Jamestown, North Dakota, a town one hundred miles west of Fargo. This game was the moment of truth for me because I knew I had to produce to keep the starting job at second base, and I wanted more than anything to prove to Simmy that he was right in naming me his second baseman. Although I had gained the trust of Simmy, I also knew he was a fickle manager and one bad day at the plate could easily sway him to change his mind. Luckily, after a lineout in my first at-bat, I had a great day at the plate, going 3-for-4 with a single, double, and a home run, totally assuring my spot as the RedHawks' second baseman. We went on to win the game in the bottom of the ninth on a game-tying home run by Tony Kunka and a walk-off home run by Darryl Motley. And as in Perham, we were treated to a sellout crowd and a rousing ovation several times during the slugfest in Jamestown. The ride back to Fargo was very gratifying, not only because

I had a good day at the plate, but more so because I had several timely hits that sparked the exciting come-from-behind win. It was easily the best feeling I had had so far in my short time with the team.

Our final exhibition game finally placed us in front of our fans at tiny Jack Williams Stadium, which we would continue to call home for a few more weeks until our luxurious new accommodations were finished. Thousands of fans packed the cramped stands, ready to rock the house. Maybe it doesn't compare to, say, a capacity crowd at Citizens Bank Park, but, believe me, six thousand folks aching to see baseball can sure make a lot of racket.

Even though this game wouldn't count in the standings, it remains one of my biggest thrills. Everyone knew that I was one of two homegrown players (Tony Kunka—Moorhead), and each time the P.A. announcer introduced me, the crowd cheered wildly. In the seventh inning, with the Winnipeg Goldeyes ahead by a run, I gave them something to really cheer about.

Pumped up from adrenaline, I sent the first pitch I saw over the left-center-field wall for a game-tying home run. The sound of the fans as the ball disappeared was deafening. I'd never experienced anything like it. We let the game slip away in the ninth, but, as in Perham and Jamestown, when the last out was made, the crowd rose to its feet in a standing ovation. It made me incredibly proud, not only to be a member of this franchise but to be able to say I was born and raised in the Fargo-Moorehead area.

★ II ★

THE 1996 regular season began in Sioux Falls, South Dakota, against the Canaries, who, despite their lightweight name, were a solid club. Several news crews from the Fargo-Moorhead area accompanied us there to cover the first professional baseball game the neighboring cities had seen since the Eisenhower administration.

Sioux Falls started right-hander Jamie Ybarra, the Northern League's 1994 rookie pitcher of the year. He'd spent 1995 playing for the Florida

Marlins' A-level team, but was back suiting up as a Canary again. Chad Akers, our shortstop, led off with a single. My job, as the number two hitter, was to advance him.

The infield was still damp from rain showers the day before, so a bunt was obviously in order. My execution was miserable—I popped the ball in the air, over the mound—but there was no quibbling with the result. The bunt-that-wasn't landed just beyond Ybarra's reach. In charged the alert third baseman, but he slipped on the wet turf and went down hard on his backside. There you had the second hit in RedHawks history. Cooperstown never asked for the ball; I can't imagine why not. We easily won the game 11–4 for our inaugural victory. The next day, though, we notched the franchise's first loss, and in heartbreaking fashion, too.

The series' third and final game would prove to be a turning point for my career. With the entire team on the bus and ready to head for the stadium, Simmy climbed on board, and he didn't look too happy. He informed us that our only catcher, Mike Crosby, had been signed by the Montreal organization and was already on a plane headed for the Expos' double-A farm team, the Harrisburg Senators. Such was the life of an independent-league manager: If a major-league organization came knocking for one of your men, that player was out the door in a flash.

The organization had been looking for a backup receiver since spring training, but it wasn't viewed as critical. Certainly we could get through the first week of the season without the starting catcher going down, or in this case, heading east.

"Okay, guys," Simmy said, "I'll be looking to get us a catcher for tomorrow's game, but someone has to step up and catch today. Who is it gonna be?" He might as well have asked for a volunteer to walk barefoot on a bed of hot coals. Come to think of it, given my previous experience behind the plate, that might be safer. Nevertheless, I hesitantly raised my hand and said in a small voice, "I'll do it."

Our manager knelt down in the aisle and clasped his hands together gratefully. "Bless you, Chris Coste," he said, beginning to weep. "I just know you're going to surprise us all and become another Mike Piazza." Just joking. Actually, Simmy just stared at me blankly. I did not take that as a vote of confidence, nor the fact that he stepped off the bus to call our general manager and pleaded with John Dittrich to track down a catcher el pronto.

The Canaries beat us again, this time 10–9, on a walk-off home run in the bottom of the ninth. I didn't commit any errors or passed balls, but I also didn't have any chances to prove to Doug that I could handle the position defensively. That would come the following day in Sioux City, Iowa.

The Explorers featured an experienced and speedy lineup. GM Dittrich was still bargain hunting for someone to replace Crosby, so I got the nod. Leadoff hitter Gerald Young got on base and tested me right away. Frankly, he must have wondered what the hell was going on. I was listed as the RedHawks' second baseman, but the last time he'd seen me, during spring training, I was standing on the mound. Now I was crouching behind home plate. Perhaps he thought I had an identical twin.

On the very next pitch, Young was winging it to second. But I got the ball off in a hurry and nailed him by two steps.

I assume the Explorers thought it was merely beginner's luck, because they attempted five steals. Only one runner would swipe second successfully. More important, I didn't allow any passed balls, and the pitchers didn't throw any wild pitches, both signs of a well-caught game. To add to my memorable day, I had two key hits to help us come from behind and beat Sioux City by a score of 8–6.

We all high-fived and slapped backs as we rolled into the visitors' clubhouse. The manager called me into his office. "Hey, Coaster," he said, "I gotta admit, I'm surprised. I caught for eight years in the minors, and I know how hard it is to catch at any level, but especially here. Great job, son. I gotta make a phone call right now, and I want you to hear it." He flipped open his overworked cell phone and punched in some numbers.

"Hi, John? Simmy here." He must have been calling the general manager. "You know how I told you to find another catcher? You can scratch that; Coste is gonna handle the job for now."

I was blown away. For a guy like Doug Simunic to put his trust in me bolstered my self-confidence like you wouldn't believe.

After a disappointing 2–4 road trip, we returned home for a three-game set against the league's other expansion franchise, the Madison

Black Wolf. It was a landmark moment for the organization and the whole community, as this was the first official home game. Unfortunately, we let down the sellout crowd by getting blown out, leaving Simmy in a terrible mood. He'd been handpicked by the RedHawks front office because of his talent fielding championship-level teams, and, simply put, he was under a lot of pressure to win the Northern League championship, as he'd done in just his second year of managing, with the 1994 Winnipeg Goldeyes. His 1993 and 1995 teams made it as far as the championship series but just missed winning it all.

He was expected to repeat that success in Fargo. Bruce Thom wasn't another George Steinbrenner—in no way was Simmy's job on the line after a mere seven games—but this was not the start that he or anyone else had envisioned. After the humiliating loss to Madison, Doug had some choice words for the team, most of them loud and profane. I mean, the man was just irate. Then he stormed out of the clubhouse and disappeared into his office with coaches Jeff Bittiger and Andy McCauley.

Now, Simmy was famous for parading around the locker room in his snug extended-leg BVDs. As he sat in his chair complaining aloud to Bitt and Andy about the team's play, he proceeded to disrobe down to his underwear. Then those came off, too. Now, that's nothing out of the ordinary, as players frequently walk around naked in the confines of the clubhouse. But Simmy was so worked up about the ugly loss that he rolled up the BVDs he'd been wearing for, oh, eight hours or so, and wiped the sweat off his face, completely oblivious that they were decorated with fresh skid marks. It sure didn't escape the attention of Bitt and Andy, who stared at their manager in awe. Finally, Doug stopped talking nonstop for the first time in probably twenty minutes, looked down at the BVDs in his hand, and shrugged. "What? Haven't you two ever seen a guy wipe his face with his ass before?"

Apparently Simmy's clubhouse scolding woke us up, as the RedHawks salvaged the last two game of the series. From there we went on a tear, winning eleven of our next thirteen while averaging ten runs per game. In one week I produced twelve hits, including two home runs, and suddenly my manager was telling anybody who would listen that I had the talent to eventually become a major-league catcher. The two of us grew so close that people started referring to me as Simmy's son. Quite a reversal from when he first met me.

Now if I could only survive physically. Catching is simply the most demanding position on the diamond. And if you're handling a pitcher with shaky control, prepare to be bruised and battered. In mid-June we were up in Thunder Bay, Canada, playing the Whiskey Jacks. Tim Smith, our top pitcher, was the starter. Tim could throw a nasty two-seam fastball consistently around ninety-five miles per hour plus a razor-sharp slider that was almost unhittable. However, the refugee from the Boston Red Sox minor-league system tended to lose command and throw a lot of balls in the dirt. The average dirt ball was not a major concern for most catchers, but Tim Smith's dirt balls were nowhere near average. If he wasn't on, you hobbled away from the field looking like you'd just gone twelve rounds with Chuck "The Iceman" Lidell.

It didn't take long to know which Tim Smith had come to work that day. In the bottom of the first inning, with a Whiskey Jack perched on third and two out, Tim peered in for the sign. Reluctantly, I put down three fingers, indicating slider. It was a risky call with a runner just ninety feet away, but it was his best pitch.

The second he released the ball, I realized it was coming in low, so I dropped to my knees, closed my eyes, and hoped for the best. Smith's slider had such movement that the batter swung mightily but missed just as the ball exploded in the dirt, kicking up shrapnel. Then it bounced up and caught me right in the chin, just below the mask. My inexperience was to blame: I should have remembered to tuck my chin into my chest, not turn away. The ball came to rest right in front of home plate—giving the appearance of a perfectly executed block. I smothered it and fired to first base in time for the final out, then hustled to the dugout.

Trainer Dave Buchholz met me just as I got to the steps. "That's a bad cut," he observed. The ricochet had opened up a bloody three-inch gash on my chin. Fortunately, it wasn't deep and wouldn't need stitches, so I was able to stay in the game. But my fun was only beginning. The leadoff hitter in the second inning fouled a ball squarely off my right shoulder, one of the few places not protected by the normally dependable chest protector. The pain was so severe that I didn't know if I would be able to throw the ball as far as the mound. But after a few practice tosses to Smith, I got back into my crouch.

Third inning, exact same thing happened involving the exact same spot. I could barely lift my right arm. The only reason I stayed in the game was that we had a commanding lead, and if a few opposing baserunners swiped a bag, so what? I soon came to realize that, once again, my lack of experience as a receiver was leaving me needlessly open to injury: I was hunched over too far, which exposed too much of the top of my shoulder.

My punishment wasn't over for the day. Not by a long shot. In the sixth inning, another Smith slider dive-bombed the dirt and came up to pop me under the chin again, drawing more blood; in fact, the umpire had to discard the red-streaked baseball. The play also cost me some enamel. I wasn't in a whole lot of pain, but when Simmy and the trainer came out to investigate, I assumed that my telling them I'd chipped two teeth would be grounds for mercifully being lifted from battle, allowing me to nurse my wounds in the clubhouse.

Nope. The front office still hadn't obtained a backup receiver. Simmy just looked at me and asked, "Well, can you finish the game?"

"I guess so." Like a trouper—or a dummy—I stayed in there. Finally, the bottom of the ninth rolled around, and I was praying for a quick one-two-three frame. No such luck. Almost made it unscathed, though. With just one out to go, the batter clipped a pitch straight into my groin. You *think* you know what pain is until you've taken a ball to the privates. The only way to describe it is to say that it felt like I put the end of my manhood up on a table and the world's strongest man took a sledgehammer and smashed it with one crushing blow. I had to jam my hand down my pants to make sure my manhood was still attached. I was so cross-eyed with pain that I overlooked the fact that my self-exam was being conducted at home plate in front of several thousand largely sympathetic yet amused spectators. At least the Thunder Bay ballpark's scoreboard didn't have a Jumbotron screen.

After the win, I practically sprinted for the bathroom to pee. It took two minutes for anything to happen. Then it felt like I was shooting fire. According to the trainer, the impact had swollen the urinary tract almost completely shut. I slowly, gingerly made my way to my locker, greeted by mocking jeers and cheers from my loving teammates. When I slid off my jockstrap, the plastic cup inside the sleeve fell to the floor in three pieces. I got some tape out of the trainer's room and taped the thing back together. I did intend to buy myself a replacement, but after one look at my first Red-Hawks paycheck—$250 or so after taxes for two weeks' work—I figured that our limited funds could be put to better use than a new nut cup. To this day, it remains the hardest-earned money I've ever made in my life.

★ III ★

WHEN the Saints came marching into town for three games in early July, we sat comfortably atop the Western Division. The series had been sold out since before the season began. However, St. Paul arrived without its two star attractions. Darryl Strawberry had just been signed by the New York Yankees, and would redeem himself and his career somewhat by helping the Bronx Bombers to their first title in fifteen years. Jack Morris decided to skip the trip because he wasn't slated to pitch; he'd retire for good before the year was out, but he still put up the lowest ERA in the league. The Fargo faithful showed up in full force anyway. These contests were to be the Northern League's version of the legendary scrapes between rivals the Yankees and the Red Sox: two teams battling it out to prove which one was the class of the league.

By this time, we had recently moved into our beautiful new 4,200-seat ballpark in North Fargo, which soon became known affectionately as "the nest." It was easily the best stadium in the league. The debut game, a 7–6 loss, remains one of the most memorable in RedHawks history on account of the on-field action—although it didn't involve baseball per se.

A rainstorm interrupted play in the sixth inning. We sat in the dugout, dispirited because we were behind at the time. But the fans? The whole stadium was dancing in the rain; it looked like Mardi Gras in New Orleans, just one big party. The team's music man, Jan Plaude, took notice of the crowd's energy and started blaring music over the P.A., everything from "YMCA" and "Sweet Caroline" to "Cotton Eye Joe" and Alabama's

"Cheap Seats." In the minors and independent leagues, more emphasis is placed on keeping folks entertained and showing them a good time at the ol' ballpark than it is in the big leagues, which is probably what so many people like about this kind of baseball experience. Accordingly, members of the front-office staff and the grounds crew ran out onto the tarp-covered field and started diving across the rain-drenched tarpaulin, getting soaked in the process. Everyone was cracking up.

Just then one of my teammates said, "Hey, Coaster, isn't that your fiancée running down the aisle?" I turned around, and, sure enough, here came Marcia. I could see where this was headed and let out an "Oh no."

My wife-to-be vaulted the barrier near the visiting team's dugout and rushed onto the field. She performed the night's best tarp slide, up and over the mound, scraping the side of her leg in the process. Then she got to her feet, with some embarrassment, and continued to go sliding on the slick, wet surface before being chased off by stadium security. "I've never seen that woman before in my life," I joked as she dashed back up the aisle. You can imagine the hard time my teammates gave me after that.

In spite of our coming up one run short, the rain delay seemed to form a kind of bond between the players and the fans, and from that day on it was clear that Fargo fans would be the most enthusiastic in the league. We were a month-plus into the season, and I'd never heard Darryl Motley, the former World Series hero, say how he felt about playing here. That night, while watching the crowd in high spirits, utterly oblivious to the rain, he remarked in amazement, "You know, Coastey, I am surprised. This is becoming one helluva good place to play! This is a big-league environment!" Coming from him, that was a ringing endorsement.

In game three against St. Paul, we trailed by one run in the bottom of the eighth but engineered a four-run comeback. I was already 1-for-2 with a double and a walk when I smacked a line drive that hugged the first-base line. The first baseman dove and got his glove on the ball, but deflected it about fifteen feet away into foul territory. While he scrambled for the errant ball, the pitcher and I were in a foot race to the bag. At the last second, I dove headfirst, in an attempt to get a hand in ahead of any tag.

They didn't get me out, but they got me, when the pitcher inadvertently stomped on my left hand with his cleat, breaking my little finger.

Blood was everywhere, and it hurt like hell, but I was more concerned about the injury possibly putting an end to my season. I was batting around .342 at the time, fifth best in the Northern League.

Dave Buchholz took me into the dugout to clean off the wound and asked if I could continue. As painful as it was, the surge of adrenaline made it somewhat tolerable, so I nodded yes. Dave wrapped up my hand, and I trotted out to first. On the very next pitch, our right fielder, Aaron Iatarola, brought me all the way home with a game-tying two-bagger to right center. When I got back to the dugout, gasping for breath, and gratefully sat down, I realized just how bad my finger was. I hadn't felt pain like this since—well, you know.

We went to the bottom of the ninth all tied. It had hurt so much to put on my catcher's glove for the top of the inning that I kept it on in the dugout in case the game went into extra innings. Which it appeared it would, as the Saints recorded two quick outs. Then Darryl Motley doubled, and left fielder Matt Rundels drew a walk. I strolled up to the plate determined to end this thing now—not only because I wanted us to win but because I couldn't bear the thought of having to try pulling that damn mitt over my injured hand. It took only one pitch for me to lace a single up the middle, scoring Motley with the winning run. The stadium exploded, and the team spilled out onto the field, ecstatic.

While everyone else celebrated, I spent the rest of the night at the hospital, where the team doctor confirmed that the pinkie had been fractured. But also, the nail bed had been torn and would have to be removed. Did you ever have stitches put in your nail bed? Ouch! When the painkillers wore off a few hours later, I couldn't *believe* the pain.

Two days later we went to Madison, Wisconsin, to play the Black Wolf. The pain and tenderness had actually intensified. When I took some swings during batting practice, not one ball left the infield in the air. I decided to change my approach at the plate. *Just make contact with the ball,* I told myself. *Don't worry about hitting it hard.* There was no need to worry about hitting it hard, because I *couldn't.*

The first pitch I saw was an outside slider, and with no ability to control my swing, I took what had to be the worst swing in my life. Strike. But I managed to get a piece of the next pitch and sent it up the middle for a seeing-eye single. Amazingly enough, despite my feeble stroke, I finished 3-for-5 with a single, a double, a three-run homer, and four runs batted in, boosting my average to .357. Only two ex–major leaguers were ahead of me in the batting-title race: Winnipeg's Terry Lee, the Northern League's 1995 batting champ and Most Valuable Player, and my teammate Darryl Motley. That night Darryl anointed me with a new nickname. He yelled across the happy locker room, "Hey, there's *hard-hittin' Chris Coste,* right there! Yep, that's your new nickname: hard-hittin' Chris Coste." And that's the handle I answered to for the rest of the season.

★ IV ★

UNFORTUNATELY, before long, the nickname no longer fit. For a righty hitter, the little finger on the left hand helps to anchor the bat. My pinkie was weak for several weeks. Unable to control my swing, I hacked wildly at bad pitches. My batting average plummeted, and my strikeout total soared. On a positive note, despite my struggles, the RedHawks kept winning. On July 18 we clinched the Western Division title for the first half of the season, assuring us a playoff spot. The Northern League divided the season into two halves of forty-two games each. At the end of the year, the two winners in each division faced off for the right to advance to the championship series.

By August, my finger felt better, but it took me a lot longer than that to get locked back in. Heading into the final fifteen games, my average had shrunk to .276, and the manager had dropped me to eighth in the batting order. Following my lucky 3-for-4 performance against Madison, I didn't manage another multihit performance for thirty games.

It all turned around during an August 21 series finale against the Saints. More specifically, in a St. Paul Chinese restaurant.

I was desperate to do something, anything, to break out of my slump. The afternoon of the Wednesday-night game, I went to lunch at a Chinese restaurant with some teammates. To tell the truth, I couldn't stand Chinese food, but I figured that, what the hell, maybe trying something new will help to change my karma. After we placed our orders, the conversation turned from cars, to hunting, to our own personal RedHawks baseball cards. Now, many of the guys had played professional baseball in the past and therefore this was nothing new to them. But I'd never had my own baseball card before, and here was another childhood fantasy of mine about to come true. I'd dreamed about seeing my picture on a card ever since I bought my first pack of Topps cards back in the late seventies, hoping I'd crack open the cellophane to find my hero, Reggie Jackson. It dawned on me that my card for 1997 would have this year's stats on it, and that made me upset. *How great would it look,* I thought, *if I could look at my card next season and see a number over .300.*

When the meal was over, not having enjoyed one bite of it, we all opened our fortune cookies. The slip of white paper inside mine read: "You may expect good fortune soon."

Ordinarily I would have tossed it in the trash; probably make a sarcastic joke. *But I was hitting only .276.* Maybe this fortune *would* be the start of good things to come. My superstitious nature getting the best of me, I immediately headed to a local mall, where I purchased two "good luck" necklaces at one of the kiosks there. They consisted of short leather ropes with a trinket attached: one a peace sign and the other a religious cross surrounded by red and black beads. If nothing else, at ten dollars each, they were sure to bring good luck to the manufacturer.

When I arrived at the ballpark, I learned that the game was to be broadcast back in Fargo, making it the first RedHawks game ever televised. *What a great time to break out of my slump,* I thought. *There will be thousands of fans watching on television.* I'd become something of a local celebrity over the season, and I certainly didn't want to embarrass myself at the plate again.

Hedging my bets, I wore both necklaces that night. My first at-bat produced a ringing double to right center. Hmmm, maybe there was something to this stuff after all. But my next two times up, I reverted back to my sorry midseason form, managing only two weak groundouts to short.

In the bottom of the eighth inning, something strange happened. With a Saint on first base and a 1–2 count on the batter, I went down to block a ball in the dirt. It found the necklace with the peace sign, breaking it into pieces and leaving only the necklace containing the cross. Also, one of the metal shards from the broken peace sign inflicted a small cut just below the neckline. We escaped the inning without any damage, and I came up to lead off the top of the ninth.

As I'm walking to the plate, wagging the bat in front of me, I notice what looks like a piece of trash on the ground. I reached down to stuff it in my back pocket, then realized that it was a playing card from one of the casinos in the area. And not just any card, but the queen of hearts, which is said to herald good news. I took this to be the final sign that I needed to turn things around: fortune cookie, lucky necklaces (all right, I admit that perhaps the peace sign necklace wasn't so lucky), and the unexpected TV broadcast back home.

The first pitch meandered outside the strike zone, but, trying to be aggressive, I lunged at it and hit a weak foul ball on the first-base side. A terrible swing. A few feet to the left, and it'd have been an easy out. I turned on the next offering and turned my season back around. There it flew, high and deep to left field. Gone! As I rounded the bases, a broad grin creasing my face, I couldn't help but think of the series of odd occurrences that day. Here's my interpretation: Perhaps the tiny cross felt that the other necklace wasn't worthy of hanging around the same neck, and so it saw to it that the metal peace sign broke apart. And the cut on my neck? A wake-up call of some kind.

Could I keep the good karma going, though? Back in Fargo, the Red-Hawks were slated to face the Sioux City Explorers, who had the worst pitching in the entire league. I stashed the queen of hearts in my back pocket, wore the necklace bearing the cross, and, for good measure, had the fortune taped inside my locker. My first time up, we'd loaded the bases. Digging into the batter's box, I silently repeated the fortune over and over: *You may expect good fortune soon. You may expect good fortune soon. You may expect good fortune soon.* On the third pitch, I cleared the bases with a booming double off the wall in right center. My good fortune indeed continued throughout the rest of the game: 4-for-4, two doubles, five runs batted in. I was back, baby! The way I felt at that moment, it seemed inconceivable to me that I would ever make an out again.

Over the next two games against Sioux City, I added five more hits, including two doubles, in seven at-bats, plus another two RBIs. For the first time in many weeks, I felt like I was once again contributing to the success of the team, which was on its way to a 27–15 second half (.643) for an overall record of 53–31, .631. Simmy's former team, the Winnipeg Goldeyes, kept pace with us all year, but we squeaked by in both halves, by one game and then by two.

I finished the regular season riding a thirteen-game hitting streak and took my average back up to a respectable .314—a number that would look pretty darn good on the back of my 1997 baseball card. Up until that day in St. Paul, I hadn't been very superstitious, at least not by ballplayers' standards. But for many years after that, I would always buy a new lucky necklace before spring training. And, years later, when I finally lost my ragged but prophetic slip of paper with the fortune on it, I replaced it with a new one. This fortune read: "Opportunity surrounds you if you know where to look." Maybe it wasn't as clear and concise as the original, but I kind of liked how it implied that we exert at least some control over our own fate. We just have to know where to look and how to spot our many positive opportunities.

In September the Fargo-Moorhead RedHawks overcame Winnipeg in an exciting divisional series. But the winners in the east, the St. Paul Saints, were just too strong and too experienced in postseason play. They swept us for their third league championship in four years. Still, it had been a great, fun season. I can remember Darryl Motley telling me at the end, "The only time I ever had this much fun playing baseball was with the Royals in 1985." The year they won it all. He admitted that he'd been bitterly disappointed when the Saints had traded him to Fargo before the '96 campaign. But now, having driven in a league-best 103 runs on a division winner playing in a brand-new stadium in front of the most appreciative fans ever to squeeze through a turnstile, he couldn't wait to come back in '97.

★ V ★

THAT'S always the big question when a baseball season ends, even a successful one: Which of your fellow teammates and coaches *won't* be back?

For that matter, will *you* be in the same uniform, or any uniform at all, come spring?

The next afternoon after our series loss to the Saints, we attended our last official team meeting of the year with Bruce Thom, John Dittrich, and the coaching staff. The atmosphere was heavy with mixed emotions as we faced the reality that many of the incredible friendships that took root at the first meeting back in May would be coming to an end. Some guys would be traded, others would decide they'd had enough of the life and retire, still others would, hopefully, catch on with a major-league organization.

Of course, you never come out and *say* that. In the locker room, as everyone's packing up their gear for the last time, you hear from all corners, "See ya next year." Maybe. Maybe not.

To lighten the mood, many of the guys reminisced about some of the funnier moments from the season. For instance, Tony Kunka told everyone about the joke Chad Akers pulled on him the first day of practice. Tony walked into the locker-room shower and started soaping up next to Akers. The shortstop from West Virginia had just gotten into town and hadn't even introduced himself to Tony yet. While Kunka is lathering up, Akers turns to him and says in a loud voice for everyone to hear: "Hey, buddy, I'm a little sore today. Do you think you can crack my back?" One can only imagine what went through Tony's mind when asked to crack a naked man's back.

Akers, who topped the league in runs scored, had his own story to tell. We were on a road trip to Thunder Bay, and our manager was in the middle of his daily pregame radio interview with broadcaster Jack Michaels. Akers, an all-star practical joker, rummaged through the trainer's bag, tore off a piece of athletic tape about six inches long, and quietly snuck underneath Simmy's metal folding chair. In stealthlike fashion, the shortstop stuck the tape under the bottom of the chair, then lit it on fire, in a variation of the traditional hot foot. As Jack kept Simmy busy answering questions, the flame made its way up the six inches of tape like a fuse and toward our manager's butt.

After about thirty seconds, the chair got so hot that smoke started to curl from the bottom of the chair, not to mention from Simmy's bottom.

The man was so busy talking, however, that he didn't realize his seat—both seats, actually—were on fire. His speech started to slur from the heat and the pain, but he assumed that he was suffering from an internal problem; maybe the burritos he'd eaten for lunch. Suddenly Simunic started to sweat profusely. Jack Michaels, who'd had to bite his tongue the whole time to keep from laughing, asked in a serious voice, "Doug, are you all right?"

"I'm not sure what's going on, Jack," Simmy groaned, "but I don't feel so good. Man, I've got a problem!" Finally he reached his boiling point, leaped out of the "inflamed" chair as if he'd been hot-wired, and yelled, "What the hell?! Jack, we're gonna have to do this some other time! I gotta go!" He raced through the dugout, into the clubhouse, and disappeared into the trainer's room to find Dave Buchholz. The entire team burst out laughing at the sight of our 250-pound manager flying out of his seat with a smoldering butt and yelling like a madman. By this time, the flame had actually burned a hole all the way through his polyester baseball pants. Only then did he realize that he'd been the victim of a clubhouse prank.

The stories could have gone on forever. Nineteen ninety-six had truly been a meaningful season for everyone on the RedHawks, from those of us who were just starting out in professional baseball to the veterans whose careers were at a crossroads. We made that final meeting last as long as we could; we didn't want the season to end.

CHAPTER 8

Big Fish in a Small Pond

★ I ★

THE first few weeks after the season were tough to handle. I'd gotten used to a wonderful lifestyle that I didn't want to end. During the season, I would usually wake up around ten in the morning, have a quick breakfast, watch some television, drive to the golf course for six to ten holes of golf, do lunch, and then drive to the ballpark, which is an incredible privilege in itself.

In the locker room, I'd joke around with the other players as we suited up for batting practice. Afterward, it was back to the clubhouse for an hour, eat a light snack, and usually laugh about Chad Akers's latest practical joke. Before you knew it, it was time for pregame warmups. Then we'd play baseball in a beautiful new stadium in front of a sellout crowd of 4,500 loyal hometown fans who begged for autographs before and after games. To top it all off, we'd find paychecks in our lockers twice a month, whether we won or lost. No, it wasn't a lot of money, but to a twenty-three-year-old, just getting paid to play baseball was a gift. Adjusting from that back to "civilian" life was, well, difficult.

One thing that helped ease the transition was the excitement of getting ready for my marriage to Marcia, on October 5. The wedding was to take place on the field at the RedHawks' ballpark. You don't even have to say it: *Why* would I want to get married in a baseball stadium, and *how* did I ever get my fiancée to agree? The answer was simple, for both of us.

Baseball had always been a huge part of my life. And now it had become a big part of her life as well, making it an obvious choice—at least, to me. Marcia, like most women, I think it's fair to say, had always dreamed of a traditional ceremony. After we discussed it, she agreed that this would definitely be more memorable. I wasn't sure if the RedHawks would go for the idea, but when I asked the team's GM for permission, he smiled and said, "I think it's great!"

In the weeks leading up to the wedding, whenever I was interviewed on radio or TV, I'd say, "Anyone who wants to come, feel free to show up." It was basically an open invitation. To be honest, I thought it would be nice if there were a lot of people in the stands, and, besides, you never know: You might get a lot more presents that way.

With my teammates gone for the winter, I enlisted a dozen of my high-school and college friends to wear RedHawks' uniforms. Didn't take much convincing: get to suit up and be on a real baseball field? Are you kidding? They were excited as hell!

Fortunately, Fargo's fickle fall weather cooperated with sunny skies and a balmy seventy-two degrees, so that about 750 people turned out. Marcia, in her white wedding gown, walked down the concrete aisle and onto the field. Then she passed beneath a canopy of twelve baseball bats, held aloft by six of my buddies on either side of her, before stopping at home plate, where her uniformed groom waited. For the record, Marcia did not slide into home.

Even the pastor worked the baseball theme into the ceremony. He drew a parallel between a successful marriage and a winning team, and how both depend on teamwork. To illustrate, he withdrew a baseball and tossed it to me. (Wonderful pastor, but not much of an arm.) Then I in turn tossed it to Marcia. Perfect.

☆ II ☆

TWO days after our wedding, I received a phone call from Doug Simunic, who'd deservedly been named the Northern League's skipper of the year. Before becoming a manager, he'd coached in the Los Angeles Dodgers' farm system. Simmy had pulled some strings with his former organization and had gotten me a chance to attend the final two weeks of the Dodgers' fall instructional league in Arizona. This was a good opportunity. Although it wouldn't lead to a contract with the club, I'd be able to work out and practice with its up-and-coming minor leaguers. Even better, the main instructor was former major-league catcher Mike Scioscia, who'd spent thirteen years behind the plate for the Dodgers before retiring in 1994.

For two weeks, I got the chance to work on my catching skills with Mike on a daily basis. Up until then, my only instruction, really, had come on the job. This was a golden opportunity to learn the finer points of receiving from one of the best catchers ever to play the position. I left Arizona a completely new baseball player, especially defensively. I still had a long way to go, but thanks to "Sosh," I now had a definitive path to follow.

Upon returning to Fargo, I took a job delivering computers for a local computer company. It was the perfect situation, because it allowed me to work out at the gym for two hours during my lunch break and was flexible enough that I could take time off whenever I needed to practice at Concordia College. Most of the deliveries were to elementary and junior high schools in the community, and since I'd become a local celebrity, every day I'd be besieged by kids wanting my autograph as if I were Tiger Woods or something. It made me feel like nothing short of a rock star. Sure, I was a big fish in a small pond, but I *liked* this pond. It didn't matter that my salary put my new bride and me somewhere around the poverty line; we lived rent free in the basement of her mother's house in South Fargo. I was content and had what I considered to be a great life. Then it got even better.

Just after Christmas, RedHawks general manager John Dittrich asked me to come to his office at the stadium. John and I had become good friends over the course of the season; truth be told, he was one of the few people in the front office who had faith in me. In fact, it was John who ordered Simmy to sign me to a contract and give me a fair shot in training camp. He was proud of my success in 1996 and believed that I had a good future with the team. But John also knew that the short season and low pay scale made it nearly impossible for someone to make a career out of playing in the Northern League.

"Coaster," John said, "I am not sure what you have planned for your future, but Simmy, Bitt, and I have come up with a good way to keep you around for a long time." Needless to say, he had my full and undivided attention. When he said that the club wanted to hire me as a full-time staff member, I was shocked.

"Here is what we have in mind," John continued. "Obviously, during the season you will play for the team, and that will be your only priority. But during the off-season, you will be here with the rest of the front office staff and help us with the continuing promotion of the team, ticket sales, personal appearances, marketing, and sales." He hadn't even mentioned the salary yet, but in all honesty, the words "When do I start!" were already on my lips. Somehow I restrained myself and managed to act nonchalant. "Okay," I said slowly, as if mulling over the offer. "What kind of pay are we looking at?"

Eighteen thousand dollars a year, said the GM, plus commissions. Still not a ton of money, but more than double my current annual income and more than I could have made doing anything else. There went my cool façade. It cost a local business $5,000 to have its ad posted on the outfield fence. For each one I sold, I would receive 10 percent. I would also be selling ad space in the program sold at home games. "Who in the Fargo-Moorhead area wouldn't want to buy something from you?" John said with a laugh. "You're Chris Coste."

This was too good to be true! Having a full-time job with the Red-Hawks made it easy to legitimize continuing to play professional baseball. Otherwise, unless I got signed by a major-league team, I would eventually have to give it up. It was a luxury no other Northern Leaguer had. I hadn't given up on the big-league dream at all, but I knew that the odds of becoming a major leaguer were less than one in a million. I was fine with that, because I still had what I considered a great path to follow.

Just before the 1997 season started, I was promoted to director of merchandising, which put me in charge of the souvenir shop at the stadium. RedHawks merchandise was a hot property around Fargo. My main duties consisted of designing and ordering new items and hiring a small staff to run the shop during the season. I didn't have to look far: Marcia, who'd just graduated from Moorhead State University with a degree in fitness and sports science, took over for me while I'd be playing baseball. It was a great situation for both of us, and we were as happy as could be.

When training camp began in May, I was in a totally different state of mind than the previous year. Then I was a nobody, a local guy who'd been signed purely because it made for a good story. Now I was a key member of the franchise: its starting catcher and number three hitter in the lineup. What a difference a year can make. The community continued to embrace the team, so that most of our games were sold out before the first pitch of the season.

The RedHawks jumped out to a strong start but faltered in June and the first half of July to finish third, eight and a half games behind our adversaries from the previous year, the Winnipeg Goldeyes. We were the model of mediocrity, winning as many as we lost. Fortunately, we had the best manager in the history of independent baseball. Simmy was able to use his connections to fill in our roster's weak spots with guys who'd once played in double-A or even triple-A ball. Right after the midseason all-star game in St. Paul, my first, the team went on a tear, playing at a .619 pace to barely slip past Winnipeg and into the divisionals.

For the second straight year, however, the RedHawks stalled in the postseason. We won the first two games against the Goldeyes, in their home ballpark, no less. Back at Newman Outdoor Field, we felt confident that we could put the Goldeyes away. We seemed to blow a tire in game number three and never regained control; Winnipeg got rolling, and we couldn't stop their momentum as they spanked us three games straight in front of our always supportive but bewildered fans. It shouldn't have happened. Not only did we hold a 2–0 advantage, but Fargo definitely had the superior club *on paper*, to use the old baseball expression. Like stock certificates following a Wall Street crash, the paper was now worthless.

For me, the season was almost a repeat of 1996: hot, cold, hot. Through the first two weeks, I was atop the league in batting average and doubles, only to slow down around the midseason mark. But a solid finish brought me back up to a .312 BA and twelve home runs. In the postseason, I was named the Northern League's best catcher. Except for our disappointing performance in the playoffs, all in all it was an excellent season. I'd pretty much put my fantasies of getting to the big leagues on a shelf; as far as I was concerned, life was as good as it could get. Besides, in Fargo, where I'd become the de facto face of the RedHawks, I already felt like a big leaguer.

★ III ★

ONCE again the off-season added another facet to my career. RedHawks radio announcer Jack Michaels invited me to temporarily fill in for an ill colleague as host of a sports talk show on an all-sports AM radio station known as "The Ticket." I was nervous, as I think anyone with no on-air experience would be. But it sounded like fun, and, besides, it was only for a few days. For me, a confirmed baseball addict, the biggest challenge would be talking about other sports. Aside from a fundamental knowledge of the goings-on in the National Football League, I was thoroughly unschooled in college football and pro basketball. I was fairly fluent in hockey, but, surprisingly, the sport had never really caught on in our part of North Dakota.

I needn't have worried. My three days on The Ticket were a blast. When the host decided not to return, Michaels asked me to take it over as a full-time gig. I was stunned. This wasn't just any time slot, it was the coveted four-to-six afternoon drive-time show, the most listened-to shift of the day. I'd thought my life was charmed before. You mean to tell me I'd now get paid to play ball in the spring and summer, and then to yak about sports on the air the rest of the year? Apparently heaven was right here in Fargo. Marcia saw only one problem with my being behind a microphone: "You're way too good-looking for radio," she kidded. "You should hold out and try to get yourself on TV."

So during the 1997–98 off-season, I juggled the roles of ballplayer, merchandising director, radio announcer, and husband. On a typical day, my first stop was the stadium, to brainstorm new designs for T-shirts and other merchandise. Maybe make a few sales calls. Next it was on to the

YMCA for a two-hour workout, followed by a leisurely lunch with Marcia. Then I'd return to the ballpark so I could watch ESPN and study the sports section to prepare for my upcoming shift. Finally I'd hurry over to the radio station and discuss sports for two hours. What a life!

From the outset, listener response was amazing. The entire two hours were filled up with callers, making it easy for me to BS my way through the time slot. Plus, I found that a funny thing happened whenever I sat behind the microphone: It was as though my brain flipped on a switch, and I became this other person who could sound reasonably well-informed and articulate about sports. Even those "other" sports.

After a few weeks of doing the show, I decided to call it "Tough Guy Radio." As in: "Welcome to Tough Guy Radio here on 1280 AM, The Ticket. I'm your host, RedHawks catcher Chris Coste . . ." Or: "We've got Mike from Fargo on line one. Hey there, tough guy, whatcha got for us today?" After a while, the callers began applying the tough-guy tag to me. People would stop me in public and say, "Hey, Tough Guy! Loved the show today!"

Of course, once the season started, I had to take a leave of absence from the show, as Doug Simunic was rightly concerned about my many off-field responsibilities distracting me on the field. "Coaster," he said jokingly, tugging at his mustache, "when you're back there catching, I don't want you worried about how many caps you're selling in the souvenir shop or what's happening in women's fast-pitch softball in Nebraska!"

There was no need for him to worry. I felt more prepared, physically and mentally, for the upcoming season than I did the years before. In the past, my motivation was to claw my way into the clubhouse of a pro team. Now that I was there, naturally I wanted to keep the life Marcia and I enjoyed. Nothing, I vowed, was going to take this away from me.

From both a personal and team standpoint, 1998 was the best season yet. My defense had improved by leaps and bounds the past two seasons, and I finished with a .328 average and 10 home runs. For the second consecutive year, I was named to the Northern League postseason all-star team, and another honor came my way when I was voted All-Independent League catcher; this was an all-star team made up of the best players from all the independent leagues in the country.

As for the RedHawks, we played at the top of our game all year, posting a 64–21 record overall. That's a .753 winning percentage, meaning that we took three out of every four games, on average. About half the Western Division all-stars wore RedHawks uniforms that July; besides me, the lineup included Chad Akers, Jeff Bittiger, third baseman Johnny Knott, and pitcher Blaise Ilsley. The pesky Goldeyes played .674 ball. Ordinarily that's more than good enough to win you a pennant in any league, but in 1998 they finished a distant second, six and a half back.

The biggest step forward, though, was the way we steamrolled through the playoffs. First we beat Winnipeg three games to one, which set us up for another series against the pride of the league: St. Paul. This time we brought out the broom, disposing of the Saints in three. And we didn't just beat them, we *punished* them. Look at these scores: 17–6, 19–13, and, in the September 12 finale, 12–3. I excelled in both series, knocking in eight runs in one of the games, and took home the MVP award for the championship face-off, while delivering a title to Fargo won Doug Simunic a second manager of the year award.

And Bruce Thom delivered on the promise he'd made to Darryl Motley back in the spring, handing each member of the RedHawks an awesome championship ring.

☆ IV ☆

A FEW weeks after the season, I received a call from Bill Bryk, a scout with the Pittsburgh Pirates. Great, right? Just what I'd hungered for all these years. Well, although I was excited to know that I'd caught the eye of major-league scouts, the thought of possibly leaving the RedHawks—and the great life Marcia and I had in Fargo—was a bit daunting. Never thought I'd feel that way, but I did. Adding to my conflicted feelings, Marcia was pregnant! We'd found out only a few days earlier.

After giving it serious thought, this is what we decided: I'd just come off my best season ever, and I knew deep down inside that I could now compete with any catcher at the double-A or even triple-A level. Therefore, my wife urged me, "You have to give it a shot."

"Chris, you've never failed at any level," she went on. "I know you'll prove to the Pirates that you're the best minor-league catcher they've got. And who knows what could happen from there?" Of course, Marcia was biased. But after three straight seasons of hitting .312 or better, I could also rely on the opinions of my peers. I can't tell you the number of times that opposing players would come up to me and ask why I was still in independent ball. "Damn, Coste, you're better than most big-league catchers. You should at least be playing in triple-A." By this time, I wasn't about to disagree.

I met with Bill and auditioned briefly at bat and in the field. He got back in touch right away to tell me that Pittsburgh would like to sign me. I could attend spring training and possibly win a catching spot at its double-A affiliate. To see what they were getting, the Pirates invited me to the final three weeks of their fall instructional league in Florida. Again, this should have thrilled me. But all I could think about was my pregnant wife being without me. Although I ultimately flew down there, my heart wasn't in it as much as it probably should have been.

During those three weeks, my defense shined; one coach claimed that I was the best receiver in the Pittsburgh system. Oddly enough, I struggled a bit at the plate. According to the encouraging coach, if I showed I could hit come spring training, he felt certain that I could climb the ladder—possibly even see action with the big club sometime during the 1999 season.

I was determined to "tear the cover off the ball," as he'd put it. So in addition to working in the RedHawks' front office, every day I'd spend two and a half hours in the YMCA weight room. By the time February rolled around, I'd gained ten pounds of hard muscle.

Leaving Marcia behind for spring training was incredibly difficult. Remember, for the past four years, I spent most of the year at home, and road trips never took me too far away. Now I was reporting with the pitchers in early March. Who knew when I'd be back again?

Once I arrived at the Pirates' minor-league complex in Bradenton, Florida, that became less of a concern. I appreciated the encouraging words of the instructional-league coach, but with so many catchers milling around training camp—I counted more than a dozen—it was immediately apparent that a guy from the lowly Northern League would have to homer practically every time up to gain serious consideration. As far as I could see, the Pirates already had their catchers for their double-A and triple-A teams. I came to find out that it was commonplace for a team to sign up extra catchers for spring training. Why? Because with so many pitchers in camp, they needed more guys *to catch them in the bullpen.*

Looking around me, I had to agree with the assessment of the coach I'd met in the instructional league: I was the best receiver there. But I think that the organization's decision-makers were blinded by my independent-league status. It's the only rational explanation for why my .420 average in thirty at-bats wasn't deemed good enough to earn me a job. Nor, apparently, was my having gunned down several would-be base stealers.

I should probably explain that each major-league organization has five or six minor-league teams, ranging from rookie ball, the lowest level in terms of skill and experience, to triple-A, one step below the big leagues. Not every player is considered a prospect, obviously, and so organizations fill in the rest of their rosters with "filler" players: guys who have to wait on the bench for an opportunity and then make the most of it. In other words, guys like me. Many times, the filler player is better than the prospect, who still needs time to develop. But since the prospect is seen as having more potential, he will receive more playing time—particularly if he's a high draft pick in whom the team has invested a lot of money. Once ballplayers reach triple-A, if they are not on the parent club's forty-man roster, it is extremely difficult to climb the final rung of the ladder to the big leagues. As in any line of work, other people's perceptions partly dictate how far you go. I wasn't on the Pirates' roster, which was another strike against me.

On the final day of spring training, I was approached by Marty Brown, the manager of the double-A Altoona Curve. He gestured at all the players on the field and said, "Coastey, you can do the math. We already have our two catchers, and our roster is all set, but I'll tell you what: I want to keep you around. You can catch and hit, and you definitely have a future in baseball as a catcher. The pitchers love throwing to you, and I don't want to lose you." Marty went on to tell me that the normal way to keep a guy like me around was to put me on the "phantom" disabled list; until June, when the rookie team's season commenced, I would belong to the club but without eating up a roster spot. So that was the choice I had to make: go to Altoona, Pennsylvania, but not be able to play, or accept my release and return to the RedHawks and my agreeable lifestyle in Fargo. And my wife, who by now was seven months pregnant.

At the time, the decision was easy. I went home, convinced it was the right thing to do. Except here's what happened over the next few months: Pittsburgh's double-A and triple-A teams both released catchers due to poor play, *and* not long after that, the Pirates' starting receiver, Jason Kendall, broke his ankle, KO-ing him for the rest of the season. Wait, it gets better: Less than a week after Kendall's injury, his backup, Keith Osik, strained a leg muscle. Pittsburgh was forced to call up a catcher from all the way down in A ball. If you heard crying coming from the basement of Marcia's mom's house, it wasn't a newborn—Marcia still had several weeks to go—it was me. Not really. But clearly I'd made a mistake in judgment, although, again, there was no way I could have known how things would unfold. I'm not saying I definitely would have gotten the call to the big leagues. However, I certainly would have gotten the chance to catch a lot in triple-A, which in turn would have put me on the team's radar and probably would have led to an invitation to the major-league camp in the spring of 2000.

☆ V ☆

AS disappointed as I was to have lost that opportunity, I was excited to be back in Fargo, especially with the 1999 Northern League season about to begin. Until then, I went back to working as the director of merchandising, and the old contentment returned. Then, on May 16, Marcia gave birth to our daughter, whom we named Casey. (No explanation should be necessary.) It was easily the most emotional and exciting day of my life and helped to put my recent career crisis in perspective. For after witnessing the birth of a child, I knew that there was nothing baseball could offer me that was nearly as precious.

Nineteen ninety-nine was a career best: I stroked sixteen home runs in addition to batting .335, and once again was recognized as the top receiver in the Northern League as well as in all of independent ball. The league had doubled in size by merging with the Northeast League. However, this was largely in name only. The long-standing Northern League now operated as the Northern League Central, with the same divisional configurations as before, while the eight former Northeast League franchises made up the Northern League East, also with two divisions of four teams each.

The RedHawks fell short of repeating as champions, but we still enjoyed an excellent year: 50–35, .588 overall. In the semifinals we flattened the Schaumburg Flyers three games to none, but then had the same fate meted out to us by our perennial adversaries (say it with me) the Winnipeg Goldeyes. They were eventually knocked off by a Northeast League club, the Albany-Colonie Diamond Dogs. John Dittrich was named general manager of the year, which said a lot about the organization and its prospects for 2000 and beyond.

After my experience with Pittsburgh, I'd made up my mind not to actively seek a job with a major-league organization. So, of course, two weeks after the '99 season ended, the Cleveland Indians got in touch. I wasn't home to take the call, which was just as well. I took two days to sort out my thoughts before calling them back. I was going to turn down any offer they might make. I had a lifetime job with a team I loved in a city I loved, I got to host my own radio show, and I still got to play baseball. There was no way I was going to uproot my wife and four-month-old Casey from our stable, blissful life.

At least, that was the plan.

I listened to what the Indians scout had to say, then respectfully declined his offer. He made it easy by admitting that the Indians hadn't even seen me play during the 1999 season, which told me that there was no serious opportunity for advancement here. Like the Pirates, they probably were just stocking up another warm body with a catcher's mitt for spring training.

A few days later I was contacted by an irate Doug Simunic.

"What the hell do you think you are doing?" he bellowed into the phone. "You turned them down? Are you joking?"

"Simmy, why bother? I would just be going to spring training, catch some bullpens, and get sent home at the end anyway. Why would I give up what I have here only to get screwed again? And you know it, too; I'll get screwed, just like always." I added that the money Cleveland offered, while representing an increase, was only for the short baseball season. In the end, it'd actually cost me money to accept the Indians' offer.

Doug was unmoved. "First of all," he huffed, "you are good enough to be in the big leagues right now, and the cream always rises to the top. You *will* rise to the top, you always have. But even with that, you are missing the point. Forget the money. The point is that this is why guys play independent baseball, to get shots like this. Any independent leaguer would die to have this opportunity."

He was right: This *was* the goal of an independent leaguer; however, I was not just any independent leaguer. My situation was different. But then Simmy said the one thing that made me rethink my decision.

"You know," he warned, "if you turn this down, you will wake up in your bed when you're fifty years old and wonder what might have been if you'd given it a shot. And you will regret it."

Aw, now why'd he have to go and lay that on me? It changed my outlook just like that. I called back the Indians and accepted their offer. Just like the previous spring training, I would report to spring training and hope to impress the decision-makers. They assured me that I would have a legitimate opportunity to win a starting job in double-A ball. I didn't buy *that;* I knew they were simply telling me what I wanted to hear. But if they were paying attention, it was realistic to believe that at least I could impress them, go to double-A, and, hopefully, play well enough during the season to make a compelling case for myself.

My off-season preparation was even more rigorous than the ones before. This year, I was doubly motivated. I didn't want to have to return to

Fargo a second spring in a row having failed to stick with a major-league organization. That was number one. Two, I felt that I represented the Northern League. *I* knew that on any given night, the caliber of play was as good as any game in triple-A ball. For me to fail would reflect poorly on the league and its players.

One thing that made spring training 2000 easier mentally than the year before was the fact that Marcia and Casey accompanied me down to Florida. My wife left her job as a physical therapy technician at a local hospital so we could all be together. I remember how alone and miserable I'd felt in Bradenton with the Pirates; with my mind now free to concentrate on baseball, I was ready for an eye-opening, mind-bending spring.

CHAPTER 9

Breakthrough Season

J UST like the Pirates, the Cleveland Indians' minor-league spring camp also resembled a catchers' convention. And, just as I'd experienced the year before, I arrived in Winter Haven, Florida, to discover that the organization's double-A and triple-A clubs had already tapped two receivers apiece for the 2000 season.

A few days into spring training, each player met briefly with the director of minor-league operations and the field coordinator, the two main guys responsible for sorting all these players into the different slots: A ball, triple-A, outright release, and so on. The purpose of the five-minute meeting was to let each player know exactly how the club viewed him and which job he was fighting for.

With me, the director quickly got to his point. "We pretty much have our catchers all set, but there is always room in the event of an injury," he said. "We like the way you swing the bat, and if you have a good spring, you will have a chance to make the double-A team."

Okay, fair enough. But then Jeff Datz, the field coordinator, caught me off-guard with the comment "We like the fact that you can play third and first base. Combine that with your ability to be a third-string catcher, and you have some value as a utility guy."

My heart sank. Third base? Third-string catcher? You've got to be kidding me. I'd never make it to the big leagues as a utility guy, because true utility players were usually middle infielders, and although I could play a capable second base, I knew they wouldn't consider me because of my lack of foot speed, at least compared to the athletes who usually play second and short. I couldn't help but feel that the Indians were blinded by my independent-league status. This was becoming old news.

I kept things interesting, though, taking off on one of the hottest streaks of my life. After roughly twenty-six at-bats, my average stood at an even .500, and the hits included a few homers and several for extra bases. As for my defense, I was nailing runners in virtually every game. However, the double-A manager, Eric Wedge, was still next door at the big-league camp and had yet to see me play.

Wedge finally arrived the final week, and his first order of business was to call us all together. He told us about himself: his nine years catching in the minors, his brief stints with the Boston Red Sox and the Colorado Rockies in the early 1990s, his managerial philosophy. He was only thirty-two, just five years older than me. One thing Eric stressed was that we could always come to him with our concerns. I decided to take him up on his word.

"Hey, Wedgy," I asked, "where do you see me fitting in around here?" Blunt and to the point.

"Well, Chris," he said thoughtfully, "I really haven't seen you play much, but from what I hear, I see you as a good third catcher option and a guy who can play a few different positions. I don't know if there will be room in double-A or not, but this last week of games will determine a lot."

"I know you haven't seen me play," I said, "but I am not a third catcher. In fact, I am not a utility guy. I guarantee you that I am better than any catcher this organization has, and that includes triple-A." Then I repeated the line I'd said to other skeptical managers throughout my career: "Just keep your eyes open, and I guarantee that I will prove it to you!" I wasn't trying to be cocky. But I was twenty-seven years old and had no hesitation about standing up for myself.

I came to find out later that another catcher in camp, Matt Nokes, had told Wedge nearly the same thing about me. I'd competed against Matt in the Northern League, where he'd gone to play following ten years in the big leagues. He made a heartfelt case on my behalf to Eric and the field coordinator, while several players listened in, telling them vehemently that "Coste is far better than anyone you guys have in camp. For him to not get a shot would be a travesty." Unfortunately, his kind words had no immediate effect, because on the last day of spring training, Eric Wedge posted a No Vacancy sign.

"Coastey, you know how things work," he began. "Right now we just don't have room for you on the roster, but I really want to keep you around on the phantom disabled list." He started to explain it to me, but I respectfully interrupted him and said that I was familiar with the concept.

"I know it doesn't seem like a good situation," Wedge added sympathetically, "but trust me, I know you can hit and you can catch, and although I can't make any promises, you will get a shot at some point. I know you have a wife and a daughter, and it might be tough to drag them around playing minor-league baseball. But like I said, I think you can be a hell of a player. Just be patient, and good things will happen."

It was frustrating to hear the same thing two years in a row. But after missing out on what could have been a huge opportunity with the Pirates in 1999, I decided to give it shot. Marcia, Casey, and I drove from Florida up to Akron, Ohio, home of the double-A Aeros, not sure what to expect. In baseball, though, you come to expect the unexpected. Before the first pitch of the season was even thrown, a player went down with an injury, and just like that, I was activated. I knew I wasn't going to play much, but if and when the time came, I would approach it like I always had, as if it were a tryout.

That opportunity arrived sooner than I thought, in the ninth inning of the final game of the Aeros' first homestand. We were getting blown out by the Bowie Baysox, the Baltimore Orioles' representative in the Eastern League, on a snowy day with the temperature hovering around thirty degrees. I was huddled up on the bench in a thick parka, trying to keep warm, when the manager yelled from the other end of the dugout, "Coste! Grab a bat and get up there and pinch hit!" Took me a few moments to extricate myself from the winter wear, but I practically ran up to the plate.

Here we go, I thought. *My first at-bat in double-A.* After falling behind 1–2, I lined a slider to center field for only our second hit. In the context of the game, the single was meaningless, but not to me it wasn't.

To my surprise, the very next day Wedge penciled me in at first base, and seventh in the order. Another audition. I made the most of it, going 2-for-5 with a double and two RBIs. However, the Aeros roster was brimming with young prospects, so playing time remained hard to come by. Three weeks into the season, I'd seen action in only a handful of games. Still, whenever I did play, I'd get my hits, so that with ten games' worth of appearances under my belt, I was hitting around .450. It was only ten games, but, nevertheless, I was making a statement. If I was going to catch the eyes of the decision-makers, I couldn't hit .300. Not even .330. I needed to put up a ridiculous number like .400.

Even that didn't cut it, at least not for a twenty-seven-year-old nonpriority player. Just as I was starting to play more, Akron added an infielder, and as suddenly as I'd been added to the roster, I found myself back on the phantom disabled list. I didn't let it discourage me, though. As Wedge had told me as we were breaking spring camp, I reminded myself to be patient, and good things would happen. I *had* to remind myself, because I can't honestly say that I fully believed it.

A week later, another player injured himself—reactivate Coste. The first day Wedge put me in the lineup, I responded with three hits. Played four out of five games, still treading .400. Injured player all mended— back I went on the PDL. After a while, some of my teammates found it hard to look me in the eye, because it was apparent that I was getting screwed. Wedge himself waved me into his office one day to try to explain the bizarre situation.

"I know this is ridiculous," he began, "and believe me, if it was up to me, you would be batting third and playing every game at catcher, first, or third base. But it is not up to me. Like before, just be patient and do exactly what you have been doing. Good things are going to happen to you, I know it." I didn't mind him saying those words again; in fact, I needed to hear them.

A conversation with one of my teammates, second baseman Jeff Patzke, helped me to stay positive. Like me, Jeff was older than most of the other guys—he'd ascended as high as triple-A ball three times in the last three seasons, with the Toronto and Pittsburgh organizations—and although he was more talented and experienced than most of the prospects, he, too, warmed the bench. We were standing together in the outfield during batting practice when I asked him, "Hey, Jeff, you've had success in triple-A. Are you frustrated at not getting to play here in double-A?"

"No, not yet," he said evenly. I guess he sensed my frustration, because he added, "Just wait Coastey, things will change. It's early May, and after a while things will work themselves out; they always do. Either some guys will get injured or certain guys won't produce. I see it every season, and by June 1, the best players always work themselves into the starting lineup."

He was right. The next day Patzke started at shortstop and had three hits, forcing Wedge to start him the next day at second base. Another three hits. Ten days of production like that, and Jeff had anchored himself into the starting lineup, hitting over .330. Then an infielder at triple-A Buffalo in the International League got hurt, just like Jeff had predicted, and he got the call.

Things started to work out for me as well. Eventually I was reactivated—make that *re*-reactivated—and Eric wedged me into the lineup, mostly at first base or designated hitter. I heated right up again, collecting two or three hits per game. By now, the manager could see that my success was not some fluke, and so he moved me up to the number three spot in the order. It was all good, although I was somewhat disappointed at not getting to catch. That changed in mid-May, when Wedge rested the starting receiver and let me don the mask. I threw out a would-be base stealer in the bottom of the very first inning. Back in the dugout, I overheard a teammate rib the skipper, "Damn, Wedgy, maybe Nokes was right about Coastey. He nailed that guy at second by a mile!" I didn't understand the reference to Matt Nokes; that's when somebody filled me in on his supportive words from spring training.

My average still hovered around .400, and I'd amassed so much playing time that I was only twelve at-bats shy of qualifying for the lead in the
Eastern League batting race. That came to an abrupt end as soon as the
Cleveland brass came to town to check out their young prospects. I arrived at Canal Park to find my name down at the bottom of the lineup
card. Pretty odd, considering I was the hottest hitter in the league. But
the Indians' general manager, assistant GM, and several other members
of the front office weren't there to observe someone like me. Only in
baseball can you be considered old and creaky at just twenty-seven years
of age, if not younger. Good thing I had the manager in my corner; otherwise I wouldn't have been in the lineup at all that night. To put it
mildly, I was pissed off. But determined.

At-bat number one produced a line drive double to right center. In the
fourth inning, after working the count to 2–0, I stepped out of the box to
gather my thoughts. *I'm the number nine hitter; I know I'm going to get
a fastball down the middle. Swing as hard as you can, and aim for center
field.* When the pitcher released the ball, I lifted my front leg high in the
air, Kirby Puckett–style, drew the bat back, then whipped it around with
the most ferocious swing of my life. I heard the catcher yelp "Oh, damn!"

The enormous blast crashed into the Miller Lite sign 430 feet away in
center, easily the farthest ball I had ever hit. Later in the game, I was
holding a runner on at first. "What the hell are *you* doing hitting ninth?"
he wanted to know. "Are you the secret weapon or something?" I had to
laugh.

The big-league decision-makers returned to Cleveland, and I resumed
my more fitting place in the batting order. As of May 30 I was leading all
Indians minor-leaguers with a .352 batting average. Two days later, my
cell phone rang. I glanced at the caller ID: Eric Wedge.

"What's up, Wedgy?" I just hoped I wasn't doomed to return to the
bogus disabled list again.

"Hey, Coastey!" he said cheerily, "I've got some good news for you!
You're going to Buffalo. Triple-A. Congratulations, man!" Eric sounded
more excited than at any time during the two months I'd played for him.
He went on to explain that someone in the big leagues had gotten hurt,
and Russell Branyan, the Bisons' third baseman, had been called up to

take his place. Since I could play third and was on fire at the plate, the organization tabbed me to fill *his* spot on the roster.

Probably no other human being has been so excited to see the Buffalo skyline as I was. We made the three-hour drive in about two hours, somehow managing to evade the notoriously vigilant Ohio State Highway Patrol along Route 90. I'd heard about what a great city Buffalo was to play in and about its beautiful 18,000-seat baseball stadium, Dunn Tire Park. But when I walked through the center-field fence, 404 feet from home plate, and looked around, I was in awe. It was way bigger than any place I'd ever played before; standing there was like stepping into a whole different realm of baseball.

The 2000 Bisons were the best club in all of triple-A, so I realized that my playing time would be limited on such a talent-rich team. The last thing on my mind was getting an opportunity to catch. Buffalo had two receivers: six-foot-four Bobby Hughes, who'd played for the Milwaukee Brewers in the past two years; and Jesse Levis, a veteran of parts of eight seasons with the Brewers and the Indians. I'd just have to wait.

In mid-June, during a game in Indianapolis, I was sitting in the bullpen as usual. Hughes was involved in a collision at home plate, severely dislocating his shoulder. Our manager, Joel Skinner, himself a former major-league receiver with the White Sox, Yankees, and Indians, called on me to replace him, as Levis was nursing a banged-up finger. I went 1-for-2, and we won, so Skinner let me start the next day as well. Indianapolis, the new triple-A affiliate of the Milwaukee Brewers, was throwing tough twenty-one-year-old right-hander Ben Sheets.

I got good wood on the ball my first time up but lined out to second. My second at-bat came with two outs and two men on. The first two pitches were a trade-off: a strike and a ball. I decided to sit back and wait for a curve, Sheets's best pitch. Good guess. The next thing the young phenom knew, the ball landed on the berm well over the left-field fence for a three-run homer. Before we notched the final out, I'd added a single and a double.

None of this, however, was going to guarantee me a start the next day. I understood that. Sure enough, the lineup was posted, and I wasn't in it.

Our DH, Jeff Manto, couldn't help but voice his joking displeasure to the manager.

"Hey, Skinner!" he hollered from across the clubhouse. "Coste gets three hits and he's not in the lineup today? You've gotta be kidding me! What's wrong with this picture?!" It made me proud to know that I was starting to earn the respect of my triple-A teammates.

Over the next month, though, I continued to hit, and as a result, Skinner let me catch more often, sometimes up to four times a week. Also, we were winning games at a record pace, mainly due to our great pitching staff. By mid-July I was hitting over .350.

Which made it hard when a healthy Bobby Hughes was activated, relegating me not just to the bench but back down to Akron. I was a little upset at first because I'd gotten acclimated to being a part of an older and more experienced team. Speedy center fielder Dave Roberts, who would soon graduate to a career in the National League, came over to commiserate.

"Coastey, I know this is disappointing and you deserve to be catching for us here, but just be patient," he said, sounding an all too familiar refrain. "I know you can play in the big leagues, and I will tell you this: You are going to make a lot of money in this game someday—I guarantee it. One thing is for sure, you will never have to go back to independent baseball again." Dave Roberts: an awesome guy.

I finished the 2000 season with a combined .325 average at double-A and triple-A, tops among all Indians minor leaguers. While it was disappointing not to get called up again, for once I could look forward to an ample pay raise. I'd been hearing what minor league free agents like me were earning, and it blew me away. Nobody got rich in the minors, but a good triple-A player could make upward of $75,000 for five months of work. Not bad for getting to play baseball. To a guy who'd never made more than $1,500 a month in independent ball, it sounded like a fortune. Not that any team was going to offer me fifteen grand a month—not yet—but a salary about half as much was certainly feasible.

Before I could even test the market, I happily accepted the Indians' first offer: $7,000 a month plus an invitation to my first *major-league* spring training camp. The money couldn't have come at a better time.

Remember, when I played in Fargo, Marcia, Casey, and I lived with her mother rent free. In Akron, the three of us lived with a wonderful host family, also for free. We occupied their comfy basement apartment, which reminded us of home. (We keep in regular touch with the family to this day, and they come to visit when the Phillies are in Pittsburgh or some other city nearby.) In Buffalo, though, we stayed at the team hotel, a Holiday Inn. Nothing fancy, but costly nonetheless. Basically, we were in debt up to our ears. Now my family could breathe easier financially. And as trying as the 2000 season was at times, it placed me right on the doorstep of the major leagues.

CHAPTER 10

Minor-League Stiff

★ I ★

As part of the agreement with Cleveland, along with the salary and the invitation to major-league spring training, I got to play for the Indians in the Arizona Fall League, a league full of baseball's best young prospects. Although I was twenty-seven, six years older than the average player, the chance to participate in the league provided an opportunity not only to boost my status with the Tribe but to play in front of scouts, managers, and coaches from every major-league organization. Basically, if a ballplayer does well in the Arizona Fall League, he is deemed ready to play in the big leagues.

Unfortunately, during the last game, I ruptured the labrum in my right shoulder while making a throw from the warning track in right field. The only remedy for a torn labrum (a rim of cartilage that stabilizes the socket joint) is arthroscopic surgery followed by a lengthy recuperation. As a result, I wound up missing spring training alongside the Indians' major leaguers. Nevertheless, I considered myself lucky: Besides making a full recovery, I came to learn that the operation I underwent was less extensive than it usually is for this type of injury. For many ballplayers, a labral tear forces them into retirement. So it could have been a lot worse.

When I came off the disabled list in mid-April, the Indians gave me a choice: I could go to triple-A and play on a part-time basis or go to double-A and catch regularly. The decision was easy. In my mind, the only way I was ever going to get to the big leagues was by becoming exclusively a catcher like I was in the Northern League. I would never be a major-league utility man, and the best way to establish a reputation as a mainstream catcher was by going to double-A. If I could hit like I did the previous season and continue to prove I was good defensively, I knew I would eventually ascend to triple-A as a starting catcher. And starting triple-A receivers almost always get a shot in the big leagues, especially in September, when the big-league rosters expand from twenty-five to forty.

Oddly enough, I only spent one week in Akron before getting called up to Buffalo. The Bisons were banged up and needed some guys that could play multiple positions and hit. It was exciting to return to Buffalo, a strong veteran team with the likes of Dave Roberts, Dave Hollins, Tim Laker, Steve Woodard, and Charles Nagy, even though I knew that I would rarely get an opportunity to catch. However, a continuing rash of injuries opened up opportunities, until I was in the lineup more than five times a week. Making the situation sweeter still: Eric Wedge, my biggest advocate in the Cleveland organization, had become the Bisons' manager over the winter.

I've always seen myself going into managing whenever my playing days are over. I figure I could make a good one, because I could look around a clubhouse and relate to practically every guy in it. I've played eight out of nine positions, I've been the best hitter on a team, the worst hitter, I speak fluent Spanish, and I've always been communicative and open-minded. The best managers, like Eric Wedge, who was awesome to play for, usually exhibit those latter two traits. You always knew where you stood with him, and you felt that his door was always open.

I got off to a rocky start in Buffalo, hitting a measly .255 with only two home runs at the all-star break. Even stars have off-years, but I couldn't afford it; just one poor season could kill the big-league dream, plain and simple. Fortunately, things changed for the better beginning with the first game following the break. My first time up, I blooped a single to center, which always feels like a gift. Then I finished the game with a blooper into the right-field corner for a triple.

They say that good luck produces its own good luck. Brimming with confidence, I went on a thirteen-game tear of two or three hits per game, which raised my average to over .290. But the last month of the season, I broke a finger on my throwing hand when a runner barreled into me at home plate, putting me out of commission for two weeks. Considering how I'd been tearing the cover off the ball, it was a major setback. I finished 2001 with respectable numbers: .288 BA, 7 HR, 50 RBI in 75 games and 271 at-bats. But, again, for someone trying to shake the albatross-like label of Former Independent League Player, respectable wasn't good enough to call attention to myself. Based on my overall performance, if I were to sign with a team other than Cleveland for the following year, I would most certainly make less money and have to prove myself all over again. At least the Indians knew what kind of hitter I was. If I was ever going to climb to the big leagues, it would have to be with them. With this in mind, I re-signed with the Tribe, earning a raise to $8,500 per month and another invitation to major-league spring training. All in all, I considered myself very, very lucky.

✷ II ✷

SPRING training 2002 would be crucial, because for the first time, I'd have the chance to play in front of a major-league manager and his coaching staff. It was common knowledge among minor leaguers that you had virtually no shot at seeing action in the big leagues without first having taken part in training camp with the parent club. No coaching staff is going to call up players it's never seen or heard of before.

Charlie Manuel, in his third season piloting the Indians, would be going with the same catching duo as the year before: Einar Diaz and his backup, thirty-three-year-old Eddie Taubensee. Meanwhile, a prospect named Josh Bard was slated to start behind the plate for Buffalo. Since being acquired from the Colorado Rockies in mid-2001, he'd taken an elevator from A ball to double-A to triple-A all in the same year. So, it appeared that I would begin the season as the Bisons' backup receiver. My hope was that with Eric Wedge as manager again, he would find other ways to get me into the lineup more than just once a week. By this point in my career,

I knew that over the long haul, things did have a way of sorting themselves out, just as my Akron Aeros teammate Jeff Patzke had preached the year before. I would be patient and wait for a door to swing open.

Just two weeks into spring training, it looked like I wouldn't have too long a wait after all. Eddie Taubensee's back flared up on him, which allowed Bard to slip in and make a run for the backup job. He was on fire, rattling off one hit after another. If he got promoted to Cleveland, then I could become the starting catcher in Buffalo. With five days left before the start of the season, I probably prayed harder for Josh's continued success than he did.

Following a long day of practice at Winter Haven's Chain of Lakes Park, I got back to my hotel room and turned on the TV. I was absent-mindedly watching some sports channel, when my eye caught these words scrolling across the bottom of the screen: "Indians acquire catcher Eddie Perez from the Atlanta Braves for . . ." Needless to say, I was heartbroken. Josh Bard, too. For weeks it had appeared he was ready to board the luxury liner to the big leagues, now he'd be rowing his way back to Buffalo by dinghy. With me right beside him.

Eric Wedge helped to ease the disappointment. The first day of the 2002 campaign, he called me into his office for some words of encouragement. "Coastey, you know how things work," he said. "I'm going to do everything I can to get you in there as much as possible, but for now it might be only once a week behind the plate. Like I've told you many times in the past, I know you can catch, and I think that you can play in the big leagues. I don't know with which team, and I don't know when, but just sit back and be patient, like always."

Every time the manager put me into the lineup, I came up with two or three hits, so that in addition to my weekly appearance as Bard's backup, I logged plenty of games at third, first, or DH. (Before the year was out, I even put in two relief stints on the mound, winning one and losing one. Now, *that's* versatility.) April ended with my average exceeding .400, high enough to lead the league. I kept it up all summer, getting named to the triple-A all-star team—as starting catcher, no less. How ironic is that?

I was positive I'd be wearing an Indians uniform before the year was out. So were my teammates. Problem was, the big club's management didn't feel the same way. Apparently, they weren't comfortable with my level of defense. This was incredibly frustrating because my teammates, the guys who got to see me play on a daily basis, knew I was an above average defensive player at every position I played. After I played third base for a few games, several teammates said things like "Wow, Coastey, you might be the best third baseman in the league. . . . It's a shame nobody knows it." Then, after I played first base for a few games, other teammates would say the same thing: "Damn, Coastey, you might be one of the best first basemen in the league. . . . It's a shame no one knows it." Finally, after I got to catch, they would say the same thing again: "You might be one of the best catchers in the league—in fact, you might be the best overall defensive player in the league. . . . How do the Indians not know it?" Believe me, I never once considered myself the best defensive player in the league, but I did know that I was a lot better catcher than the Indians thought I was.

I've always believed that a player who can capably man several positions suffers from the old perception "jack of all trades, master of none," and once a player gets labeled, it can be extremely difficult to transcend people's perceptions. Like I said, frustrating. I also faced the same vicious cycle you find in any field, that of not being able to gain experience because of a lack of experience.

Looking back over my whole career, not just the 2002 season, I think that my somewhat unorthodox style turned off a lot of decision-makers. By that I mean that I was not what you'd call a textbook player. Take hitting, for example. As a kid, I'd never really been coached on the finer points of hitting, so I taught myself and developed a few odd habits. I enjoyed plenty of success, but whenever I'd hit a rough patch—and everybody does—it might make a scout assume that I couldn't handle major-league pitching. The same was true of my defense. Since I became a catcher relatively late, my mechanics weren't always sound. Therefore I didn't fit the typical profile of a major-league catcher.

Several of my managers, including Eric Wedge and Doug Simunic, had a similar comment about me. Basically it went like this: If a scout came to watch me for only a game or two, he probably wouldn't be all that impressed, because I'm not flashy like Manny Ramirez or physically imposing like his teammate David Ortiz. But if they stayed to watch me over the course of, say, thirty games, they would certainly see my value as a major-league-caliber player.

Clearly the Indians brass didn't stick around that long. Buffalo finished second in the International League, 87–57 (.604), four games behind the Scranton/Wilkes-Barre Barons. Despite my .318 average, 8 home runs, and 67 runs batted in, in 124 games, *and* being named team MVP, the parent club bypassed me and called up several other guys instead. It was confusing, and a little depressing, too. I didn't realize how much until Marcia, Casey, and I went to see the Tribe play against the Minnesota Twins at the Metrodome in late September.

I was excited to get to watch some of my former Bisons teammates in the big-league environment; during the season, we'd become like brothers. However, I have to admit that once I saw everyone out on the field, while I was sitting up in the stands, my happiness for them turned to despair. Of the ten players in the starting lineup for the Indians—including DH—seven of them were in Buffalo with me at some point during the season. What more could I do? How much better could I play? Why was I not down there with my buddies, having the time of my life?

At that moment, I felt as though this was probably the closest I would ever get to the big leagues: as a spectator. I couldn't hide my emotions from the person who knew me best. As tears began welling up in my eyes, Marcia leaned over and whispered, "I know you deserve to be out there. All those guys on the field know you deserve to be out there, too.

"But just remember," she added resolutely. "All these setbacks you've faced will make you appreciate it that much more when it does happen. And it will happen. You will make it!" Could any ballplayer possibly have a more sensitive, selfless, understanding, wonderful wife?

☆ III ☆

IT was flattering that the Indians wanted to re-sign me. As much as I loved playing in their organization, especially Buffalo, I felt that in order to become a major leaguer, I needed to go elsewhere. I mean, if being named an all-star and the Bisons' Most Valuable Player wasn't enough to earn me at least a September call-up, what would? And looking ahead to 2003, the Indians now had three catchers vying for two jobs. Down in triple-A, a prized catching prospect from Venezuela, Victor Martinez, was being groomed to take over the starting job, while first base and third base would belong to a pair of promising youngsters. Given all that, I'd be lucky to play once a week.

Fortunately, I could afford to contemplate taking my chances on finding another team. My successful 2002 season all but ensured that I would hear from several major-league organizations. And maybe one of them would view me as a legitimate catching candidate. In October I heard from Theo Epstein, assistant general manager of the Boston Red Sox. Only twenty-eight years old—the same age as me—he was just a month away from getting promoted to full-fledged GM, making him the youngest person in baseball history to hold that position.

"I wanted to know what your plans were for the 2003 season," he said, adding that he'd heard great things about my catching. "According to our scouting reports, you're more than capable of being a backup catcher in the big leagues." By no means was Epstein handing me the job of second-string receiver behind Jason Varitek; that role belonged to Doug Mirabelli. He was simply showing confidence in my ability behind the plate. If I signed with Boston, he continued, at the very least I would begin the season as the starting catcher for its triple-A affiliate in Pawtucket, Rhode Island. It was exactly the kind of offer I was seeking. Eleven thousand dollars a month plus a ten-grand signing bonus made it look even better. Without any hesitation, I signed with the Red Sox.

A few weeks later, I also inked a contract to play in the Mexican Winter Baseball League.

☆ IV ☆

MOST U.S. baseball fans aren't familiar with winter ball, so let me give you a rundown on what it's all about. Briefly, there are winter baseball leagues in Mexico, Puerto Rico, Venezuela, and the Dominican Republic.

The level of play is considered to be as good as or better than triple-A, and each league boasts the presence of several high-profile current or recent major leaguers such as David Ortiz, Vinny Castilla, Miguel Tejada, Tony Batista, Bobby Abreu, Ramon Hernandez, and Johan Santana. The other players in the league are made up of better-than-average triple-A players from the United States and Canada, or one of the other winter baseball countries.

Players sign on to play winter ball for a number of reasons. Some are looking to gain experience. Others, like Castilla and Tejada, do so because they are from the country in which they're playing. Also, since the caliber of play is high, and team rosters include several big names, the Latin American fans treat all of the players like big leaguers, especially the good American players. They support their teams through thick and thin and are as die-hard as any fans in the world.

In November 2002 I signed a contract to play third base for the Obregon Yaquis of the eight-team Mexican Pacific League. No, not *Yanquis*. Yaqui is the name of a river in northern Mexico, as well as a Native American tribe (no, not Cleveland) indigenous to the region. The MPL is structured much like the Northern League was, its season divided into two halves. I arrived just as Obregon was finishing up the first half. The team's two main catchers soon went down with injuries, so I volunteered to fill in behind the plate. At first this was hard for the players and fans to accept, as it is incredibly unusual in the MPL for a non-Mexican to play that particular position, on account of the language barrier. But in the end, the Mexican pitchers loved the way I caught and demanded that I remain the everyday receiver.

Obregon had stumbled to a sixth-place finish in the first half, prompting the front office to engineer some radical roster changes. We went on to win the second-half title, which put us in the playoffs as the number three seed. Fans all over the city treated us like celebrities everywhere we went. My Mexican teammates kept telling me that the city would go absolutely bonkers if we won the league title, for it had been over twenty years since the Yaquis had even made it to the league finals.

Bonkers? That had me a little concerned. I'd briefly played winter ball in Venezuela following the 1998 and 2001 seasons. During my first game there, in Caracas, I looked around the ballpark bulging with thirty thousand shrieking fans. Then my eyes caught sight of a dozen or so soldiers, dressed in army fatigues and clutching semiautomatic machine guns, stationed on the field. At their heels dutifully sat some of the meanest-looking German shepherds you've ever seen. I remember feeling alarmed not so much by the fact that I was surrounded by men with guns and attack dogs but by the fact that a baseball game in Caracas *required a military presence*. What would happen if you struck out?

Thankfully, the Mexican fans were every bit as passionate but non-threatening. The Yaquis narrowly won the first two rounds before coming up short in the third. Nevertheless, it was an awesome experience. During the playoffs—a total of seventeen games—I hit at a .385 clip, with seven home runs and eighteen runs batted in. The performance vaulted me into the Mexican equivalent of Michael Jordan, to the point where I couldn't walk down the street without being mobbed. Just the sight of me strolling out to the bullpen before games used to incite the crowd to start chanting my name—*"Coas-tey! Coas-tey! Coas-tey!"* the volume building slowly. I'd thrust my arms in the air as if conducting a human orchestra, and the sound would break like a storm. Sometimes there'd be something like seventeen thousand frenzied spectators chanting *"Coas-tey! Coas-tey! Coas-tey!"* Does wonders for your self-esteem, let me tell you! I couldn't wait to step onto the field each day, so I could get to experience what it must feel like to be a rock star.

Following a dramatic victory in the first playoff round, jubilant fans paraded through the city streets all night. Several of my teammates and I went into a restaurant to celebrate. When the crowd spotted us, they stormed into the place and started dancing on our tables. It was pure anarchy. But fun! We finished eating really, really late and walked back to our hotel. Roughly one thousand rabid fans were there waiting for us. Upon seeing me, they rushed up, surrounded me, and broke into song: *"Ole! Ole! Ole! Ole, Chris Coste! Ole! Ole! Ole! Ole, Chris Coste!"* This went on for about ten minutes. If only U.S. baseball scouts felt the same way.

Even after the Yaquis were stopped in the third round, the city treated us like kings, hosting a parade in our honor. Several thousand fans came out to show their appreciation. In eight years of playing professional baseball, my time in Obregon was the best experience I'd had.

Which is why I've gone back every winter since. Each year, my popularity there continues to rise. Go figure. At one point during the 2003 MPL season, my Mexican and American teammates kept joking that if I walked through downtown Obregon accompanied by the president of Mexico, the people would ignore him and crowd around me asking for autographs. I'm proud to say that I immersed myself in Mexican culture and learned to speak Spanish, becoming nearly fluent. Back in the States, my Hispanic teammates would force me to use what I'd learned, conversing with me only in Spanish.

Another thing I learned playing winter ball was how to throw out base runners from my knees. During a game against the Hermosillo Naranjeros, I was up at bat when their catcher, Iker Franco, gunned a throw to second from his knees, extinguishing the speedy Alfredo Amezaga. Whoa! I'd always been good at throwing from a standing position, but I realized at once that I needed to expand my repertoire defensively if I was going to attract attention. It took a while, but eventually it became one of my trademarks in the minor leagues.

The biggest benefit from playing in Mexico was that it prepared me for spring training in a way that working out in a gym could not. In 2003, for instance, I finished winter ball the first week in February—just in time for my thirtieth birthday. Red Sox camp opened in the middle of the month, so I was able to arrive more ready for baseball than many of the other guys.

On the negative side, being a Yaqui took me away from Marcia and Casey. If my U.S. and Mexican teams both made the playoffs, I would be home in Fargo for not even three weeks in an entire year. Sometimes I'd miss Thanksgiving *and* Christmas. So it was definitely a strain on our family at times. Now and then Casey would say to my wife, "I miss Daddy. I wish he was home with us." Marcia, though, helped her to understand that Daddy had to be away for long stretches. I think that because my wife was so supportive of my career, it made it easier for Casey to accept the circumstances. And remember, this was the only life our daughter had ever known. She wasn't in school yet, either, so the two of them could join me for all of spring training and come on road trips relatively close to home. We're fortunate to have a great extended family in Fargo, on both sides, so there's always been lots of family for them to lean on.

✸   V   ✸

I WAS excited to get to camp with the Bosox, although going abruptly from celebrity in Mexico to anonymity in Fort Myers, Florida, was a weird transition. Here I was just another minor-league free agent sharing a clubhouse with the likes of Jason Varitek, Manny Ramirez, Pedro Martinez, Tim Wakefield, Derek Lowe, and Nomar Garciaparra. I didn't care, though. For me this was the opportunity of a lifetime. If either Varitek or Doug Mirabelli got hurt, I was next in line to take his place. The thought of making the big leagues was awesome enough, but to achieve that as part of a team like the Boston Red Sox was beyond description. They'd played bridesmaid to the New York Yankees five years in a row, and the mood in camp was that 2003 was going to be their year for winning the American League East.

Playing time was hard to come by, as Jason and Doug wanted to get in lots of work. I wasn't worried, though. My measly eighteen at-bats were still more than any other catcher not named Varitek or Mirabelli, and I was ready to go to triple-A as Pawtucket's starting receiver and the big club's catcher-in-waiting. I would be like Prince Charles—except that he doesn't ascend to the throne of England if his mother the Queen happens to pull a hamstring.

Everything changed with one phone call from my agent, Pat Arter. I could tell from his subdued tone of voice that I probably wasn't going to like what I was about to hear.

"Chris," he said, "we have a problem. I just got off the phone with Theo Epstein, and I think you should call him.

"He wants to look for another catcher for triple-A."

What the—? Wanting answers, I immediately phoned the Boston GM. I can't remember word for word what he said to me, but the gist was that although I had *exceeded their expectations* and was a *much better defen-*

sive catcher than they'd thought, the organization didn't feel comfortable with me as the guy to step in should either Varitek or Mirabelli get hurt. "We want someone with more big-league experience." That much I recall. Also the fact that I wanted to reach through the phone line and shake Theo Epstein by the shoulders. I felt like a person who knew the answer to the World's Most Important Question but couldn't get anyone to listen. *Grrrrrr!* I flashed back to our conversation from the fall, when Epstein had told me that his scouting reports described me as a good defensive receiver who was more than capable of filling the role of a big-league backup catcher. Although I'd barely touched a bat all spring, I'd sparkled on defense, throwing out several runners and blocking the ball well.

Needless to say, I was confused and mightily pissed off. How did "You exceeded our expectations" and "You're much better defensively than we thought" square with "We want someone with more major-league experience"? I wanted to pull my hair out, although if this kind of thing kept up much longer, there'd probably be little need for that. Who cares about experience? Experience is nice, but what about actual production? When I got off the phone, I was as frustrated as I had ever been in my baseball life. And there was absolutely nothing I could do about it.

It became all too clear that I had made a mistake by signing with Boston, and there was nobody to blame but myself. Regardless of all the compliments that Theo Epstein paid me when he was pitching me on signing with the Sox, I should have known that a team as good (and as moneyed) as Boston would never call up a guy like me, especially to sub for a star like Jason Varitek. Imagine the bad press that would ensue if he went on the disabled list, and a thirty-year-old who'd spent his entire career in the minors—and two independent leagues, no less!—walked out from the wings. The fans would be calling for Epstein's head on a five-sided plate. Public perception matters in baseball just like in any other form of entertainment, so that a contending team with a sizable payroll would rather add someone with a major-league pedigree, even if he's less talented. Got that? Me neither.

My only hope was that Boston wouldn't be able to find a veteran receiver right away. Maybe I could get off to a ferocious start with Pawtucket, and the powers that be would realize, if belatedly, that I was their man.

That bubble burst like a wad of Bazooka, as the Sox picked up another catcher right away. Okay, on to plan B: I'll prove myself in triple-A—put up my best numbers ever!—the new guy won't work out as expected, and *then* they'll see the error of their ways and promote me. Brilliant!

Wrong again. *Nothing* went according to plan in 2003. On the second day of the Pawtucket Red Sox's season, Rochester Red Wings third baseman Shane Andrews banged into me while tagging up from third. He didn't hit me very hard, but he did land on top of my ankle, spraining it severely enough for me to miss three months of the season. (But you shoulda seen the other guy.) By the time I finally returned, I was odd-man-out; manager Buddy Bailey put me in occasionally at first base and as designated hitter, but rarely behind the plate.

The season mercifully drew to a close, forcing me to live with the ugliest statistics of my life: 98 AB, .188 BA, 1 HR, 8 RBI. Most painful of all was how far I'd fallen in just one year. The previous autumn, I'd enjoyed my best all-around season and appeared to have a lock on the starting-catcher's job with the Pawtucket Red Sox, who, as it turned out, topped their division in the International League.

Now I was thirty years old, coming off an injury-riddled season with numbers more embarrassing than an atrocious driver's license photo. What team would give me a chance now? I truly feared that my baseball career was on the ropes.

★ VI ★

RETURNING to the Mexican Pacific League, my main goal was to prove to baseball organizations at home that not only was I healthy but still a quality player. One of the many advantages of playing winter ball is that many major-league teams dispatch their scouts to Latin America to fill in their minor-league affiliates with free agents.

A good first month back in Obregon attracted the interest of the Milwaukee Brewers, who'd seen me play the past few seasons in triple-A and in Mexico. The organization wanted to sign me to a minor-league contract to play for its triple-A team in Indianapolis at $14,000 a month. I was shocked by the offer, in a good way. After my brutal 2003 season, I was just hoping to hang on in the minors, so I accepted at once. Signing with a National League organization would give me an edge: Since the senior circuit didn't have the designated-hitter rule, its teams would need more guys like me who could hit and play a few different positions—especially catcher.

Spring 2004 was a carbon copy of my preseasons with the Indians and the Red Sox, as I rarely got to play. However, I was fortunate once again to have a booster in manager Cecil Cooper, who'd been a fixture at first base for the Brewers in the 1970s and 1980s. He promised me that I was going to be an everyday player for him, including two or three starts behind the plate weekly. With that kind of opportunity, I had high hopes for the 2004 season and knew that I would not only make him a believer but the Brewers, too.

For the second year in a row, the injury bug bit. No matter how much you keep yourself in shape, the older you get, the more likely you are to break down. This time I strained an oblique, one of the deep abdominal muscles on the side of the stomach that help control breathing. Cost me five weeks. I'd been hitting around .295, which wasn't great, but it definitely put me in contention for a call-up in the event of an injury to a Brewers receiver. After the strain healed, however, the Indianapolis Indians decided to keep the catcher who'd arrived from double-A to take my place, giving us three catchers. Since I could play elsewhere on the diamond, Cecil started me mostly at first and third. In essence, I was a victim of my own versatility because if I could *only* catch, he would have been forced to give me time behind the plate. I finished 2004 at .294, yet the Brewers summoned one of the other Indians catchers to the big leagues, a guy who was hitting nearly fifty points less than me. But he had what most clubs look for in a backup catcher: major-league experience. Sigh.

After the season, it was back to Mexico with the hope that a major-league team would be interested in signing me to a minor-league contract. This time the Philadelphia Phillies, another NL team, came along. Their proposed salary constituted a $1,000-per-month pay cut, but at age thirty-two, I was in no position to haggle. And why would I? Just a few years earlier I was making less than $2,000 per month with the Indians, not to mention the small salaries I pulled in during my independent days.

My prospects with the Phillies seemed dimmer than they had been with the Brewers organization. Philadelphia had receivers Mike Lieberthal and Todd Pratt ready to be unwrapped for 2005. Lieberthal, a two-time all-star, had spent eleven seasons in a Phillies uniform; Pratt was a thirty-eight-year-old veteran. Even the catching contest at triple-A Scranton/Wilkes-Barre had already been won, by Carlos Ruiz, a twenty-six-year-old Panamanian, and A. J. Hinch. A.J. was about the same age as me and although he had never hit well in the big leagues, his experience provided great insurance for the Phillies should either Lieberthal or Pratt get hurt.

For the first time since establishing myself in 2000, I seriously worried whether or not I would make it out of spring training without getting cut. After all, Red Barons manager Gene Lamont had a twenty-five-year-old named Ryan Howard anchored at first base, while another prospect, Juan Richardson, from the Dominican Republic, would most likely start the season at the hot corner.

I focused on the one thing I could control: namely, my personal performance. Midway through camp, the Phillies realized that the twenty-four-year-old Richardson needed more seasoning in double-A. Here was my opening to plant myself at third and play so well that no one would be able to budge me.

Manager Gene Lamont, who'd guided the Chicago White Sox to two division titles before moving on to helm the Pittsburgh Pirates, played me every day and hit me in the middle of the batting order. He was very honest with me, which I appreciated. "I'd love to have you catch, but my hands are tied," he said candidly. The Phillies wanted to showcase Ruiz, a highly talented prospect who was being prepared to one day succeed Mike Lieberthal with the big club. Between him and Hinch, a quality backup, there just wasn't room for me to get any significant time behind the plate.

I had two main goals for 2005. One of them was fairly modest: just stay healthy! The other was to bulk up my home run total. Since the 2000 season, I'd earned a reputation as one of the better hitters in triple-A—always hovering around .300—but I'd never hit more than eight home runs in the minors. And although I drove in my fair share of runs and usually ranked among the league leaders in doubles, let me ask you this: If you're a fairly serious baseball fan, there's a pretty good chance that you can name last year's home run leaders. Okay, who took top honors in doubles? I think I've made my point. Well, home runs excite baseball scouts, too, not just those from the major leagues but from Japan, where I'd been looking to get a cleat in the door.

I vowed to try to hit a home run every time at bat, regardless of the count. In the past, if I had two strikes on me, I would shorten my swing and focus on putting the ball in play. Not anymore. The new approach paid off with fifteen round-trippers by the all-star break, to go along with a .285 average. It turned out that I didn't have to sacrifice hits for homers. And the Red Barons played in Scranton's cavernous Lackawanna County Stadium, one of the toughest parks in triple-A for smacking the long ball. For the second time in my career, I was named to the triple-A all-star team, but as a third baseman.

To tell you the truth, I'd rather have obtained the honor as a receiver. I considered 2005 my finest season so far—.292, 20 HR, 89 RBI—and yet unless I established myself primarily as a catcher, I would probably never play in the major leagues. I contemplated that reality after the season while lounging in my La-Z-Boy back home in Fargo. There I was, thirty-two years old, a career minor leaguer, faced with the decision of whether or not to play winter ball in Mexico. The thought of having to leave Marcia and Casey yet again for three more months was really gnawing at me, and for the first time in my life, I actually considered walking away from the game.

Baseball had given me a lot of joy, and since I'd reached the triple-A level, it had kept my family and me financially comfortable. But was that still enough to offset the frustrations and disappointments, and the interminable time away from home? I had to decide.

Toward the end of September, I was watching my favorite team, the Minnesota Twins, on TV. The catcher looked familiar, but it wasn't the team's regular, Joe Mauer.

I finally recognized him. "Hey! That's Chris Heintz!" Chris was a catcher-infielder I'd played against in triple-A, and I kind of identified with him. Like me, he was in his early thirties and had bounced around the minors a lot. He, too, had just come off his best season in triple-A, hitting .304 for the Rochester Red Wings of the International League, but he didn't get to catch very often because the parent club considered two other Red Wings receivers higher priorities. The difference between the two of us was that Chris got the September call-up, and I was at home watching him on TV. I felt a combination of happiness for Chris, and resentment for the way I had once again been overlooked as a catcher.

Suddenly Heintz laced an RBI double to left-center, jolting me out of my daze. In fact, I leaped out of the chair and pumped my fist in excitement. Now, I'd never talked to Chris Heintz off the baseball field. Yet I felt connected to him, as if we were brothers. While he was standing on second base in the middle of a major-league diamond, I was on the phone to my agent.

"Pat," I told him breathlessly, "we need to find a team like the Twins that would reward a successful triple-A season with a big-league call-up. We also need to find a team that would let me catch on occasion."

It was soon after this, in the winter of 2005–2006, that I received the offer to play in Korea. No, it wasn't the big leagues, but it represented the chance of a lifetime to finally become financially secure, and to play in a country known to have one of the premier foreign leagues. It could also lead to an opportunity to play in Japan in the future. At age thirty-three, it looked awfully good.

As you know, separate conversations with Pat and Marcia brought me to my senses. Then the Koreans rescinded their offer anyway. The Phillies wanted me back, and I decided to re-sign with them. I'd get to attend the major-league camp, and hopefully this time I'd get a legitimate chance to prove I could be a major-league catcher.

Throw in the towel now? No way.

CHAPTER 11

Getting the Call

As fate would have it, during spring training 2006 I came the closest I ever had to heading north with a major-league team.

For the record, I *did* accompany the Phillies to Citizens Bank Park in Philadelphia for two exhibition games against the Boston Red Sox in early April. It was there, just two days before the start of the regular season, that the ax fell when the club traded for David Dellucci, swallowing up my spot on the twenty-five-man roster. I had the kind of spring training that players in my situation only dream about: .463 BA, 3 HR, 11 RBI, with big hit after big hit.

In my eyes, I didn't just come close, I'd made the team. I *earned* the right to be on that team. But as in the past, even that standout performance wasn't enough for me to stick.

I chewed on all of these thoughts as I tossed my bags in the back of my Mitsubishi Endeavor and prepared to make the long—really, *really* long—drive to Scranton. The hardest part was knowing that I'd come so close. It felt like I'd been holding a winning lottery ticket in my hand, only to have it snatched away. At age thirty-three, what were my odds of ever putting together a spring training that spectacular again? Probably never. And still it wasn't good enough. The best word to describe my state of mind as I drove up the Pennsylvania Turnpike was *numb*. And tired.

To take my mind off things, once I arrived in Scranton, I headed for the golf course with my spring training roommates Clay Condrey and Brian Sanches, plus Sal Rende, the Red Barons' hitting coach. As Sal and I walked to our golf cart, I noticed the number on the side: 67. My original spring training number with the Phillies. Too bizarre. I immediately phoned Paul "Red" Brower, the Red Barons' clubhouse manager.

"Red," I asked, "could you please do me a favor and change my uniform number from ten to sixty-seven?" Apparently the lower number, more worthy of a big leaguer, just wasn't in the cards for Chris Coste. Maybe it had even jinxed my chances. I don't think that Red fully comprehended the odd request, but he said haltingly that he would take care of it.

A few days later, the entire team attended the annual banquet in our honor, along with eager fans and supporters from the local business community. One of the good things about playing in Scranton, just a hundred miles away from the City of Brotherly Love, was that most folks in the area were Phillies fans. So the Red Barons were just as beloved as their big-league brethren. Well over two thousand people crowded into the banquet at the Pittston Convention Hall. Apparently most of Scranton had been following my personal drama throughout the spring, because the warmth they showed me through the evening was incredible.

Then one of the key speakers stepped up to the microphone. "It's great to see all the fans and the Scranton players here tonight," he said, "but the one person who we all agree should not be here is Chris Coste."

Huh? *Did he just say my name?* I thought to myself.

He continued: "We all know that Chris should not be here. He deserves to be on the big-league team in Philly right now!" With that, the entire room erupted in applause. Then they stood as one, giving me a standing ovation. I was . . . blown away.

The next day we got on a plane for Columbus, Ohio, to open the season against the New York Yankees' triple-A Columbus Clippers. More than ever, I wanted to get off to a good start to prove that my spring num-

Mom and I in 1979.

A shot of me from my days in Fargo's Babe Ruth baseball league.
My swing was a whole lot better when I was thirteen.

Proof that I was once a pitcher, from my days with the amateur team in Glyndon, Minnesota, in 1992.

The Concordia College team in 1995. I'm in the front row, second from the left, with my hat on backward. We're smiling because we had clinched the conference title earlier that day.

The earliest photo of me catching. Our catcher had been signed by the Expos, and I volunteered to catch even though I'd caught only one game in my entire career. Talk about on-the-job training.
Julie's Photography

My wedding to Marcia in October 1996 on the field of RedHawk Stadium. The guys holding the bats are former college and American Legion teammates.
Julie's Photography

My Fargo teammates liked to play practical jokes. Here Chad Akers lights manager Doug Simunic's chair on fire while he's giving a radio interview.
Julie's Photography

In 1996 I developed my unorthodox style of hitting and had a breakthrough year. The catcher in this picture is Hector Villanueva, who had played in the majors for many years.
Julie's Photography

Me (second from left) with (from left to right) teammates Chad Akers, Johnny Knott, and Darryl Motley in 1998. We were the unofficial leaders of the RedHawks that year.
Julie's Photography

People were always confused about what my best position was, and the scoreboard operator at Citizens Bank Park was no exception.

I had always dreamed of playing in Fenway Park, and nothing, not even a rain delay, was going to keep me off the field. Shortly before my teammate Shane Victorino snapped this photo of me by the Green Monster, I spent a good twenty minutes running barefoot around the outfield in the rain. I felt like the luckiest fan in the world.

Shane Victorino

After every save, Tom Gordon would look up and thank God and then rub the catcher's head.

Miles Kennedy

Phillies fans often form small fan clubs for individual players. Here I am in 2007 with two members of the Coste Guard.

Rosemary Rahn

Tagging out Matt Kemp at the plate in 2007.

Miles Kennedy

When I started getting more popular, Reebok sent me a pair of custom spikes with my number on them, something usually reserved for more established players. My teammates David Dellucci and Abraham Nunez teased me that in their combined sixteen years they hadn't received this honor. So I got some stickers and custom-made a pair for each of them.

Here is one of my #27 spikes surrounded by one each of theirs.

I started my annual tradition of burning my bats in the family campfire in 1996 after my breakout year, and have done it every year since.

Marcia, Casey, and I at the Phillies' family day in 2007. Casey is always excited to get on the field because, as a girl, she can't go into the clubhouse the way the sons of players can.
Elizabeth Condrey

Four generations of the Coste family at home in Fargo. Gramps is holding the bat I used to get my first hit, Casey is holding my first home run ball, and Mom is holding the ball from my first hit.

bers weren't any fluke. After grounding out in my first at-bat, the next time up I doubled off the top of the center-field wall. Yep, this was going to be a great season. *Maybe I'll hit .400.* Given my track record, I had damn well better.

My solid start continued in Toledo, where we faced the Detroit Tigers' triple-A affiliate, the Mud Hens. I wasn't killing the ball like I had down in Florida, but I was getting my hits. The main disappointment, as always, it seemed, was precious little playing time behind the plate. Manager John Russell played me at first base, while Carlos Ruiz did all of the catching.

Then I fell into a horrendous slump. My strikeouts multiplied like never before. It was a struggle to get the ball out of the infield. Having been so locked in throughout the spring, I suddenly felt everything slipping away. I reminded myself, *I am a career .300 hitter! If there was ever a time* not *to go into a slump, it is now!* I didn't want to give the organization any ammunition that might reinforce its belief that I didn't belong in the big leagues. But I was trying so hard to blast five-hundred-foot home runs every time up that I wound up having the worst month of my career.

A few weeks into the season, Phillies starter Mike Lieberthal pulled a leg muscle, and Ruiz was called up to take his place. As frustrated as I felt with my lack of hitting and lack of opportunities to demonstrate my catching skills, I was incredibly happy for Carlos, who'd become a good friend.

In mid-May, things started to turn around, although it sure didn't seem like it at first. We'd had an afternoon game in Rochester, New York, against the Red Wings. I returned to my hotel room to find that it had been broken into. The thief had made off with over $2,000 worth of video and audio equipment. He might as well have stolen my catcher's mitt, too, because it sure wasn't doing me much good. But two days later I cracked my first homer of the season off righty J. D. Durbin. I'd almost forgotten what it felt like.

The next day, back home against Pawtucket, I did it again on a 3–1 count. Just as the pitcher was going into his windup, a spectator sitting right behind home plate yelled out, "Hey, pitcher, let's go, throw a strike! This guy has only one home run all year!" It made me mad as hell! I shut him up by connecting for one of the longest homers I'd ever hit. Then I collected two more hits, inching my average up to a robust .177.

The next morning, the ringing of my cell phone woke me from a sound sleep. I let the call go to voice mail, then checked caller ID. The digital readout said "John Russell." What on earth could he want? I keyed in the numbers and listened to his message.

"Hey, Coastey, this is J.R., John Russell. Give me a call back when you get a chance. We've got some things to talk about."

Oh no. J.R. spoke in a flat monotone voice, so I had no idea how to read him. But when you're hitting .177, and the manager calls, you immediately assume the worst. Had I been traded? That wouldn't be too terrible. Uh-oh, what about released? That could spell the end of my career.

I must have paced back and forth in my room for about twenty minutes, working up the courage to call John back.

"Hi, J.R.," I said calmly, and held my breath. "Coste here. What's up?"

Not wasting any time, he blurted, "Well, get your bags packed. You're going to Philadelphia."

"*What* was that?" Philadelphia? I honestly had no idea what he was talking about.

"You're going to Philadelphia," he repeated. "You're going to the big leagues!"

"What?! You're freakin' kidding me! Philadelphia? The big leagues?"

"Yes!" You could practically hear him smiling. "But you've got to hurry. Their game is at one thirty-five, and if you get going now, you can make it by game time."

I was convinced I was in another one of those dreams of mine. Why would the Phillies be calling me up now, when I was mired in such a slump? "What happened?" I asked. "Did someone get hurt?"

"Well, Fasano got a foul tip in the groin, and they're not sure if he is going on the disabled list or not, so they need a catcher to be there just in case."

That tempered my excitement a little bit. Oh, so I probably wouldn't be activated. I was officially in a "holding pattern." That's the term used by triple-A players to describe just this kind of situation, where a big leaguer is banged up, and someone from the minors joins the parent club in case the sidelined player goes on the DL. More often than not, the minor leaguer winds up commuting back to where he came from. Furthermore, Sal Fasano was plenty tough. No way would he ever be put on the disabled list unless he'd broken a bone or torn a muscle. Hit in the groin with a foul tip? It'd happened to me plenty of times. Ah, well, it looked like my trip to Philly would be a short one. Still, to know that I was on the organization's radar in spite of my poor start made me feel great.

Thirty minutes into my drive to Philadelphia, I decided to give Marcia a call to let her know what was going on. Only problem was, I didn't know how to tell her the good news without her getting too worked up and excited.

"Hi, Marcia," I began, "now, don't get too excited, but I am on my way to Philly. Fasano got banged up last night, so I am going on the holding pattern for him. I'll probably get there and have to turn right back around, because there is no way he will go on the disabled list."

Before she could answer, my call-waiting started beeping impatiently. I didn't recognize the number. "Honey, hold on for a second; let me get this."

"Hey, Chris, this is Ruben Amaro." The Phillies' assistant general manager. "First of all, congratulations. How much longer before you get to the stadium?"

"I should get there just before game time," I responded. I didn't even process the fact that he'd said "congratulations." You don't say that to someone who isn't even going to be activated.

"Okay, well, make sure you come in and see me before you put your uniform on and head to the dugout," he instructed. "You have to sign your contract first."

"Wait, what do you mean? Am I officially on the team?"

"Oh, no one told you? We had a guy retire today. You are officially a Philadelphia Phillie."

I had to brace my hands on the steering wheel, because otherwise I might have gone swerving right off the road.

Infielder Alex Gonzalez was the player who'd decided to retire after thirteen productive years in the big leagues. Now that he wasn't playing much, though, he wanted to get on with the next phase of his life. Ironically, I was two months older than Alex, so at the age of thirty-three, I was just beginning my big-league career, while his was just ending.

Oh, crap, Marcia was still on the other line. I clicked back over.

"Who was that?" she asked.

"That was Ruben, the assistant general manager," I said, trying to play it cool in order to build up the suspense. Yeah, right. The emotions were so overwhelming that I couldn't hide my excitement.

"Well, what did he say?"

"You are not going to believe this: I just got traded."

"Traded? What? To who?"

"To the Phillies!" I screamed. "We are going to the big leagues! I am a big leaguer!"

All I could hear on the other end of the phone was Marcia screaming with excitement. Just . . . screaming. Then she yelled out, "You did it! You did it, baby! I am so proud of you! You finally did it! You're a big leaguer!"

She continued to scream, cry, and laugh all at the same time. Hearing the emotion in her voice uncorked my own feelings, and the magnitude of what had just happened truly sank in. I had made the big leagues! After all this time, and countless heartbreaks. No more falling through the cracks. The day that I thought would never happen had finally come to pass.

Marcia cupped her hand over the phone as she relayed the news to our families. Coincidentally, Casey had just finished first grade, so the two of them were about to join me in Scranton for the rest of the summer. It just so happened that both of our families were throwing them a going-away party at a local hotel. My mom was there, Marcia's mom, my gramps, my sister-in-law, grandma, and four nieces.

At first, seeing the tears in her eyes, everyone worried that she had just received some horrible news. Far from it. "It's Chris," I heard her say. "He's calling from the car. He's going to Philadelphia! He's made it to the big leagues!" The room erupted in cheers and applause.

Just then my daughter yelled out, "Mommy! Mommy!" getting everyone's attention. "Mommy, that's what I wished for last week when I blew out the candles on my birthday cake! I wished for Daddy to get to the big leagues!"

Well, you can imagine what the scene must have looked like. Marcia swept up Casey in a big hug, tears were falling. I was crying, too. My wife and I had lived the dream together for exactly half our lives—seventeen years. And Casey was part of it, too. The exhilaration I felt at that moment could be matched only by the day she was born.

I had to laugh, though. Ever since my daughter was two years old, any-time that we wanted to dissuade her from asking for a certain toy, we'd always say, "If Daddy gets to the big leagues, we'll buy that for you." For more than five years now, she'd been programmed to correlate my making the big leagues with more toys for her. So for her to wish that Daddy would get to the big leagues couldn't have been more perfect.

As I neared Philly, I thought back to the last time I'd driven this same highway, but in the opposite direction. Then I was a minor leaguer, depressed and discouraged, thinking that perhaps I was on the road to oblivion. Now, just a month and a half later, here I was returning to Philadelphia as a bona fide major leaguer. What's more, the entire theme of my career had changed. Instead of fighting to make it to the big show, from now on my goal would be to succeed so that I'd never have to go back.

CHAPTER 12

The 2006
Big-League Season

★ I ★

THE drive from Scranton to Philly took ten hours. At least, that's what the two hours felt like. I pulled up to Citizens Bank Park just twenty minutes before game time. As I cruised around trying to find the players' parking garage, I took in the sight of thousands of fans piling into the stadium. Having been a player for so long, sometimes you forget what it's like to be a fan and immerse yourself in all the buzz and excitement of attending a baseball game. I had to smile at the fact that all these people were here to watch a major-league game that *I* was going to be a part of.

When I finally found the garage, I was stopped by Fred, the main parking attendant. In an intrusive tone of voice, he demanded, "Do you have a pass to get in here?"

"No. I am Chris Coste. I just got called up from the minor leagues."

"Well," he said, "if you don't have a pass, I can't let you in. That's the rules."

"What? I don't *have* a pass. You've got to have some sort of record, or somebody must have told you I was coming."

"No sir, no record of a minor leaguer coming in today, and I can't let just anybody in. For all I know," he added suspiciously, "you're just some fan trying to get into the stadium."

"You have *got* to be kidding me!" It took me a dozen years to make it to the big leagues, and when I finally get there, they don't believe that I'm a big leaguer! It was comical, sort of, but at the time, I wasn't laughing.

Fred's face split into a wicked grin. "I'm just giving you a hard time. *Of course* I know who you are. Welcome to the big leagues, Chris."

Funny. Very funny.

After parking amid the many Mercedes, Hummers, and Escalades, I heaved my three bags over my shoulder and made the long walk to the clubhouse. *I wonder how many other big leaguers have to carry their own bags like this,* I jokingly thought to myself.

When I reached the clubhouse, I was greeted immediately by Ruben Amaro Jr., contract in hand. The assistant GM had patrolled the outfield for the Phillies, Indians, and Angels in the 1990s, while his father, Ruben Amaro Sr., ate up ground balls as Philadelphia's starting shortstop three decades before that.

"This is one autograph I am sure you don't mind signing," he joked.

"No question about that!" I exclaimed. "You just tell me where to sign." I could have been consigning my soul to the devil for all I knew, given my excitement. Fortunately, it was a standard baseball contract calling for the major-league minimum annual salary of $327,000, prorated at a daily rate.

With the game only minutes away, I hurried to the clubhouse to suit up and make my way to the dugout. I wanted to soak it all in. After all, for all I knew, my call-up could be a short one, and each game had the potential to be my last.

And there it was! My official big-league jersey hanging on the outside of my big-league locker. What a beautiful sight! On the back, in bright red numbers: a 2 and a 7. Not 67, but 27, just as Frank Coppenbarger had promised on April 1 when it looked like I would claim the final spot on the roster. I couldn't help but appreciate the irony that the locker next to mine belonged to David Dellucci, the outfielder acquired from Texas later that same day, bumping me to the minors. April 1. April Fool's Day. I should have known.

I threw on my uniform in record time, then tore through the club-house, down the steps past the indoor batting cage and video room, and up the tunnel. The light from the brilliant afternoon sun grew brighter and brighter, and the clamor of 44,000-plus fans buzzed in my ears. Then it was up three steps and into the dugout, where the May sunshine hit me right in the eyes, practically blinding me. I stared into the farthest depths of the upper deck filled with cheering fans as Cory Lidle struck out Manny Ramirez with a fastball to end the top of the first inning. Just like the last time I'd been here, we were playing Boston.

Hitting coach Milt Thompson was the first person to see me. "Coastey!" he yelled, and with that, most of the players jumped off the bench and made their way over to offer congratulatory hugs and handshakes. Aaron Rowand lifted me up in a crushing bear hug. Then it was Jimmy Rollins's turn.

"Congrats, Coastey!" he said. "It's about time! This is a day that was long overdue!"

A TV cameraman picked up on the dramatic moment and panned the dugout, so that the congratulatory scene was broadcast on the stadium video board as well as on the air. Thousands of fans, seeing what was going on, began applauding, and I heard shouts of "All right, Chris Coste! Welcome to Philly!" and "Congrats, Chris! Welcome to the big leagues!" What a feeling. I can't tell you what happened the rest of the day, except that we beat Boston by a score of 10–5.

Our next game took us, by bus, to Shea Stadium to face the division-leading New York Mets. I couldn't help but think of the irony of the situation—after all the bus rides I endured throughout my minor-league career, my first big-league road trip was on a bus. When I walked into my Manhattan hotel room, I stared out the window at all the people and cars twenty-three stories below. I had stayed in some nice places in triple-A, *but this*—this was a big-league room in a swank hotel right in the middle of Times Square. I called Marcia back home in North Dakota. My stammering attempts to describe the view couldn't do it justice. I just hoped that I would stay in the big leagues long enough for her and Casey to get a taste of what it was like.

The next morning I ordered room service. Thirty bucks for a simple ham-and-cheese omelet seemed outrageous by minor-league standards—and certainly Fargo standards—but flush with $82 in meal money per diem, I figured I'd earned the right to overpay for breakfast my first day on the road. I really wanted to go out and explore Times Square, but never having been there before, I was afraid I might get lost. Next time, I promised myself.

Later in the afternoon Carlos Ruiz and I headed for Shea Stadium on the No. 7 train, the same train that Atlanta Braves reliever John Rocker had once made famous with derogatory remarks about its multicultural passengers. Although I had played baseball all over the planet, I felt like I had stepped into a totally different world, and I loved every minute of it.

During infield practice, I made sure to take ground balls deep behind first base—the very spot where a routine grounder off the bat of Mets outfielder Mookie Wilson slipped through Boston first baseman Bill Buckner's legs during the 1986 World Series. The once-mighty Mets had finished in the cellar in 2002 and 2003, and next to last in 2004. But under Willie Randolph, who'd never managed in the big leagues before, or anywhere else, for that matter, they climbed above .500 in 2005 and now were vying with the Atlanta Braves as Philadelphia's chief rivals in the National League East.

The Mets outlasted us in sixteen innings, 9–8. My nerves were on overdrive the last seven innings in anticipation of making my major-league debut as a pinch hitter. We'd run out of position players, so as soon as our reliever tired, I would undoubtedly go up to hit for him. Except that Ryan Madson went seven strong innings before finally giving up a game-ending home run to New York center fielder Carlos Beltran. Our bullpen had been depleted, aside from closer Tom Gordon. Therefore, if the game had gone on a few more innings, I might have been pressed into service on the mound, making my major-league debut as a pitcher. We didn't get that far, thanks to Beltran's blast, but I'd have been raring to go. In fact, only one week earlier, I'd thrown a scoreless inning for the Red Barons.

I had no illusions of seeing much action, especially since the guy I'd replaced on the roster, the now-retired Alex Gonzalez, could barely get into a game. But, as best as I could tell, my limited role as third-string catcher and right-handed pinch hitter, with sporadic duty at first and third, was safe for at least a few weeks. That assumption was reinforced after a

May 26 home game against the Brewers, when the club welcomed Aaron Rowand back from the DL and sent down outfielder Chris Roberson to triple-A. They could have sent me down after just five days in the big leagues but opted to keep me instead, undoubtedly because of my ability to catch.

I made my major-league debut in that night's game, a seesaw battle. We tied the score with two runs in the bottom of the ninth, but now trailed by one. Charlie Manuel sent me up to bat for Tom Gordon with one out and no one on. As I stood in the on-deck circle, the crowd started making some noise, and when I made my way to home plate, the stadium filled with cheers.

You know how nowadays stadiums blare a batter's favorite song over the public address system as he's stepping in? I had the perfect song chosen in advance: "Let Me Blow Ya Mind," by Eve with Gwen Stefani. Back when I was playing for the Buffalo Bisons, I made a deal with a teammate of mine named Anthony Medrano. The two of us had traveled similar paths, spending many years in the minors. We agreed that whichever one of us reached the major leagues first would have that song played before our first big-league at-bat. The lyrics go like this: "Now I got my foot through the door, and I ain't goin' nowhere / It took a while to get me here, and I'm gonna take my time."

As the song echoed throughout the ballpark, my main thought was to take the first pitch. I had a reputation in the minor leagues for being a notorious first-ball fastball hitter, but since this was my first major-league plate appearance, I thought it would be a good idea to see a pitch or two before cutting loose. However, the pitcher was flame-throwing right-hander Jose Capellan, brought in from the bullpen to face me. Since he was blessed with a fastball that regularly hit ninety-six miles an hour, sometimes higher, plus a wicked slider, I decided I'd better hack at the first fastball that came my way. I sure didn't want to tangle with that slider of his. He'd probably try to get ahead right away with a fastball, so why let the best pitch of the at-bat go by untouched?

I was right. Capellan reared back and blazed a fastball right down the heart of the plate, where my bat met it squarely, force against force. The center fielder raced back, looking up, but settled under the hard shot just short of the warning track. A 370-foot out. That's always discouraging, to be right on top of the ball and just not get it all. In an odd way, sometimes you prefer striking out to hitting one a mile in the air, in the same way that a blowout loss is sometimes easier to swallow than a one-run heartbreaker. Although my approach had been correct, I wished I hadn't swung at the first pitch. After all those years in the minor leagues, to make an out so quickly made it seem almost anticlimactic. Minutes later Milwaukee sealed its 6–5 victory.

After the game, Marcia and Casey were waiting for me in the family room located just off the players' parking garage. They'd flown in that afternoon and made it to the stadium right before the start of the game. I'd spotted them in their seats and waved from the dugout, but now we got to share our first group hug as a major-league family. As soon as I saw them burst out the doors of the family room and come running toward me, I dropped my bag and prepared to be bowled over by the two most important people in my life. We hugged one another tightly for over a minute—a minute filled with the happiest tears we have shared since Casey's birth—then walked to our car.

The first words out of Casey's mouth were: "Daddy, just how rich are we now?" Once again, Casey associated the big leagues with instant riches.

✮ II ✮

THE next night I got in the game as catcher by way of a double switch in the top of the fifth inning. I'd been down in the batting cage preparing for another possible pinch hitting opportunity, as our starting pitcher, Gavin Floyd, was due to lead off the bottom half of the frame. But with the Brewers already ahead 6–2, and Floyd running into more trouble, Charlie pulled him in favor of reliever Geoff Geary. At the same time, he inserted me into the pitcher's spot in the batting order.

I scrambled frantically to put on my catcher's gear (first I had to find it), then jogged out to the mound to discuss the situation with Geoff. I'd seen him pitch on many occasions in the minors and knew exactly what kind of stuff he had. On the other hand, when he told me something about the signs he would use if a runner should get to second base, I had no idea what he was talking about.

"*What* signs with a man on second?" I'd assumed that, as is typically done, he would use the old "second sign—shake to the first sign" routine. I'll explain: Usually, if I flash three fingers, then one finger, then two fingers, the second one—one finger—is the hot sign. But if the pitcher shakes his head no, then the first sign of the next group becomes the hot sign.

"We'll do touches," Geoff responded.

"Wha—? What is that, exactly?" I knew that several of the Phillies' relief pitchers used a complicated system of "touches." Here the catcher signals the pitcher by touching one of three predesignated places on his body. More often than not, the head signifies sign one (whatever sign one is; say, fastball); the chest for sign two; and the knee for sign three. It's just another way for the battery to communicate in code, while making it harder for the opposing team to steal your signs and therefore know which pitch is coming. Now you know not only how signs work in baseball but why most sane folks never want to play catcher. The problem was, I'd never done touches in the minors. Since each reliever did it differently, there was no way I could learn Geoff's system right then and there.

"We'll do touches, but they will just be fakes," he said, determined to stay with his system.

"Hey, this is my first inning behind the plate in the big leagues! Let's just keep it simple. Go with the second sign, and if you shake, then it will be the first sign. After the inning, we can go over the signs again, but for now, there is *no way* my mind is going to understand anything you say!" I was stressed out enough, and the last thing I needed was more confusion.

Geoff went on to strike out Brewers catcher Damian Miller for the second out, bringing up outfielder Brady Clark with a man on first base. On the second pitch, the runner took off for second. Thinking that Clark wasn't going to swing, I reached out to catch the ball, which quickens your release by a millisecond or two. To my surprise, he swung and clipped the end of my mitt, grounding the ball weakly to third base for what should have been the third out. Our team headed for the dugout.

But since Clark's bat caught my glove, the umpire called catcher's inter-
ference and awarded him first base.

The scoreboard lit up "E2." Great. After just two hitters, my major-
league fielding percentage dropped by half to .500. You can imagine what
it felt like to be a rookie catching in the big leagues for the first time and
having to stand there while confusion reigned in the stands and my teammates had to return to their positions. It was easily the most embarrassing moment of my career.

Not a good way to start out, I thought to myself. Thankfully, the next
batter, Milwaukee's pitcher, rolled a squibbler to third for out number
three. No harm done. Except to my ego.

I led off the bottom of the fifth, hoping to vindicate myself. I got on,
not by hitting the pitch but by getting hit *by* the pitch. I'll take it. One
pitch later I was trotting home ahead of Jimmy Rollins, who'd homered
to cut the deficit in two. My first run scored in the big leagues.

In the sixth inning, with the Phillies still behind 6–4, I came up with
runners in scoring position and one out. A fly ball would bring home a
run. So would a grounder to the right side. A base hit would tie the game.
Just don't strike out, just don't strike out, I admonished myself as I took
some practice cuts. Jose Capellan was on the mound again. This time the
tall Dominican elected to open with his slider. Strike one. Next pitch,
fouled down the third-base line. Then I blistered an 0–2 slider to the
third baseman. Although I hit the ball hard, I didn't advance the runners.
I didn't do my job. Then I struck out my last time up. A Ryan Howard
home run tied the game in the seventh, but we wound up on the short
end of a 9–6 game. I was still looking for my first major-league hit after
three at-bats.

The typical player doesn't have to worry that he's 0-for-3. When you're
a thirty-three-year-old rookie third-string receiver, however, 0-for-3
could equal two weeks' work. I didn't have the luxury of taking too much
more time to start hitting. Now that I'd made it to this level, I was not
about to return to the minors—at least not because my performance was
lacking. I frequently thought back to something that Eric Wedge used to
tell us again and again. He'd say, "A lot of players will get to the big

leagues, but it takes a real man to *stay* in the big leagues." I wanted to stay for the next ten years if I could.

When you're the twenty-fifth man on the team, the season resembles an obstacle course, with barriers placed here and there at random. My next major hurdle was Mike Lieberthal's coming off the disabled list. The Phillies had called up Carlos Ruiz to take his place when Mike was side-lined on May 5. So the front office had to decide which third-string catcher should it keep: Ruiz or Coste. Well, Carlos was still fairly young and considered a prospect. Therefore the thinking was to return him to triple-A, where he'd get to play regularly. Spending six days a week warming the bench could have a damaging effect on anyone's develop-ment. So I cleared this particular hurdle and got to remain in the big leagues.

At the beginning of June, we made the long trip west to face the Los Angeles Dodgers for a four-game series. It was my first official plane ride as a major leaguer (when you're new to it all, you keep a running tally of all the different "firsts," or at least I did), and I enjoyed every second of the five-hour chartered flight. Baseball still subscribes to certain proto-cols, and rookies have to know their place. Sometimes literally, as when you're traveling by plane. One of the veteran players told me that be-cause of my advanced age, I could sit wherever I wanted. "But," he added pointedly, "if you wanna play it safe, sit near the middle of the plane." I plopped down in the spacious exit row, where you get all that extra leg room. I popped a movie into my DVD player, then looked around the plane and promptly felt guilty over getting to ride in such a luxurious craft. I chuckled as I thought back to my last plane ride with the Red Barons just two weeks earlier—a commercial flight, which I spent in a middle seat, crammed between two random passengers.

We split the series. Can't tell you much about it, except that I extended my hitless career to 0-for-5. What I remember vividly was being handed my first bimonthly big-league paycheck. Even though it was prorated for one week, it was the biggest check I'd ever seen. And although I noticed the amount taken out for taxes, I didn't care. I'd promised myself long ago that if I ever made it to this point, I wouldn't complain about the tax-man. I'd been around enough major leaguers and coveted draft picks bitching and moaning about how Uncle Sam took too much of their hard-earned pay. Imagine being me, a guy who was once making $700 per month in the independent league, having to listen to some young hotshot whine about how $2 million of his $5 *million signing bonus* had gone to the government. I sure wasn't going to be that guy.

The next series took us to Arizona to face the Diamondbacks, and although I didn't play at all during the series, another injury to Mike Lieberthal further solidified my status. Not that you ever want to see a teammate get hurt. Instead of calling up Carlos Ruiz this time, the club brought back outfielder Chris Roberson. I reflected happily on how I should get a start behind the plate in the near future, as Sal Fasano, now the first-string catcher, would need a rest sooner or later.

That day came on June 10 against the Washington Nationals, with my spring-training friend Cory Lidle scheduled to pitch. The day before, we stood on the top step of the dugout, talking. "I'm gonna tell Charlie that I want you to catch me," he said. Although he thought Fasano was a better-than-average catcher, apparently the two of them just couldn't get on the same page during Cory's previous start, for whatever reason. Remembering our good professional rapport during the spring, he thought we'd work well together.

He was right. Cory threw six strong innings, surrendering two runs, his best outing in quite a while. Lidle, a native Californian, was in his tenth season and with his sixth big-league team. While never a star, he made for a capable third or fourth man in the starting rotation, regardless of the uniform he wore. He'd won thirteen games for the Phillies the year before, matching his career high from 2001. That year, playing in Oakland alongside his high-school buddy Jason Giambi, Cory put up a 13–6 record to go with a 3.59 ERA, as the A's made it to the postseason. I helped him out against the Nationals by throwing out Ryan Zimmerman on an attempted steal, snuffing a Washington rally.

Didn't help with the bat, though. Before the game, I'd joked to Fasano that I'd better go 3-for-3 if I didn't want Charlie to lift me for a pinch hitter in a crucial late-inning situation. Instead I took the collar, giving the manager little choice but to send up David Dellucci in the seventh. All he did was smack what turned out to be a game-winning two-run double for our only victory in the four-game set. I'd like to think I did my part by failing to get on base three times (although twice I lined out hard with runners aboard, and off Livan Hernandez, no less), so that Dellucci could get up there and win the game for us.

To tell you the truth, I wasn't too worried about my hitting. Charlie Manuel let me know that he had confidence in my bat, based on what he'd seen during the spring and the spring before that, when I hit .313 in limited action. So long as I handled the pitchers well and cut down runners on the base paths, he'd be satisfied. For now, at least.

As disappointing as the Washington trip was in terms of how the team fared and my lack of hitting, it remains one of my favorite memories. For the first time, Marcia and Casey came on the road with me. They'd joined me on dozens of trips in the minors, and although we'd stayed in plenty of nice hotels, the Grand Hyatt Washington, just a few blocks from the White House, was no "mere" Radisson or Crowne Plaza. The first time Casey wandered into the elegant multistory atrium and looked around at all the restaurants, escalators, and glass elevators (so much glass, in fact, that it resembles the glacial Fortress of Solitude from the movie *Superman*), she turned to Marcia and said, wide-eyed, "Mommy, I can get used to this!" Now, where had she heard *that* before?

★ III ★

A JUNE 15 home game against the Mets presented me with my next big opportunity to prove my value. Brett Myers, already the ace of the staff at age twenty-five, was pitching. Working with him can be a challenge because Brett calls his own game and is very intense. The guy knows what his next pitch should be before he's even gotten the ball back from his catcher. So while you don't need to call the game, you do need to think like Brett. He's got an assortment of quality pitches, and if you're not attuned to his philosophy of pitching, the big right-hander will shake you off until he sees the sign he wants. That may not seem like a big deal, but it is, in that it can disrupt a pitcher's rhythm.

Which is exactly what happened against the Mets. I'd hoped to have a great chemistry with Brett, who is very particular about his receiver. If he enjoyed pitching to me, perhaps I could become his personal catcher, much like Eddie Perez and perennial Cy Young winner Greg Maddux with the Atlanta Braves in the 1990s. Unfortunately, Brett and I were never able to get on the same page that night. Lose your rhythm, your location suffers, and balls start flying off the opposition's bats. Charlie had to go to the bullpen after only a few innings. It was Brett's poorest outing of the year, and I couldn't help but feel like it was my fault.

To make matters even worse, the game was televised on ESPN, so the whole country got to see me go 0-for-4, including hitting into a game-ending double play. Just a brutal night. The only bright spot for me was throwing out Mets shortstop Jose Reyes, the fastest man in baseball. In 2005 he swiped sixty bases in seventy-five attempts; this year he was on his way to sixty-four steals. Plus, I made the throw from my knees in the style of Tony Pena, the all-star catcher of the 1980s and 1990s, and later a coach and manager. Before the game started, I'd made it a point to inform the rest of the guys in the bullpen, "I'm going to throw out Reyes tonight. *From my knees.* Just watch me!" Judging from their eyeball rolling, they thought I was full of it. What they didn't know was that in the minors and in Mexico, I'd thrown out lots of runners that way the past few seasons. It helped that the pitcher at the time was Brian Sanches, who tends to be fairly quick to the plate. He gave me the perfect pitch: a fastball high and away in the strike zone. As soon as the ball left my hand, I knew I had him. Jimmy Rollins was there to make the perfect tag, and Reyes ran off the field looking slightly stunned. *I can't believe I just did that on ESPN,* I thought to myself.

"Damn! That was pretty impressive!" said the batter. It was none other than Paul Lo Duca, the Mets' all-star receiver. Pretty awesome.

Still, we lost, giving us our sixth defeat in our last six games. Granted, it was only mid-June, but the Phillies were falling far behind the Mets and the Braves in the division race. Philadelphia fans are notoriously . . . *direct,* and they let me know in no uncertain terms that they were losing patience with my failure to hit.

"Hey, Coste, you suck!" one screamed. "You don't deserve to wear a

major-league uniform! You'll be back in Scranton by tomorrow!" Ah, my
public.

I can handle any razzing a fan throws at me, but what made that hurt a
bit was the fact that Casey had left her seat and made her way down
toward the dugout, where she listened to this attack against her father,
which was to include several colorful obscenities.

Afterward, in the locker room, I was talking about my lack of offense
with several reporters, one of whom pointed out an interesting fact.
"You know, Chris," he said, "if I remember correctly, Willie Mays started
out 0-for-12 in his career as well." I responded by reminding them that
the Say Hey Kid was only nineteen years old at the time, not thirty-three
like me. I tried making light of my miserable start at the plate, but suddenly I was overwhelmed by the thought *What if I never get a hit in the
big leagues?*

Intellectually, I knew it was just a matter of time. But psychologically,
I seriously began to wonder if it would ever happen. That's a pretty common neurosis among hitters, even some of the best. When you're hitting
the ball real well, you can't imagine ever making another out. But when
you're stuck in a slump like a cat in quicksand, you start to worry that
you're never going to climb out of it. I'd never felt that way before, but I
did now.

Thank God the next day was payday. My first *full* major-league paycheck. Now, *this* was the biggest check I had ever earned, and I still was
not going to complain about the taxes. In the clubhouse before game
time, Brian Sanches and Clay Condrey, my roomies during spring training, marveled at all the numbers.

"Hey, Coastey, check this out!" Clay said as he proudly handed me his
pay stub.

I turned and gave mine to Sanches. "Hey, Brian, check *this* out!" Right
on cue, Brian cracked, "Hey, Clay, I got paid, too! Check *this* out!" The
three of us, longtime minor leaguers, could have kept it up all day. We
were making the major-league minimum, but as far as we were concerned, to earn that kind of money playing a game we loved was incomprehensible. It was crazy! We were all quickly humbled, however, when

Bobby Abreu, whose locker was next to mine, thrust his paycheck in our faces.

"Hey, guys," he said grinning, "check *this* out." I honestly can't remember the exact figure, but Bobby was making around $13 million a year, so use your imagination. Just be sure to imagine lots of zeros.

★ IV ★

THE first full round of interleague play was upon us. For the series opener against the Tampa Bay Devil Rays, I got the call to start behind the plate. Rookie Cole Hamels, a twenty-two-year-old lefty, didn't have his best stuff, and we fell behind early. It was almost enough to give a catcher a complex, especially when I lined out to center my first time up. The Philadelphia reporter who'd told me about Willie Mays going hitless in his first twelve at-bats made it a point to stress that in his thirteenth time at the plate, the New York Giants outfielder cracked a home run. No such luck for me.

I practically tiptoed into the batter's box in the fifth inning, by now convinced that I should tie a white flag around my bat and surrender. The score was seven–zip, with one out and Aaron Roward and David Bell on the bases. James Shields, the Rays' rookie right-hander, possessed a deceptive two-seamer that induced lots of ground balls. *Don't let me hit into a double play,* I prayed. Yep, really setting my sights high.

After working the count to one ball and two strikes, and fouling off a few tough pitches, I knew that Shields was eventually going to come in with the two-seamer. As he released the pitch, I pulled my hands in, swung down on the ball, and connected for a line-drive single up the middle, scoring Aaron from third. When I saw the ball bounce safely into center field, I felt as though a huge weight had been lifted off my shoulders and smacked my hands together in excitement. I wasn't even at first base yet, and I hoped that no one saw me do that. It doesn't looked good when you're down by six runs.

When I reached first, I looked up and saw my face filling the scoreboard. I did my best to suppress a smile. The umpire rolled the ball into the dugout, where Jimmy Rollins intercepted it and faked throwing it into the stands. If he had, I would have sprinted from first, dove into the sea of fans, and pried the ball loose from whoever had caught it. I was going to bring that sucker home and put it on my mantel. I couldn't believe it. I'd finally gotten a hit in the major leagues. And not just after thirteen at-bats but nearly thirteen years.

Then it dawned on me: I was still hitting just .071. Not even halfway toward the legendary Mendoza line. With that scary thought as motivation, I singled to left field my last time up. As heartening as the evening was from a personal perspective, we'd taken yet another loss. Furthermore, I felt badly about Cole Hamels's early exit. It was clear that the kid was destined for great things, and I hoped that I would get a chance to catch him again soon.

As you know by now, I've spent most of my career trying to prove myself to various coaches, scouts, and decision-makers of the front office. Add to that lengthy list Bill Conlin, veteran sportswriter for the *Philadelphia Daily News*. I was reading one of his columns when I came across an item suggesting that Sal Fasano and Chris Coste were the worst catching duo in Phillies history, or something like that. You try not to let that sort of thing bother you, but it's hard to develop a thick skin when you're looking to *climb* your way to .100. No one likes seeing themselves put down in the press, and it pissed me off. Which wasn't a bad thing. I wanted *so bad* to show everyone, not just Conlin, that I could be an asset to this team, not its weak link. People had doubted my ability before, and I'd always proved them wrong. I was determined to do so again.

With the season approaching the midway point, we traveled to Boston. I had been eyeing this trip on the schedule since getting called up on May 21 and just hoped that I would still be a Phillie when the time came, so I could get to play in historic Fenway Park—one of three ballparks I'd always wanted to visit. The other two were Yankee Stadium, not on the calendar for 2006, and Chicago's Wrigley Field. We'd be playing the Cubs there in late August.

So here I was at Fenway, which opened the same week as the sinking of the *Titanic*. Now if I could only get inside. I'd taxied to the ballpark with Scott Palmer, the team's director of public affairs. Problem was, neither of us knew where the players' entrance was, so for more than thirty minutes, the cabby circled the stadium (right on Lansdowne Street, right on Ipswich Street, right on Yawkey Way, right on Brookline Avenue, then repeat—see? I've got it memorized) in a pouring rain. Finally Scott and I jumped out of the taxi and ran from gate to gate, getting drenched in the process, until we finally stumbled on the cleverly hidden players' entrance. "Wow, Coastey," said Scott, pausing to catch his breath, "you spend all this time fighting to get to the big leagues, you finally make it, and you still had to fight to get into Fenway Park."

I laughed. "I wouldn't have it any other way. Besides, look how wet my shirt is. This is perfect."

"What do you mean?"

"Hey, not only is this shirt soaked with big-league rain, it is soaked with *Fenway Park* rain! I may never wash this shirt ever again!" So what if we were waterlogged? I was a major-league ballplayer standing in the locker room of the oldest ballpark in baseball. When I got called up, I promised myself that no matter how long or short a time I spent in the big leagues, I would remember to savor every moment. Each day, when I arrived at whatever stadium we were playing in, I would reflect on how lucky I was to be playing baseball and to be part of the game's history. With that in mind, I changed into a T-shirt and shorts and ran barefoot all over the soaking-wet outfield grass for something like twenty minutes. Anyone watching me probably thought I was an idiot, but I felt like the luckiest *fan* in the world. And despite playing the national pastime for a living, I still consider myself one of its biggest fans. How many people would have traded places with me at that moment?

I stopped before the Green Monster, the 37-foot wooden wall in left field, a mere 310 feet from home plate. (Some say 308 feet, others, 304 feet.) I had no idea it was covered with some kind of plastic (since 1976; before that, tin). As a result, the Green Monster is pockmarked with dents from the thousands of balls that have pelted it over the years, making it baseball's version of Grauman's Chinese Theatre. I mentally compiled a list of some of the greats who'd left their imprints: Wade Boggs, Don Mattingly, Thurman Munson, Mark McGwire, Cecil Fielder, Jim

Rice, and, of course, Hall of Famer Carl Yastrzemski, who stood sentry in front of the wall for twenty-three seasons, applying a geometry professor's skill in deftly playing caroms off its crazy angles.

The Phillies continued our losing ways, getting stomped 10–2 in the series opener. Game two produced another loss, but at least we were original about it. I'd taken over for Fasano, who'd come out for a pinch hitter. With the contest tied at three in the ninth, I came up against the Bosox's ferocious young closer, Jonathan Papelbon. I could see that he was throwing lots of fastballs early, then finishing off batters with his split-finger fastball, which was all but unhittable. My best bet, I figured, was to sit on the fastball. You've probably seen the way Papelbon holds the glove over his face on the mound, peering over the top for the catcher's sign with a sniper's intense gaze. On a 1–1 count, in came a ninety-six-mile-per-hour fastball, which I promptly laced up the middle for a single, my third big-league hit.

Jimmy Rollins, not wasting any time, stepped up and nailed a deep fly ball halfway up the Green Monster in left center. I was 95 percent sure that it was going to hit high enough not to be caught, but I halted for a half second to be sure. The pause led third-base coach Bill Dancy to stop me there. It may have looked as though I'd fallen for the fake from Red Sox center fielder Coco Crisp, but the truth was that I never even saw him. I'm just slow. Not Molina brothers slow, but close enough. When the next batter, Chase Utley, grounded to short, I broke for home. Jason Varitek was waiting for me, ball in hand, so I pulled my own fake-out. I made it appear as though I was going to barrel into the Boston catcher, who stood up to brace himself. Then I dropped down as low as possible and slid right between his legs, touching home plate before he applied the tag.

Out!

Out?!? No way! Either the umpire was blocked from seeing the play, or maybe he couldn't believe that someone so lead-footed on the base paths could sneak past an all-star receiver like Varitek. Especially given that he'd had me dead to rights. Damn! There was no point in a rookie's arguing the blown call, though. We went on to lose in the tenth on a two-run walk-off bomb to center field by David Ortiz. Big Papi hit the ball so far that ESPN must have shown his violent swing at least fifty times the rest of the season. There I was, watching helplessly from behind home plate as the pitch never made it to my mitt.

When I walked into the clubhouse the next day, I was pleasantly surprised to see that I'd be catching and batting ninth against the veteran knuckleballer Tim Wakefield, but much to my dismay, the game was rained out. I thought for sure that Charlie would insert Fasano back in the lineup, since he was well rested. However, when I got to Fenway the next day I found my name still penciled in the number nine spot.

As had been our pattern of late, we fell behind early. Down by six? The facial expressions in the dugout seemed to be saying "Not again!" That's how it is when you're losing. However, we constructed a five-run seventh. I was right in the middle of it, stroking a bases-loaded RBI single to right off longtime reliever Rudy Seanez. I added two more hits before the day was done, including my first extra-base hit, a double down the left-field line off Mike Timlin.

I was feeling pretty cocky. When lightning-fast Coco Crisp reached first on a swinging bunt, I informed the home plate umpire that I wasn't about to let the Red Sox center fielder run on me.

"You know what?" I said to him as Crisp stood alertly on first base, obviously looking to go. "I think I'll throw him out from my knees this time." The ump just smirked and slipped his face mask back on.

Sure enough, Crisp took off for second base on a hard slider from Ryan Franklin. Ordinarily the pitch comes in low and away, making it tough for a catcher to throw out a base stealer. But since I was throwing from my knees anyway, it turned out to be the perfect pitch, allowing me to keep low to the ground. The momentum from throwing jerked my head all the way to the left, so that I couldn't see the play. But when I heard the collective groan from the Fenway faithful, I knew we'd caught Crisp.

"Told ya!" I said to the ump nonchalantly. He mumbled a compliment under his breath. Just as when I'd thrown out the Mets' Jose Reyes from my knees, another first-rate catcher happened to be at bat: Doug Mirabelli. "That was pretty impressive!" he said, nodding his approval.

At long last I was beginning to redeem myself. It was hard to bask in the good feeling, though, as David Ortiz continued our downhill slide, this time chipping a game-winning RBI single in the bottom of the twelfth. I remember sitting dejectedly on the team bus back to the hotel, as disappointed as could be.

That was until I got a call from a friend back in Fargo named Greg Salvevold. He'd once played in the Devil Rays' farm system as well as various independent leagues around the country.

"Wow, what a day!" he enthused. "You must be on top of the world!"

"What do you mean?" I asked. "We lost again."

"I understand all that," Greg said, "but take a step back and think about it. You just played against the Red Sox at Fenway Park. *Fenway Park!* And you had three hits, all later in the game when it was important, *and* you threw out Coco Crisp from your knees! Are you kidding me? You're a big leaguer who had a great day! You played in the same game as Manny Ramirez, David Ortiz, Ryan Howard, Chase Utley, and Jason Varitek, and you, Chris Coste, were more productive than any of those guys!"

I understood where Greg was coming from. As a ballplayer himself, he would have given anything to be in my major-league shoes. And he was right. I'd just played in a big-league game at Fenway Park? It *had* been a great day, regardless of the final score.

☆ V ☆

OUR next series took us to another great baseball stadium, Oriole Park at Camden Yards, in Baltimore. Opened in 1992, the Orioles' home launched the trend of designing new stadiums with a traditional feel. I loved its red-brick façade and awesome playing surface—the antithesis of all those soulless cookie-cutter ballparks that sprang up in the 1970s. If I was down following the three-game sweep at the hands of the Red Sox, I was even more depressed after the O's won both ends of the opening day-night doubleheader. I contributed a quiet 2-for-4, raising my average to a respectable .296. But there was nothing respectable about the team's recent performance: seven losses in a row, and fifteen in our last eighteen games.

We flew from Baltimore to Toronto on June 30, not sure if we'd be al-

lowed back into the country. Sal Fasano started against the Blue Jays' talented right-hander A. J. Burnett. He sprained his left knee while running
out his second single in as many at-bats. Charlie Manuel called over to
me. "Coste! You're in." I took Sal's place at first base, still feeling stiff
from the night before. Jimmy Rollins gave me a chance to loosen up my
leg muscles by doubling me home two pitches later. I finished the day
2-for-3, one of the hits a key RBI double off Burnett in the fifth. More
important, we came away with an improbable 11–6 victory. I say "improbable" because the Phillies were short a starter, on account of the previous day's twin bill. Therefore it fell to the relief corps to work all nine
innings. In the end, A. J. Burnett was beaten by a parade of Aaron Fultz,
Geoff Geary, Ryan Franklin, Rheal Cormier, Arthur Rhodes, and Tom
Gordon.

To make the day even more memorable, we received our paychecks
after the game; my second full big-league check. I ripped open the enve-
lope and smiled in amazement when I saw the amount, just like I had
done the previous two times, only to catch myself as a thought entered
my mind—*Holy crap, look at the freaking taxes on this thing! Whoa, wait
a second, I promised myself I would never complain about the taxes, ever.
I am not going to start now. I am lucky to be getting this check!*

Fasano's sprained knee landed him on the DL, leaving Carlos Ruiz and
me as the only two catchers. I'd figured to start more often, but that wasn't
the case, as Carlos got the nod in all three games of a home series against
the Padres. Then I started the opening game of a weekend series against the
Pirates, our final three games before the all-star break.

I didn't make the most of the chance, going 0-for-4 in a 3–2 loss. Owing
to a mental condition I call "Twenty-fifth man paranoia," I worried that
perhaps Charlie would lose faith in me. After just one bad game? That
wasn't likely. But when you feel your future rides on every game, it's easy
to place too much importance on a single poor outing. To the manager's
credit, he put me right back in for Saturday's game. In the number six
spot, too, right behind Ryan Howard. This time I took full advantage by
going 2-for-3 with three RBI and propelling us to a 6–2 win.

When I got back to my hotel in New Jersey, just ten minutes from the
stadium, I turned on ESPN. For the first time since arriving in the big

leagues, I got to see highlights of myself on national television. (The Ortiz home run footage hardly counted as a highlight.) It was . . . *surreal.* Most unbelievable of all: The *SportsCenter* anchors pronounced my last name correctly. Casey was sitting next to me. She glanced up at the screen and saw the line score. "Coste, 2-for-3, 3 RBI."

"Daddy!" she yelled out. "That's our name right there! It said Coste right there on the screen!" It was definitely a proud moment for the Coste family.

Sunday morning I got to the stadium fully expecting Ruiz to be starting, the usual custom when a night game is followed by a day game. There was my name again, in the number six hole. Cole Hamels pitched well enough to earn the second win of his major-league career, while I had another big day at the plate, connecting for two big hits and driving in two runs including the go-ahead tally. For the second night in a row, I got to watch myself on ESPN.

Suddenly the media frenzy that had surrounded me in spring training revved up again. Down in Florida, I'd attracted lots of attention because the public and the press both love stories about underdogs. That certainly described me: a thirty-three-year-old rookie trying to make the major leagues after an eternity in the minors. Now that angle was old news. However, the fact that I was hitting a productive .311 at the all-star break was deemed newsworthy.

As good as things were going, there was still the chance that I could be living on borrowed time in the major leagues. After all, both Lieberthal and Fasano would be coming off the disabled list soon. I sidestepped one of those hurdles when Lieberthal was activated. The team opted to return Carlos Ruiz to Scranton/Wilkes-Barre for the same reason as before: He was Philadelphia's catcher of the future and needed steady work. So, for the time being, I was the backup to Lieberthal.

Little changed after the all-star break. We continued our losing ways, dropping the first two games against San Diego. In the finale, I caught Jon Lieber. Mike Thompson, a right-hander with a good two-seam fastball, was on the hill for the Padres, with my old buddy from Buffalo, Josh Bard, behind the plate. He knew that I liked to swing away at fastballs on the first pitch and therefore would never call for one. So when I saw

Thompson shake off Josh's first sign, I thought to myself, *Here comes a fastball*. And there it came. I kicked my front leg higher than usual and stepped into the ball, meeting it solidly. Off it rode into the second deck in left field to cut San Diego's lead to 3–1. It was one of the few times in my life that I knew the moment I'd hit the ball that it was destined for the seats. I dropped my bat and started my home run trot. It wasn't until I'd passed first base that I realized: my first major-league homer! I hoped that the fans at Petco Park observed the recent tradition of throwing the opposition's home run balls back onto the field. It's meant as an insult, not a courtesy. Darn. No such luck.

But as I headed for home, my back to the outfield, I heard the crowd cheer wildly. I looked over my shoulder and saw the ball bounce to a stop in the outfield. As I crossed home plate, I marveled aloud to Bard, "I didn't think that was *ever* going to happen." Not getting the ball back from the stands, but hitting a major-league homer. Josh and I had stayed in touch since I'd left the Indians organization; he was one of the guys who always encouraged me to keep plugging away at catching the dream.

San Diego's lead held going into the sixth inning. Then, with David Bell on first, I sent another Mike Thompson first-pitch fastball into the gap in right center for a long double. My teammate came all the way around to score the tying run. The next batter hit into a force-out at second. I jogged back to the dugout and sat down near the watercooler. This was unbelievable: my first major-league homer, two ribbies, my average up above .330. Out of habit, I pinched myself. Outfielder Shane Victorino couldn't help but notice.

"Coastey . . . *what* are you doing?" he asked.

"Oh, nothing," I replied, then quickly tried to change the subject. "Hey, aren't you supposed to be on deck right now?" The last thing I needed was for my teammates to catch me pinching myself in the corner of the dugout.

We overtook the Padres 5–4 with a two-run rally in the ninth, and once again I got to see myself included among the game highlights on ESPN. There it was, my first home run in the major leagues. I could have watched it over and over again all night.

July 20 was a travel day, as we flew back home to go head-to-head against the Atlanta Braves. I was driving to Citizens Bank Park for game one when my agent called me on my cell phone.

"Hey, Coaster, nice homer last night!" Pat said. "By the way, do you know who you guys are facing tonight?"

"Well, we play the Braves, but I don't know who's pitching for them," I responded.

"John Smoltz. Man, I hope you are playing. You are hot right now, and if there was ever a time to face Smoltz, it's now."

"I don't know if I want any part of John Smoltz," I said, only half joking. "I may be hot right now, but if there is one pitcher in all of baseball that can humble a guy, it's Smoltz." The thirty-nine-year-old righty was a starter again after four stellar seasons in the bullpen, and was on his way to a 16–9 record.

"No way, you'll be fine," Pat insisted. "You'll get him. I just hope you are playing."

Charlie Manuel, deciding to go with the hot hand, started me against Smoltz. Just as anyone would have predicted, I struck out on a nasty slider in my first at-bat. In the fourth inning of a scoreless game, I came up with David Bell on first and two outs. I knew Smoltz would try to deceive me with the slider at some point. Our pitcher was due up next, so there was no need for him to give me anything hittable. I wasn't able to get around on a first-pitch fastball right down the middle and fouled it off. Damn. That was my pitch to hit. Another fastball came in high for a ball. I stepped out of the box and came up with a plan.

Smoltz was going to throw a slider here. I was sure of it. If it was a good one, I'd keep the bat on my shoulder. *But if he makes a mistake over the middle of the plate,* I told myself, *attack!* I was in such a groove and so confident that I felt invincible up there. Probably the same way John Smoltz feels almost every time he steps on the mound.

I was right. Here came a hanging slider that was heading right for the middle of the strike zone. *Holy crap!* I thought to myself. *He hung the slider!* Maybe I'd willed it.

With the crack of the bat, I heard Smoltz yell "Dangit!" He knew he'd served up a gift to me.

The ball sliced through the air and landed in the seats. I stood in the batter's box unable to move. I couldn't believe I'd just homered off Smoltz, an all-star seven times over. It might have looked as though I were showboating, standing there admiring my handiwork. That wasn't the case at all. Apparently I'd forgotten how to work my feet. My brain gave me a scolding: *Run, dummy, run!* Finally, my legs started in motion. I put my head down and let them carry me around the bases.

My amazed teammates met me in the dugout with high fives and hugs. When the commotion finally stopped, Pat Burrell walked up to me with a smile. "That is ridiculous!" he said with mock indignation. "I've faced Smoltz probably fifty times, and I'm not sure I've ever gotten a hit off of him. And *you* hit a home run in your second at-bat against the guy! Unreal!" He paused for effect. "I think I want to throw up!"

John Smoltz wasn't too happy about it either, but for real. I was reading his comments on the Phillies' website the day after our 5–4 win against one of baseball's best. "It's very frustrating for me personally," the pitcher was quoted as saying. "One bad pitch to the number eight hitter." I thought to myself, *I might be the number eight hitter, but make that a number eight hitter who's batting over .330.* For the first time since getting called up to the big leagues, I felt like I'd finally earned the respect I deserved.

Making the home run most memorable of all, my grandfather happened to be in the stands, seeing me play in a big-league uniform for the first time. Oddly enough, even though we're both irrational Minnesota Twins fans, John Smoltz happened to be Gramps's favorite pitcher. This goes back to the tension-filled seventh game of the 1991 World Series between the Twins and Braves, when Smoltz matched zeros with Jack Morris for seven-plus innings. Minnesota finally pushed across the contest's only run in the bottom of the tenth to win the Fall Classic. Ever since, Minnesotans had regarded Smoltz with a grudging respect.

★ VI ★

NEVERTHELESS, I came to the ballpark for the third of four games against the Braves knowing that I might be back in Scranton before the end of the day, as Sal Fasano was due to exit the disabled list. One of us had to go. Since I had options left on my contract and could easily be sent down, I was sure it would be me. So I was surprised to learn that the Phillies decided to designate Fasano for reassignment, not me.

When someone you like leaves a team, even if his misfortune saves your own job, you wrestle with mixed feelings. Naturally I was happy about what the move meant for my future. But at the same time, Sal and I were good friends; I had a huge amount of respect for him as a man as well as a ballplayer. What kind of a guy is Sal Fasano? The next day, I heard him being interviewed on the radio. I can't remember his exact words, but basically he said that while he was sad to leave the Phillies, if there was one guy who had to take his place, he was glad it was me. I felt happy for him when just a few days later the Yankees acquired him for a minor leaguer, giving Sal a ticket to the 2006 postseason.

As July came to a close, it didn't look like Philadelphia had a prayer of getting into the playoffs. We were so far out of first place—fourth place, fourteen games in back of the New York Mets, and seven games below .500—we needed the Hubble telescope to be able to see that far ahead in the standings. In the weeks leading up to the July 31 trading deadline, rumors swirled about which Phillies might be leaving town for a contender. The names mentioned most often were Bobby Abreu, David Dellucci, Cory Lidle, and Jon Lieber. On July 30 the club announced that Abreu and Lidle were going to join Sal Fasano as New York Yankees.

Now, Lidle was an 8–7 pitcher on a sub-.500 team; Abreu's numbers had cooled slightly compared to previous years—particularly his power—but how do you replace a guy who was hitting .277 BA, 8 HR, 65 RBI, and seemed a cinch to notch a fourth consecutive year with 100 or more RBIs? All the Phillies received were three minor leaguers and a pitcher with twelve innings of major-league experience. Clearly the front office was closing the books on 2006 and looking ahead already to next year. In July.

I hadn't, though. Maybe it was the youthful naïveté of a rookie, even a thirty-three-year-old rookie. The day of the trade, I was telling reporters that the team would surprise a lot of people and make a run at the wild-card spot. Frankly, they all looked at me like I was crazy. I wasn't crazy, just hopeful. I knew a run at the wild card with me behind the plate might help erase some of my minor-league status and would convince the Phillies management that I could help the team win when it mattered.

August was a far kinder month to us than June and July had been. On August 1, in St. Louis, I hit a solo homer off the Cardinals' Jeff Suppan for an insurance run in a 5–3 victory. Our promising rookie Scott Mathieson picked up the win, his first in the big leagues.

I didn't start the next night, but in the eighth inning of an 8–7 squeaker, Charlie Manuel called on me to pinch hit. We had a man on second courtesy of a sacrifice bunt. I battled reliever Braden Looper through a ten-pitch at-bat, finally placing a ground ball past Albert Pujols down the first-base line for an RBI double. My teammates then added four more runs in the frame on our way to a 16–8 victory.

Afterward Charlie Manuel came up to me in the locker room. "You know, Coastey, that was probably the biggest at-bat of the game right there," he said. "If you don't get that hit in that situation, we might not win that game. And I'll tell you one more thing," Charlie added. "I am pretty sure that's the first time since I have become the manager here that we bunted a runner over and got him in with a hit. Nice job, son." It was a proud moment for me. I'd already proven that I could catch and swing the bat, but to show that I could come off the bench to get a hit in a clutch situation could only improve my standing.

The next day, we completed a three-game sweep over St. Louis with an 8–1 victory. I had one of my best days in the big leagues, collecting four hits and two RBIs to raise my average to .375. Almost *double* the Mendoza line! Since my awful 0-for-13 start, I was hitting at a .462 pace. Meanwhile young Cole Hamels was awesome, surrendering only two hits and striking out twelve Cardinals. St. Louis didn't put many men on base, but when one of them, speedy David Eckstein, took off for second, I gunned him down.

Just like that, we were just two and a half games behind the Cincinnati Reds and the Arizona Diamondbacks in the chase for the National League wild card. No fewer than seven other teams were in the hunt along with us, but considering how futile everything had looked earlier in the season, we were beginning to feel like we had some momentum on our side and that anything was possible.

★ VII ★

BY the time of a three-game home series against the division-leading Mets on August 15, we'd crept past Atlanta and Florida into second place—albeit a distant second. As for the wild card, Cincinnati still maintained a two-and-a-half-game advantage over us; Arizona, one and a half games. Forty-two thousand Phillies and Mets fans filled up Citizens Bank Park for the opener, which pitted Jon Lieber and New York's number two starter, Tom Glavine. The forty-year-old left-hander was closing in on three hundred career wins, most of them authored in the uniform of the Atlanta Braves.

I came up for my first at-bat with only one thought in mind: Look for the changeup, and if it comes in over the plate, crush it. Although Glavine is destined for the Hall of Fame, his style of pitching perfectly suits my odd style of hitting. Glavine fell behind in the count 2–0. Then, just as I expected, he threw his changeup at the knees, but right down the heart of the plate. I lowered by arms and laid into the pitch. Gone! Knew it as soon as I hit it. Before I'd even dropped my bat, fans in the left-field stands were scrambling after the souvenir. There was a runner on first at the time, so the homer put us up 2–0.

As I rounded the bases to a swell of cheers, I had to laugh to myself. Had I just homered off Tom Glavine, the five-time twenty-game winner? Didn't these people know I was just a minor leaguer who had no business being here? My mind engaged in a vigorous self-debate. *Wait a minute! I'm hitting over .350 in the freakin' major leagues! I belong here as much as anybody!* Yeah, shut up, Coste.

David Dellucci came up to me as I was strapping on my shin guards. "Damn, Coastey," he said. "Now that you've got Smoltz and Glavine under your belt, who's next? Maddux?" That would be Greg Maddux, the third member of the Atlanta Braves' elite pitching trio of the 1990s. He was now helping Los Angeles stay atop the National League West.

"I hope so," I responded, "because if I face him this year, it would mean that we're playing the Dodgers in the playoffs."

For my second at-bat, I went with a different approach. I'd noticed that throughout the game, Glavine followed the same pattern with right-handed hitters: If he fell behind 1–0, he'd come in with an inside fastball. Well, his first pitch to me was a ball. So I opened up my stance and sent the inside fastball screaming off the top of the wall in left, just missing another home run by inches. A single in the seventh gave me a perfect 3-for-3 against Glavine, whom we beat 3–0 behind Lieber's complete-game shutout.

The next morning, the *New York Times* carried a full-length profile about me by Ben Shpigel, "Dishing from Behind the Dish: Phillies' Coste Continues a Journey." Until then, my story of making the big leagues had been confined to Philadelphia and back home in Fargo. But after the *Times* article appeared, I began fielding calls and e-mails from book publishing companies, literary agents, and even movie producers about possibly turning my life story into a book and/or film. It was mind-boggling, to say the least. For me, though, the most exciting call came from ESPN's *Cold Pizza,* asking me to come on the show as a guest. Now, I'd watched *Cold Pizza* on a regular basis, so to receive an invitation like that was totally awesome.

Coincidentally, the day of our final game against the Mets, a new pair of Reebok spikes turned up in my locker. But these weren't just any spikes, they were custom shiny red *suede* spikes with my number stitched on the sides, a privilege usually reserved for more famous players like Chase Utley and Ryan Howard. My locker-room neighbor David Dellucci was the first to notice the shoes and didn't waste any time razzing me.

"You have got to be kidding me!" he exclaimed. "Am I seeing this right? Reebok sent you spikes with your number on them?" He shot a meaningful look at infielder Abraham Nunez, who was sitting a few feet away. "Abe," he asked, "how much time do you have in the big leagues?"

"Almost eight years," Nunez responded. "Why?"

"Well, I have almost nine years. That means between the two of us, we have over sixteen years in the big leagues. Have you ever gotten your number stitched on your shoes?"

"No, never," said Abe, playing up the hurt in his voice. "In fact, I can barely get Nike to send me one pair per season."

"I've never gotten a number on my spikes, either," huffed Dellucci. "Now, Coastey here has been in the big leagues, like, a month and a half, and look at these; he already has his number on his spikes. Unbelievable."

"Wow, Coastey," Nunez responded with a smile, "some people sure do change."

I knew they were yanking my chain. I got up, walked to the back of the equipment room, and found some numbered stickers that normally get slapped on the back of batting helmets. I applied a number 27 to the back of Dellucci's spikes.

"Hey, Dellucci," I yelled, holding up his shoes, now bearing the number 27. "Here you go. Now you've got a number on your spikes! *My* number!"

✯ VIII ✯

IN the month after Philadelphia had dealt Bobby Abreu and Cory Lidle on July 30, seeming to raise the white flag of surrender, the club played 18–11 baseball, good enough to move past Arizona and close to within a half game of the San Diego Padres in the wild-card race. But when you're fighting for that fourth playoff position, the ground can suddenly shift right from under you.

Over the next two weeks, San Diego crept up on the division-leading Dodgers until they were just half a game back. Now we had Los Angeles to worry about, too. We completed a sweep of the Astros in Houston on September 16. With just two weeks remaining in the regular season, we sat two games behind L.A. and one and a half behind the Padres. The Florida Marlins and San Francisco Giants weren't out of it by any means; their .500 records put both teams two games in back of us.

During the Astros series, Cole Hamels flirted with a no-hitter. Having caught several of his previous starts, it came as little surprise to me. The young lefty's stuff is that good. In fact, before the game, I went to him with a proposition.

"Cole," I said, "I have an idea. If I ever catch a no-hitter of yours, instead of the typical Rolex watch, how about you buy me a new car—maybe a Ford Expedition or something like that?" It's something of a baseball tradition for authors of no-hitters to reward their catchers with a nice present.

"Absolutely!" he agreed. "In fact, not only will I buy you an Expedition, but if it happens to be during the playoffs, I will make it something like a Cadillac Escalade or Lincoln Navigator."

"Are you serious?"

"No question! Absolutely!" Cole thrust out his hand, and the two of us shook on our "deal." We were only kidding around, really. Or were we?

Just two days later, Hamels carried a no-hitter into the seventh inning. Believe me, when Adam Everett broke up the no-hitter with a double to right center, no one was more upset than me. Not even Cole himself. I ran out to the mound to make sure he was okay following the hit. You know what he said to me? "Sorry, Coastey. I guess the Expedition will have to wait."

A sweep of the Marlins in front of our own fans propelled us into the wild-card lead by a half game on September 24. The series finale was one of those dramatic games that remind you why baseball is the most attended spectator sport in America. Florida jumped out to a 4–0 lead against Jamie Moyer in just the first inning, which can put a dent in a team's confidence. The Phillies never flinched. With the way we'd been playing, we looked at the scoreboard and shrugged. Home runs from Jimmy Rollins and Chase Utley tied the game in the third. Then, after a pair of two-out singles from Jeff Conine and Pat Burrell, I came up against starter Scott Olsen, a rookie left-hander who won twelve games that season.

The count went full, then I fouled off three tough pitches. I strode into the next pitch from Olsen and lifted it to left field. Would it go out? The whole stadium seemed to hold its collective breath. Then the ball vanished over the wall by just a few feet. A tie-breaking three-run homer, easily the highlight of my career up to that point. The win was our fifth in a row. Since September 1, the club had gone 15–7. Around midseason, a few reporters had questioned the Phillies' desire. Not anymore. For the first time all year, we controlled our own fate.

September 25 was to have been an off day, but due to a rainout against Houston earlier in the year, we had to play a makeup game. The day off would have been preferable, as the Astros edged us 5–4. Then the Nationals beat us in similar fashion, 4–3. The loss in Washington was especially painful because a decision by the umpires took away a Chase Utley home run that, as the replay showed, clearly brushed the foul pole. Afterward, in the clubhouse, we all gathered around the TV watching Los Angeles play Colorado. By now San Diego had vaulted past the Dodgers, who were now our sole competition for the wild card. The mood inside the locker room shifted like the Santa Ana winds based on what happened on screen. Los Angeles pulled away, clobbering the Rockies, 11–4, and went up on us by one full game with five left to play.

We weren't discouraged at all, especially after we came out on top in yet another one-run nail-biter, 8–7 in fourteen innings against Washington. Jimmy Rollins provided the winning blow, a two-run triple. I was on base at the time, my fourth hit in seven plate appearances. Just like the night before, though, we had to suffer through another Dodgers victory.

The finale in D.C. went the Nationals' way, 8–7. Coupled with Los Angeles's fourth win in a row, this one a 19–8 blowout over the Rockies, we entered the final weekend of the season trailing by two games. The math was simple: We had to sweep in Florida and hope for the best. The Marlins had it in for us; a few weeks earlier newspapers had quoted Scott Olsen as saying that he "hated" the Phillies because of the way we'd dominated his club all year. (Um, isn't that what we're *supposed* to do?) Some of our guys responded in kind, and just like that a rivalry was formed.

The Marlins always seemed to give us trouble, but in the opener we played against type and beat them 14–2. Now if the Dodgers would only lose one. But they didn't, beating San Francisco 4–3. The best we could hope for was to win our last two and for L.A. to lose its last two, forcing a one-game playoff.

We did our part, escaping a late Marlins rally to win 4–3. As the team bus took us back to our Miami hotel, everyone was tracking the progress of the L.A.-S.F. contest on their cell phones. Before we even arrived, we learned that the Dodgers had won *again* by a score of 4–2. With that, we'd officially been eliminated from the playoffs. It was a sad feeling,

made even sadder by the fact that we lost the race not while on the diamond but while sitting passively on a bus. Everyone trudged into the
hotel, not really sure what to say to one another. After having come so
close, emotions ranged from anger to despair. But we had nothing to be
ashamed of. The 2006 Philadelphia Phillies made an incredible run,
starting the day of the trading deadline, well after everyone had written
us off.

Following the meaningless last game of the season, we flew back to
Philadelphia. The thought that we'd let a postseason berth slip through
our fingers still stung. However, as I packed up my car for the long ride
back to Fargo, I was able to step back and appreciate how lucky I was to
even be in this position. After spending all those years in the minors, I
could now sit back and relish my first off-season as a major leaguer. Better still, a major leaguer who'd hit .328 with seven home runs and thirty-
two runs batted in in 198 at-bats spanning sixty-five games. If someone
asked me, "What's your lifetime average?" I could say .328. At least until
next year. Take that, Joe DiMaggio (.325), Pie Traynor (.320), Frankie
Frisch (.316), and Mel Ott (.304). Bring on Ty Cobb.

To me, the 2006 season felt like several different seasons in one. There
was my incredible spring training; the horrendous start in Scranton; taking the collar for my first thirteen big-league at-bats; then coming into my
own at the same time that we made an incredible wild-card run. With
those thoughts in mind, I was able to look back fondly on all of the great
experiences I got to be a part of . . .

I got to play a big role for the Phillies during an incredible comeback
season.

I got the opportunity to finally prove that I could catch in the big
leagues.

I got to witness Ryan Howard's MVP season, in which he hit fifty-eight
majestic home runs, and also held my breath as Chase Utley authored a
thirty-six-game hitting streak.

I got to become the personal catcher for Jamie Moyer and Cole
Hamels. Cole, a future Cy Young Award winner, I am convinced. (And
hopefully I will one day be tooling around in a new Ford Expedition, or
better yet, a Cadillac Escalade.)

I got to hit against the likes of Roger Clemens, Pedro Martinez, Tom Glavine, John Smoltz, Jonathan Papelbon, and Brandon Webb, and actually hit homers off of Smoltz and Glavine, both of whom will one day be inducted into the Hall of Fame.

Also, I got to compete against position players such as Albert Pujols, Barry Bonds, Derek Jeter, Alex Rodriguez, and Ken Griffey Jr.

I got to play in many beautiful stadiums, including Wrigley Field and Fenway Park, two of the most historic ballparks in baseball.

I got to become a fan favorite and hot topic for the media—and, let's not forget, a guest on ESPN's *Cold Pizza*.

I got to regularly order room service at fancy hotels, including that $30 ham-and-cheese omelet. (Well, it *was* good.)

I got to fly from city to city with a major-league team on a major-league plane while eating steak and lobster.

Yes, I was a lucky man.

Most important, I got to catch the dream that had been so elusive my entire career. But, I have to admit, sometimes I'm still waiting to wake up from the dream.

I WISH I could say that after my breakthrough 2006 season I went on to become a major-league star, or at least locked up a role as a back-up catcher. Unfortunately, it was not to be, at least not right away. In the off-season, the Phillies signed another catcher to back up Carlos Ruiz, and once again I found myself starting a season in the minor leagues. Apparently, my .328 rookie season hadn't quite overcome the idea that "there must be a reason why Chris Coste spent so much time in the minor leagues."

Though I had prepared myself for it mentally, getting sent back to the minor leagues proved more difficult than I could have ever imagined. The Phillies had moved their triple-A team from Scranton to Ottawa, way north in Canada. Although the Ottawa team was only one level removed from the big leagues, it felt far, far away, like a Foreign Legion outpost in the desert. Once I'd tasted the big-league life and played in front of cheering Philadelphia crowds at the height of a pennant race, I felt lost in the frozen tundra of Ottawa. I can remember sitting in a bar-restaurant in downtown Ottawa with reliever Clay Condrey, who had also experienced the pennant race the previous season, watching the Phillies on an overhead television. To watch the Phillies—a team that I felt I should be playing for, my team—on TV and not at least be in the dugout was almost unbearable. It brought me back to the many moments during my long minor-league career when playing in the big leagues felt like an unattainable dream.

I had, however, received a sign from above earlier that year that things would eventually work themselves out. When I was sent down I broke the news to Marcia and Casey in our rental car in the parking lot of the Phillies' spring-training facility in Clearwater, Florida. After a brief moment of silence—a moment filled with confusion, anger, disappointment, and sadness—Casey began to shed a few tears in the backseat. As I reached for the radio button to break up the tension, Marcia broke the silence: "It just doesn't make any sense!" Just as she finished speaking, the radio kicked in and a country/western singer blared out: "*It just don't make no sense!*" We all looked at one another. This must be a sign that everything would be okay; we'd had this kind of thing happen before.

Sure enough, the Phillies did call me up in May, though it was a temporary situation that was set to end when Ryan Howard came off the disabled list. Thirteen days later, I found myself playing not back in triple-A Ottawa but in double-A Reading, Pennsylvania. At the time, many fans wondered what I'd done to be kicked down even further. But the truth was, the decision had been mine. I'd asked to go to Reading for two different reasons. Number one, the only position I'll ever play in the big leagues is catcher, and one of the Phillies' hottest prospects, Jason Jaramillo, was catching almost every day in Ottawa. In Reading, I would be able to catch three or four times a week and stay sharp in case one of the major-league catchers got hurt. Second, Ottawa was not a baseball town. Our games were more like two churches getting together on a Sunday to play a friendly softball game, and I missed the excitement generated by passionate baseball fans.

As I prepared for my first game for the Reading Phillies, who were playing in Portland, Maine, against the Red Sox' double-A team, I was feeling really discouraged. I had played in the big leagues the night before and even had two hits, and most of my previous six years had been played in triple-A. For the first time in my career, I seriously considered hanging up the cleats. If I hadn't needed the steady paycheck, I might well have bought a one-way ticket back to Fargo and retired. For the first time, I hated the game of baseball. Fortunately, those feelings were erased only a few short days later when we returned to Reading.

I came to find out that Reading was a lot of fun. I got to start catching again and, just as important on the mental side, I got to play in front of fans who cared about baseball, fans who actually knew who I was and knew my story, and not just the Reading fans, either. One time while playing the Yankees' double-A team in Trenton, New Jersey, I received a standing ovation from the crowd. I actually had to step out of the batter's box and tip my cap before they would sit down.

Overall, my experience in Reading was phenomenal and made me feel like a big leaguer once again, simply because the fans treated me like one everywhere I went. The level of support I received, in the form of letters, emails, and crowd reaction, was like nothing I could have ever imagined and made it easier to continue on my path. The fans reassured me that in their opinion I belonged in the major leagues, and that I'd surely get back there soon. And they turned out to be right.

I was sitting in the visitors' clubhouse at the stadium in Harrisburg, Pennsylvania, during a rain delay when Reading manager P. J. Forbes called me into his office to tell me that Jayson Werth, one of Philadelphia's outfielders, had hurt his wrist. I'd be going back to the big leagues. Just like the first time back in May 2006, I felt as if I had won the lottery, and although I wasn't going to the big leagues to catch, for some reason I felt that this was going to be more than a temporary call-up. When I called Marcia to tell her the news (while she was out in the Harrisburg stadium parking lot with Casey), she was so excited that she immediately backed our Mitsubishi Endeavor straight into a wooden parking post, causing a medium-size dent in the right rear fender. Under normal circumstances I might have been mad, but that dent will never be fixed and will forever signify the Coste family going back to the big leagues, together.

Unlike the previous season, it didn't take me fourteen at-bats to get a hit. In fact, I had a pinch-hit home run in my first at-bat back, got hot at the plate, and suddenly found myself backing up Ruiz again. It was sweet redemption, particularly when the team got hot and the Mets went into free fall the last two weeks of the season. We would charge into first place on the final day of the season—perhaps avenging the franchise's own collapse way back in 1964. And the last day was one of my most memorable days as a player.

With the Mets/Marlins game starting thirty minutes before our game against the Nationals, Citizens Bank Park was at capacity and eagerly awaiting any changes on the out-of-town scoreboard. It was simple to do the math: If both teams won or lost, there would be a one-game playoff the next day, but if one team lost and the other won, the winning team

was the division champ and would move on to the playoffs. I wasn't playing that day, so I sat in the video room next to the dugout watching the
first inning of the Mets/Marlins game. As the Marlins drew first blood in
the first inning, putting up one run, then another, I ran to the dugout for
the crowd's reaction. Thirty seconds later, when the scoreboard operator
put up the score, there was absolute anarchy, as the fans cheered and
waved the white towels they'd been given, making all of us proud to have
such passionate fans in our corner. After the loud cheers quieted down, I
headed back into the video room and watched the Marlins score a few
more runs to make it 7–0 at the end of the first inning. I turned and ran
back into the dugout so I could once again feel the energy from the
crowd, and sure enough, thirty seconds later, when the scoreboard
showed the score, there was even more bedlam. It was honestly the loud-
est twenty seconds I had experienced over the past two seasons at Citizens Bank Park, and our game hadn't even started yet.

Things got crazier as we took a lead early and Jamie Moyer threw a
great game; the excitement reached a peak as Brett Myers took the
mound to close out the game. We were up by five runs and the Marlins
were up big on the Mets. When the scoreboard showed one out at Shea
Stadium, our crowd once again erupted in loud cheers. Then out number
two—more cheers. At that point, Myers had recorded one out against the
Nationals, and after recording strike one to the second batter, he was
forced to step off the mound because the crowd had erupted in cheers far
surpassing anything any of us had ever experienced—the scoreboard
showed an F, signifying the final score in the Mets game. All we had to do
was get two more outs and the division was ours.

The storybook twist (I was no longer surprised by anything) was that
though I had not started the game, I found myself behind the plate for
the last five innings after Ruiz was hit by a pitch on the left elbow. So
there I was, preparing to catch the final pitch. Myers wound up and
threw, striking out Wily Mo Pena and jumping into the air. I vividly remember telling myself before the final pitch to make sure to get out to
the mound as fast as I could, and to keep the ball. However, when I
squeezed the final pitch, I was so excited that I ripped off my mask, threw
it high into the air, and then for some reason I paused and dropped the

ball. But the worst part was yet to come. In those moments of slight hesitation, Pat Burrell (the slowest man in major-league baseball) beat me
(the second-slowest man in major-league baseball) to the mound! Still,
that would turn out to be the highlight of our season, as we were quickly
dispatched by a white-hot Colorado Rockies team in the playoffs.

As rewarding as the 2006 season was for me, the 2007 season was even
more special because I felt I had erased any lingering doubt that I belonged in the big leagues.

For all that happened in 2007, it wasn't until the off-season that I heard
the most important news of the year. We found out that Marcia was pregnant; we would be having our second child in June.

★ 2008 SPRING TRAINING ★

We showed up to spring training in 2008 with great confidence. As exciting as the 2007 season had been, we knew we had only scratched the surface of what we were capable of, and getting swept in the first round by
the Rockies left a sour tasted in everyone's mouth. Also, it just seemed as
if it was our time—we now had playoff experience under our belts, and
we'd become stronger with some key additions, including Geoff Jenkins,
Eric Bruntlett, and closer Brad Lidge. There was only one thing on every
player's mind: Anything less than a trip to the World Series would be
considered a failure. And there was no question that the fans felt the
same way.

As for me, it could not have been any more different from every previous spring training I'd attended. For the first time in my life, I was pretty
much locked into the job as back-up catcher to Carlos Ruiz. As long as I
stayed healthy, the job was mine.

★ 2008 REGULAR SEASON ★

The start of the 2008 regular season brought another first for me: a spot
on a major-league roster on opening day. That was followed by yet

another, as my book came out in hardcover and I discovered how much work it is to publicize a book. The day after opening day, our first off-day of the season, I made my way from one local radio or TV show to another and, best of all, did two book signings in the Philadelphia area. I have since learned that every author lives in great fear of having a book signing where nobody shows up, and I was no exception. In fact, I even considered canceling these signings. I arrived thirty minutes early to the second signing at a Barnes & Noble in Willow Grove, Pennsylvania, and decided to scope out the scene and get a quick bite to eat at a restaurant across the parking lot from the store. As I sat alone at my table, about to take the first bite of a ham and turkey sandwich, I noticed a continuous stream of people walking through the parking lot and into the bookstore. It soon dawned on me that nearly all of them were dressed in red Phillies clothing and many were carrying my book! Literally hundreds of people walked through the parking lot in a very short time, so many, in fact, that a line had started to form outside. A few minutes later I received a phone call from the manager of the B&N telling me that I should prepare for a long night. Needless to say, the longer the better, as far as I was concerned.

As I was finishing my sandwich and signaling for the check, I found myself presented with an opportunity frequently available to professional athletes: the chance to make someone happy just by saying hello. I noticed a man with his young son at a table on the other side of the restaurant. They were both wearing Phillies shirts and there were two copies of my book on the table. I stood up, walked over to their table, and sat down. The dad, suddenly aware of a stranger at his table, looked up in annoyance. I smiled, and his eyes grew wide as he realized who was sitting across the table. His nine-year-old son suddenly caught on and sat up in his chair. For a full ten seconds they stared at me; their jaws hung low. I finally broke the silence: "I can sign those books for you right now if you want. That way you guys won't have to wait in line like everyone else."

The dad finally regained his voice. "That would be great! We have already read the book and it is great. We would have waited in line for as long as it took to have you sign them." Then he went on to explain what big fans he and his family were of the Phillies, and that they had been looking forward to the signing for a long time. Then he became a little prophetic. "I loved the book, but I can't wait for the next one."

"What *next* book?" I asked.

With a big grin he replied, "After you guys win the World Series this year, you are gonna have to write another book, or at least another chapter." He would not be the last Phillies fan to make this prediction.

I had made another appearance earlier in the day, this time at the Borders in downtown Philly. Again, I had a huge crowd of happy Phillies fans who told me how excited they were for the season; this was going to be the year we broke through and won it all.

Things took off for me almost immediately in the 2008 season; I homered off the Nationals' Jason Bergmann on the first pitch of my first at-bat of the season. It was a solo homer that seemed almost insignificant at the time (it cut the deficit to 5–1 in the third inning), but it was our first run scored in more than thirteen innings and put us on track for an eventual 8–7 come-from-behind win, our first of the year. Here are some other personal highlights from the season:

April 17 (10–2 win versus the Astros)

With my eight-year-old daughter, Casey, in school back in Fargo, I hadn't seen my family since spring training. I would guess that over the course of my career my stats have been considerably better when my family has been with me, and this day was no exception. They were scheduled to arrive that day for a one-week visit around game time, but the flight was slightly delayed. I made an out in my first at-bat while they were still in the air and came to the plate for my second at-bat just after they had landed in Philadelphia and were taxiing to the gate. Welcoming them to Philly, I proceeded to hit an RBI double off the wall in left field. I entered the game hitting in the neighborhood of .267 and had yet to find my stride at the plate. By the end of the game I had raised my average to .400 with four hits, including a double, a home run, and three RBIs, all with them in Philly. I still wonder what I was thinking not homeschooling Casey so they could be with me all the time.

Another side note to that game was the lunch I had a day earlier at a local restaurant with Astros outfielder and fellow North Dakotan Darin Erstad. It was quite an honor for me, and even though he has made far more money in baseball than I could ever dream of, I insisted on paying. The reason was simple: For the bulk of my minor-league career I watched Darin have incredible success at the big-league level and represent our state with pride. If you had told me ten years earlier that I would have the opportunity to buy him lunch, in the big leagues no less, I would have thought you were crazy. So it only made sense that I take advantage of the situation. Also, I ordered the grilled salmon and broccoli while Darin ate a cheeseburger and fries, and we joked that my healthy eating was not going to make me hit any better—I guess we were wrong because, on my salmon-filled four-hit day, Darin went 0-for-4 on a cheeseburger and fries. A few hours after the game I received a text message from Darin: "NEXT TIME I'M GETTING THE SALMON AND I'M PAYING!!"

April 25 (6–5 win in Pittsburgh)

With that April 17 game a week earlier under my belt, Charlie Manuel felt comfortable putting me in there more often. I was never going to take Carlos Ruiz's starting job, nor was that ever my goal, but Charlie had always made it clear that production could lead to more playing time. But I was shocked when I got to the clubhouse in Pittsburgh and saw that not only was I in the starting lineup but I was also batting fifth in the order, a spot that was usually reserved for Pat Burrell. With Zach Duke, a tough lefty, on the mound, Charlie had decided to give Ryan Howard a day off, moving Chase Utley to first base and Burrell to the cleanup spot. I was so surprised (and excited) that I got out my cell phone and snapped several photos of the lineup to savor the moment. In my situation, I have incentive to succeed in every game I play—we all do—but batting fifth for the Phillies provided as much incentive as I can ever remember. And I was tested in my first at-bat. With two outs and Jayson Werth and Chase Utley on the bases, we were at risk of not taking advantage of a good scoring opportunity. After working the count to 2–2, I eventually sent a line-drive double into left field, scoring both runners. By the time the game ended I had two more hits and finished with three RBIs, raising my average to .406.

May 10 (8–2 loss in San Francisco)

This was more of a notable situation for me than a major highlight, and it was very simple—I hit an insignificant home run off Tim Lincecum in the eighth inning when the score was 8–1. When I hit the home run it seemed like no big deal and it stayed that way until after the season, when Lincecum won the Cy Young Award. I had hit some home runs off a few other Cy Young Award winners, but never during the season in which any of them won the award. Also, Lincecum gave up only eleven home runs the entire season, and to that point I believe it was less than five. Believe me, I am not trying to brag about this home run, and I will reemphasize that it took place in the eighth inning of a game that was already decided. Lincecum fell behind, two balls and no strikes, and was forced to throw a fastball down the middle. Knowing this, I got my momentum started early, gave a higher-than-usual leg kick, and let it fly. Luckily, he threw it right into my bat path and the stars aligned.

June 11 (6–2 loss in Florida)

No game highlights, just life highlights for the Coste family on this night. I wasn't in the starting lineup that night, so five minutes before the game I went in to check my cell phone for messages. Normally, this is against the rules in a baseball clubhouse, especially so close to game time, but I had an exemption because Marcia was pregnant and only ten days away from her due date. When I saw that I had a message, I really didn't think much of it. Here is how the message went (in a calm and monotone voice): "Hi, Chris, it's me [Marcia]. . . . It's about ten minutes before game time and I didn't want to bother you, but I am in labor at the hospital. Call me when you get a chance."

I froze. It was ten days before her due date, and I was in Miami, while Marcia was way up in Philly. There was no way I would be able to make it back in time. And I'm afraid that's what happened, as Marcia gave birth to our second daughter, Camryn Marie Coste, less than three hours later, while I nervously paced as I waited for a plane in the Miami airport. I think the only Phillie as nervous as I was that night was Jayson Werth, since he became the temporary backup catcher by default.

For one day, I forgot about baseball. But the next day I became a fan all over again as I sat with Camryn in my arms, watching Jamie Moyer carve up the Marlins for eight shutout innings. I guess a sign of how much baseball has penetrated my existence is that while watching that game, holding my daughter, who was less than a day old, I began to focus in on something. I had become Jamie Moyer's main catcher and knew the elaborate system of catcher's signs he used to prevent the other team from stealing them. As Carlos Ruiz gave signs, I realized it was the only time in my life that I watched a live baseball game on TV and knew every pitch that was about to be thrown. And there were several times when I almost jumped out of my recliner yelling, "*No!* Don't throw that pitch!" probably making Camryn wonder what the heck was going on, only to watch Moyer strike the guy out with a perfectly located pitch.

Every season, no matter how good or bad your team may be, is a bit of a roller-coaster ride, and the 2008 Phillies' season was no exception. From the first week to the last, we were constantly trading first place with the Mets and the Marlins. Although we were the defending division champs, the addition of Johan Santana seemed to make the Mets the favorites, at least according to many experts, and many of those same experts picked the Braves ahead of us. The Marlins were overlooked and they played with a chip on their shoulder the whole year. But in the end, it came down to us and the Mets once again. We traded blows all year long and, unlike the previous year, they won the season series, and we did not expect them to collapse at the end of the season. That being said, things didn't take shape until around August 14, when we were swept by the Manny Ramirez–led Dodgers in L.A., which put us a full game back of the Mets and a game and a half ahead of the Marlins in the division, not to mention a full five and a half games behind the Brewers for the wild card. Just four days earlier we'd had a two-game lead in the division, and we had chances in each of the four games against the Dodgers, only to let them slip away in the end. But we told ourselves that we were too good a team to let the season get away from us.

Just a week later, the Dodgers came into Philly for another four-game series. We needed wins, and we had our work cut out for us in game one, as Greg Maddux took the hill for the Dodgers. Maddux may not be the dominant pitcher he was in his prime, but there was no doubt that he was quite capable of shutting us down. In fact, just a week earlier he had allowed only a solo home run to Pat Burrell in seven innings of work. But this time would be different. He escaped major damage for the first five innings, but in the sixth we put up four runs, knocking him out of the game and putting us on the path to an eventual 8–1 win. And it was a memorable game for me. I started and had my first hit off Maddux. I had already homered off his former teammates Tom Glavine and John Smoltz back in 2006; my friends and teammates reminded me constantly that Maddux needed to be on that list. Now, I can't sit here and try to convince anyone that I knew I was going to homer off Maddux, but I always believed I had the potential to have success against him, simply because his finesse-and-control style of pitching has always been the kind of pitching that I have had success against. After going 1-for-2 with an RBI single, I stepped to the plate in the sixth inning with two outs and two men on base and a 4–1 lead—the perfect chance to put the game out of reach. With the count 1–1, I looked for his patented sinker on the outer part of the plate, a pitch that is normally tough to handle because it has a lot of movement, making it look well outside the zone before it ultimately darts back out over the plate for a strike. By the time the hitter realizes that it's a strike it's too late—the ball is already by the hitter and in the catcher's mitt. Instead, he went with the changeup out over the plate and at the knees, also known as *my wheelhouse*. The end result was a line-drive three-run homer to left field, making the score 7–1. The win was big and the momentum put us on a path to a four-game sweep of our own. At that point, we trailed the Mets by half a game, but we were five ahead of Florida for the division lead and four back of the Brewers in the wild-card chase.

Now, I cannot verify this from Maddux personally, but before the series started he apparently had a conversation with David Yamamoto, the Japanese-English translator for one of our infielders, Tadahito Iguchi. Iguchi had played with Maddux and the Padres earlier in the season. Here is how the conversation went:

"Hey, David, you were with the Phillies last season—any good scouting reports you can give me on some of their lesser-known hitters?" Maddux asked.

David replied, "The only thing I can tell you is to be careful with Chris Coste, the backup catcher. He may be a backup, but he is a really good hitter."

"Yes, I know all about Chris Coste—he is a good hitter. In fact, I have him on my fantasy baseball team."

This story was told to me by David, and he promised me that he did not make it up. Greg Maddux, if you're reading this, I'm glad I could help you out that day. For those who didn't see the game, I had two hits, a home run, and four RBIs on the day.

The following series was a two-game set against the Mets, and one of those games will forever hold a place among my best memories. We had closed the gap to a half game with only thirty-one games to play. In the first game, the Mets stormed out to a 7–1 lead, and it looked as if we were going to be blown out. Improbably, Clay Condrey, a relief pitcher, led off with a double, sparking a four-run inning. I was still riding the pines at that point; I wouldn't make it into the game until the eighth inning, when I pinch hit and managed a seeing-eye single. With two outs in the bottom of the ninth, Eric Bruntlett tied the game with a double, which was arguably the most important hit of our season to that point.

It wasn't at all unusual for me to enter a game late, but in this case there was a twist. I was pinch hitting for Greg Dobbs, our current third baseman, and with Pedro Feliz already out of the game, they had to decide who was going to play third base. I was a possible choice, since I had played all over the infield my entire minor-league career, including well over one hundred games at third base. The only other choice was Carlos Ruiz, who was originally signed as a second baseman; however, he hadn't seen game action in the infield in more than six seasons. I was lucky enough to be standing behind Charlie and Jimy Williams when the decision-making process began to take shape. Jimy could sense that Charlie had apprehensions about taking Dobbs out of the game for defensive reasons, but with a tough lefty on the mound, he preferred a right-handed hitter. Jimy had a suggestion: "Charlie, you can pinch hit Coste for Dobbs, keep Coste in as the catcher, and put Ruiz in at third base."

Yes, do that! I thought to myself. Although I had played third base many times in the past, I had never played there in the big leagues, and I hadn't taken one practice ground ball all season. Ruiz, on the other hand, had taken ground balls with Pedro Feliz nearly every day since opening day, not because he ever expected to get in at third, but because it got his legs loose and the extra throws kept his arm strong.

When Charlie heard Jimy's suggestion, the confused look on his face was priceless; he had been leaning toward putting me in at third. Putting Ruiz at third never crossed Charlie's mind. He knew that I had played the infield a lot throughout my career, so it only made sense that I go to third. When Jimy saw the look on Charlie's face he explained his reasoning: "Ruiz has been taking ground balls at third all year—he can do it!"

As the inning started, I glanced over at the odd sight of Ruiz standing near third base and witnessed the first practice grounder thrown to him by Ryan Howard. It was just a simple slow grounder that Ruiz could have fielded in his sleep, but his nerves got the best of him and the ball bounced off his wrist and into his chest, then hit him square in the chin before finally coming to a stop in front of him on the infield dirt. It was one of the funnier moments of the season and it seemed that everyone on the team had seen it. Needless to say, such a moment would not be wasted. As the dugout burst into laughter, someone held up Ruiz's catcher's mask, jokingly offering to run it out to him for protection.

I stayed in the game behind the plate, and as the game went into extra inning after extra inning, I found myself 3-for-3 when I came up in the thirteenth inning. With one out and the bases loaded, I lined a ball over Carlos Beltran's head in center field to win the game, and I was mobbed by my teammates. We were starting to feel as if we had destiny on our side. And I had done something relatively rare, getting four hits in a game, and even rarer, four hits after pinch hitting in the eighth. I'll never forget it.

As a side note to that amazing comeback against the Mets, an interesting bit of foreshadowing had taken place near the batting cage during batting practice. While I stood next to Charlie talking about the previous games against the Dodgers, one of the Mets' coaches, Sandy Alomar Jr., walked out of the dugout and toward the batting cage. He had played for Charlie back in their Cleveland Indians days and wanted to say hello to his former skipper. As they exchanged their pleasantries, the subject quickly changed to Charlie's managing style and how he determines whom he puts in the lineup on a given night. Alomar looked over at me and asked, "Hey, Coastey, do you know when you are going to be in the lineup or does Charlie usually make it a surprise?"

"Every now and then he might tell me the night before, but usually he leaves us guessing," I replied.

"Is there ever a method? Like say, for example, if you have a good game, does he let you play the next day?"

"That does happen from time to time, but after having been with Charlie for parts of three years, I have learned to stop trying to figure out how he makes his lineup decisions." At that moment Charlie looked at me and smiled, so I took it one step further. "In fact, I have had four hits in a game three times in my major-league career and didn't make the starting lineup the day after any of them." Ironically, I got four hits that very night (off the bench, no less), and I *did* make the lineup the next day.

In a season of ups and downs, we soon experienced another up. As we approached a four-game set against the Brewers at home, we found ourselves three and a half games behind the Mets and four games back of the Brewers for the wild card. Things did not look good for us. With only sixteen games remaining, we were getting desperate, and for the first time all season, a sense of urgency began to creep into the picture. Once again, we responded. Jamie Moyer pitched an unbelievable first game and we went on to sweep the Brewers, which pulled us into a tie for the wild card and only one game back of the Mets with only twelve to play. We clicked on all cylinders after that, and with three games remaining we had a one-and-a-half game lead in both the division and the wild-card race. The Mets and Brewers had identical records, meaning that two of the three teams were going to the playoffs.

The first game saw us beat the Nationals while the Mets lost to the Marlins, shrinking our magic number to one. It was simple: With two games remaining, we had clinched at least a tie in the division, and we needed to win only one more game to get to the playoffs. The emotion and excitement ran high and we could almost hear the champagne being popped and the cheer of the crowd as we raced to the mound for a celebration. It became almost comical how we would avoid saying and doing the wrong things, because until it actually happened, until the champagne was popped, we knew there was work to be done, and we had come too far to count our chickens.

That second game against the Nationals turned out to be one of the most exciting games of the year, especially at the end. With a two-run lead going into the ninth inning and Brad Lidge entering the game from the bullpen, those last three outs seemed to be just a formality, especially after Lidge struck out the first batter of the inning. At that point, most of the players in the dugout, myself included, left their seats and jockeyed for position near the top step of the dugout for the inevitable celebration. My only goal was to get out of the dugout as fast as possible so I could beat Pat Burrell to the mound. However, after a walk and a few hits, the Nationals scored a run, loaded the bases, and were threatening to score the go-ahead run from second. Slowly and shamefully, all the players who had assembled near the top step of the dugout returned to their seats. For the moment it appeared as if we had jinxed Brad Lidge's perfect season and our shot at the division title. Then Ryan Zimmerman, the Nationals' star third baseman and number three hitter, strolled to the plate with only one out. He promptly lined a one-hopper up the middle that seemed destined for center field, a heartbreaking go-ahead single. But out of nowhere Jimmy Rollins, the two-time Gold Glove winner, snared the liner with a partial dive from his knees, and all in one motion made a perfect toss to Utley covering at second, and before we could exhale, Utley completed the improbable and division-clinching double play to Howard at first. And just like that we were division champs headed for the postseason.

The next step was the celebration. The only problem was that we were a bit confused as to how much we should celebrate, because in our minds, as great as it was to clinch the division and be in the playoffs, there was a lot more to be done. The previous year we had celebrated like crazy and were ousted in the first round, and now we were in the same situation. However, after a few moments of hesitation, the emotion kicked in and the celebration was unavoidable. Even with the previous year's disappointment in mind, the battle and roller-coaster ride of the entire regular season came to an end. After almost not making the playoffs, we had won the division. This was too much of a reward for us to suppress our excitement.

We had mixed feelings about the Mets not making the playoffs. They were our biggest rival and we had had incredible battles with them all season long, so it was nice to see them packing it in for the season while we were moving on. But at the same time, we would have loved for them to make the playoffs just for the possibility that we might play them in the second round with a trip to the World Series on the line.

Now the only question was what team we were going to play in the first round. We played the Brewers. Since adding CC Sabathia, whom we had been fortunate to miss in the four-game series during the regular season, the Brewers looked to have an edge in any five-game series, especially because CC had shown the ability to come back on short rest and still dominate. Also, although we had recently swept them in that four-game series at Citizens Bank Park, the Brewers had other pitchers capable of shutting down our offense. We won game one with an incredible pitching performance from Cole Hamels. In game two, we faced the formidable Sabathia. There were many highlights that night, including a Shane Victorino grand slam, but it was another at-bat that most fans and players will remember.

Until the bottom of the second inning in game two, it's safe to say that Brett Myers was far from the most feared hitter on the team. And for the first two pitches against Sabathia, it seemed that nothing had changed. But over the previous few weeks, Myers had been working on his approach at the plate. Instead of trying to hit the ball as hard as he could, he had lowered his stance and concentrated on hitting line drives up the middle and to right field. After Myers took a ball on the third pitch, he began to foul off pitch after pitch. I found myself getting more and more excited and so did the fans, who cheered louder with every pitch spoiled. When he drew a walk after what seemed like an endless number of pitches, they went crazy. It must have been the best at-bat ever by a pitcher in a playoff game. One batter later, Shane Victorino would hit the grand slam off the Brewers' ace, and we never looked back.

With the 2–0 lead in the series, we traveled to Milwaukee and the loudness of Miller Park. We had all played in some loud places before, including Citizens Bank Park, but the Milwaukee fans showed up in full force, and the Brewers managed to scratch out the win in game three. At that point, we certainly were not looking past the Brewers. Even though we'd had a 2–0 lead earlier in the series, we knew that any playoff team is capable of winning three straight games, and the Brewers were no exception. We could taste the series victory, but until that final out was made in our favor, we were taking nothing for granted. Fortunately, an incredible performance by Joe Blanton and key home runs by J-Roll, Jayson Werth, and Pat Burrell, who had two, allowed Brad Lidge to shut the door in the ninth to earn the series victory.

Once again the celebration was on, just as it was after we clinched the division a week earlier, and once again we were confused as to how much we should celebrate. There was no question that we were all incredibly excited to get past the Brewers and advance further than we had the previous season, but it was obvious that there was still work to be done. Further, we were in the opponent's ballpark, so we didn't have the fans there to pump us up. Yet the celebration was certainly memorable, not least because, unlike many of my teammates, I still hadn't learned my lesson, forgetting to bring protective goggles to shield my eyes from the sweet sting of champagne.

Bring on Manny Ramirez and the Dodgers! To be honest, before the first game had even begun, we were incredibly tired of hearing Manny's name. Every player and coach on our team constantly fielded questions from the media, and it seemed that every reporter's first question had to do with Manny, as if it were nine against one. I wish I had a nickel for every reporter who uttered this exact line: "Chris, how do you guys stop Manny Ramirez?" What the media and many fans forgot is that the Dodgers had a very well-rounded team. With Derek Lowe, Chad

Billingsley, Hiroki Kuroda, and a bullpen that rivaled our own, combined with an explosive and dynamic offense featuring Russell Martin, Matt Kemp, Rafael Furcal, Casey Blake, Andre Ethier, and James Loney, they were capable of scoring runs off anybody. And they showed it by dominating the Chicago Cubs' ace pitching staff in the previous series. So to worry only about Manny would have been stupid.

Fortunately, we were able to control Manny and the rest of the Dodgers offense with great pitching of our own, winning the series 4–1. There were many highlights, including many awesome pitching performances from Cole Hamels (who was the championship series MVP) and the rest of the pitching staff, but the most memorable highlights came in the eighth inning of game four.

We were up two games to one, but down 5–3, a mere five outs away from losing game four and allowing the Dodgers to tie the series. Shane Victorino tied it up with a two-run homer, drawing a stunned silence from the L.A. crowd, but that was just the beginning. A few batters later, with two outs and one man on, and fireballing closer Jonathan Broxton on the mound, Charlie sent Matt Stairs to the plate. If I am not mistaken, Broxton hadn't given up a homer to anyone since early in the 2007 season, a streak that would have been incredible for even the best pitchers in the history of the game. While he probably knew that Stairs could hit the long ball, he didn't know what I knew, which was that Matt Stairs had as good a chance as anyone of breaking his streak. I knew it because I had often taken batting practice alongside Stairs since he had joined us late in the season, and of the hundreds of former and current teammates I have had, he has the most impressive home-run-hitting batting practice I have ever seen. Most hitters, even the strongest ones, usually takes a few swings to get loose before aiming for the seats, but Stairs hits bombs from the first pitch to the last. After working the count to 3–1, Stairs knew he was going to get a hundred-mile-an-hour fastball for a strike, and most of the dugout realized this as well. You could feel the anticipation as he stepped into the batter's box. What happened next will certainly be among the most unforgettable and important images of this postseason. Broxton unleashed a sizzling fastball and Stairs connected. The moment he did, the entire team jumped up, probably before the ball even left the infield. There was no doubt about it, as Harry Kalas would say. The ball rocketed up and out of the stadium, traveling well over four hundred feet. It's hard to explain how powerful the energy and excitement of this moment were for the team; I can only say that I very nearly had to wipe a tear away, and I wasn't alone. As he entered the dugout, virtually every player on the team reached out to pound him on the back. This home run completely changed the momentum of the NLCS and ultimately sent us to the World Series, making it, in my opinion, one of the biggest home runs in Phillies history.

When Carlos Ruiz squeezed the final out of the NLCS, a pop foul from Nomar Garciaparra, officially sending us to the World Series, the celebration was on, and it is safe to say that the small amounts of guilt we may have felt from overcelebrating after first clinching the division and then beating the Brewers were totally gone. This is what we were fighting for all season long: to earn the chance to win the World Series. And once again I felt the sting of champagne, having forgotten once again to bring goggles. Of all the teams in baseball, we were now one of only two that had a chance to win it all. It almost felt too good to be true. Four wins away from Philadelphia's first major sports championship since 1983, and its first World Series title since 1980, entirely too long a period of time for a city that was starved for success, a city that deserved much better.

The next thing on our minds was who our opponent was going to be, the Rays or the Red Sox. I really don't think we ever had a preference because both teams were equally tough. Having said that, I was happy to face the Rays because of what their success meant for the sport. I have always been and always will be a fan of baseball, and the success of the Rays not only made for a great story but also reinforced the idea that every team has a chance every single year. Sure, the teams that spend the most money year after year give themselves a better chance by constantly rebuilding their teams with free agents, but in any given year a team like the Rays can break through and surprise people. And the way the Rays were playing and the way their roster was stacked, they certainly seemed to be set up for winning for at least a few more seasons.

Having extra days off can both help and hurt. One theory is that extended days off can cool a team, which is what some people thought had happened to the Rockies against the Red Sox in 2007. And it's true that not too many people outside of the Denver fan base would try to argue that the Red Sox were not the better team and not deserving of winning the World Series. An alternate theory holds that a layoff can help rest a team that might be beat up a little and can also allow that team to set up the pitching rotation exactly the way they want it. Although we had a lot of momentum going into the Series, I think we preferred having the time off and starting off with a rested pitching staff, led by Cole Hamels.

Much was made about the oddity and noise of Tropicana Field, and rightly so, given the high winning percentage the Rays had at home. I believe that Matt Stairs was our only player to have played more than a handful of games in the dome, so it was a good thing that we were allowed into the dome for a pre-Series practice. It was a chance to check out fly balls and how they might get lost in the roof, and, more important, to check out the turf and other field conditions. As we came to find out, the significance of the field conditions, noise, and roof was more of a media creation and fan perception than actual reality.

The next piece of personal excitement was the possibility that I might be the designated hitter for game one. With lefty Scott Kazmir throwing, there were a few different possibilities that Charlie could have gone with, one of which was putting Eric Bruntlett in left field and DHing Pat Burrell. In my mind, this was the option Charlie was going to choose. For one thing, although I'd been very solid on offense earlier in the year, I'd had a horrible finish to the season and had had only one at-bat in nearly a month. Another reason was that using Burrell as the DH would give Charlie an excuse to put a better defensive team on the field. As much as we would have liked to know his decision well in advance, we knew Charlie would not tell us until the last possible moment. I have been with Charlie for several years now and I know that he likes to keep people hanging because he believes shorter notice makes them play better, and from my personal experience this system has been very effective.

I woke up in my Tampa hotel room the morning of game one and ordered some breakfast. By 11:00 a.m. I had already received dozens of text messages and phone calls from friends and family wondering if I had heard any news—nothing yet. In the next two hours I received about a dozen more inquiries. Finally, around 1:00 p.m., as I prepared to get in the shower, my cell phone began ringing with yet another text, only this time I didn't recognize the number. Here is what the message said: "Hi Chris, this is XXX XXXX from *ESPN First Take*" (I had been on the show a few times over the past few years and they still had my number). "I see that you're in the lineup tonight. If you guys win can you come on the show tomorrow?"

And there it was. Could this be true? Is this how I am going to find out that I am starting a World Series game—through a text message from ESPN? And how does he know? What if it is someone joking with me? I immediately turned the TV to ESPN and began flipping back and forth between ESPN, ESPN2, and ESPNEWS to see if they were showing the lineups on the ticker tape at the bottom of the screen, as they had in the past. Nothing.

Thirty minutes later, I jumped in the back of a taxi with Clay Condrey, Chad Durbin, and Shane Victorino. "Hey, guys . . . I think I am in the starting lineup tonight." I said.

"You *think* you're in the lineup?" Durbin asked.

I explained the text message I'd received from the producer at *First Take* and immediately Victorino responded, "I could have told you that you were starting—I saw the lineup on my phone over an hour ago." Shane was a fixture in the lineup, so it never occurred to him that it might be a big deal for me to be in the lineup. Ten minutes later, I received confirmation when we arrived at the clubhouse and the ESPN ticker tape showed my name in the starting lineup.

Oddly enough, I wasn't the least bit nervous when it hit me that I was indeed in the lineup. Having fought so hard to get to the majors, I already perceived every major-league game, whether it was a typical regular-season game against the Florida Marlins, an interleague game against the Yankees or Red Sox, or a pinch hit appearance in the NLCS against the Dodgers, as being like the World Series. So I felt as prepared as any World Series first-timer in the history of the game. The only reasons I felt odd were that I hadn't played much over the past two months and I was DHing, something I had never done at the big-league level. DHing is hard because there is only one thing on your mind—hitting. Normally, playing a defensive position is a nice distraction. As it turned out, when I came to the plate in the top of the second inning with two men on and no outs, there were no nerves whatsoever, just an easy and confident feeling that overcame my mind and body. Unfortunately, I popped up weakly to right field for out number one. Looking back, I wish I had been more nervous—maybe I would have done better than my eventual 0-for-4 on the night. Fortunately, the fact that we eventually won game one erased the pain of a hitless night.

All in all, playing in the confines of Tropicana Field had no effect on either team. It was a lot noisier in Milwaukee during the division series, though I think the fans' insistence on ringing cowbells had the effect of taking voices away from the cheering.

Back to Philly. Our fans were annoyed by the level of attention the Tampa fans were getting, especially when those Tampa fans were given some of the credit for Tropicana being a tough place to play for visiting teams. As would soon be clear, all of the forty-five-thousand-plus fans in Citizens Bank Park for each game made it their personal mission to be the most intense, passionate, and vocal fans in the history of baseball. They succeeded, and they'll never know how grateful all of us players were for it. If anyone doubted the impact the Philly fans had on opposing teams, our eventual undefeated home playoff record should be proof enough.

The Final Game

With Cole Hamels on the mound to start game five, our confidence was pretty high. We could taste the champagne and feel the thrill of a World Series title brewing. At the same time, everyone made sure not to count our chickens until that last out was made. After all, other teams had come back from worse deficits in the past, and we didn't want to jinx ourselves—not to mention that the Rays had proven to be a resilient team all season long and were quite capable of getting hot and winning three straight games against anyone. It soon became a joke around the clubhouse that we were not allowed to say the word *parade*. Instead, it was "the 'P' word."

The weather forecast had called for rain that night, though what we got was a little more than your average rainstorm. It started slowly enough that the game was allowed to begin, and for the first few innings it wasn't too bad. But then the temperature dropped and the wind picked up. Being from Fargo, and having been in hundreds of minor- and major-league games in the Northeast in April, I had played in rain, wind, and cold weather at different times, but never all at once like that night. I wrapped myself up in two jackets and did not have to leave the comfort of the dugout, but something happened as our team left the field in the fifth inning that told me just how bad it was. Chase Utley, walking in from the treacherous field and weather conditions, walked by and whispered in my ear, "These conditions are absolutely unplayable!" It wasn't until that moment that I realized how bad things had become. As Phillies fans know, Chase Utley is as tough as they come and likely the last guy on the team to complain about anything.

An inning later, the game was suspended, coincidentally just after Tampa had tied the score. It may have appeared that we were upset with the umpires and Major League Baseball for the timing of the suspension, but honestly, the most prevalent emotion was confusion, especially when Bud Selig held his press conference and stated that the game would be continued when he felt that the weather and field conditions were acceptable. So how would they let us know when that was? Through a text message, or perhaps an email or voicemail? We were confused because no one had ever been in that situation before. Do we go home and wait for a call, or do we camp out at the stadium? And what about the fans? If they all go home and the weather miraculously gets better, will we continue the game without the fans? Lots of confusion.

Finally we were told that we could leave, and the next night proved too rainy again. When the weather subsided on the next day, excitement flooded the city. Nine outs stood between us and "the 'P' word." The question was what kind of attendance we were going to have for those last three innings. With the weather still a potential deterrent and the possibility that some fans might have lost their tickets or simply couldn't attend for whatever reason, the intense atmosphere that we had grown accustomed to throughout the season and especially the playoffs was in question. But as we came to find out, those concerns were ridiculous. So many fans showed up and the energy level was so great that it felt as if the stadium officials had simply opened up the gates and let the entire city into the stadium. And how could we expect anything less? This was Philadelphia, after all.

If you were watching the game on TV, you might have noticed that I was standing behind Charlie Manuel and Jimy Williams almost every second during those last three innings. Well, it wasn't because I wanted more face time on national TV. I was simply being superstitious. A few weeks back, just before the end of the regular season when we were still battling the Mets and the Brewers for a playoff spot, I was running from the batting cages and up the steps that enter the dugout. Just as I got to that particular spot behind Charlie, I heard the crack of the bat—one of our guys had just connected with a pitch. Since I was late getting to the dugout, I didn't even see the pitch, nor did I see where the ball was hit; all I could see were the heads of Charlie and Jimy Williams jumping up to follow the ball. It was a deep home run late in the game, which turned out to be the deciding moment of the game. I viewed it as one of those opportunistically superstitious moments. So for the next month, at each and every home game I would choose only one or two offensive innings (I didn't want to overdo it) to stand in that spot in hopes of re-creating the magic. And it worked. We scored at least one run in all but one of those situations. So with only three innings to play and the World Series on the line, I planted myself in that spot with high hopes. And when Geoff Jenkins led off the inning with a crucial double to get things rolling, I took it as a sign that good things were about to happen. Add in the heroics of Jayson Werth to knock him in, the incredible defensive play by Chase Utley to nail Jason Bartlett at the plate, Pat Burrell's double in the eighth inning that set up Pedro Feliz's game-winning RBI single (in my opinion maybe the biggest and most overlooked hit in Phillies' history), and the typically lights-out job by the bullpen (Ryan Madson, J. C. Romero, and Brad Lidge), and the World Series was ours!

✯ RUNNING ONTO THE FIELD AGAIN ✯

As Brad Lidge stood ready to throw that final pitch to Eric Hinske, the players, the city, and the fans watching on television held their collective breath. The tying run stood on second base. Although Lidge had been perfect all season long, even something as simple as a bloop hit could tie the game. But Lidge delivered and the place exploded. The players, too, could finally let loose. There were no more games to play!

I hadn't given up my goal of beating Pat Burrell to the mound, but once again I had been afraid of jinxing the team, so I stayed in my spot near Charlie and Jimy. What followed is a blur; if you saw me on TV, you probably know what happened better than I do. My only real memory of storming out of the dugout was yelling alongside my teammates in disbelief as we approached the pile. My next memory was jumping in and then being jumped on, all while not being able to fully believe the situation we were in. In a way, winning the World Series and being in the middle of that pile was a microcosm of my entire career—it was a dream, and I was worried that I was going to wake up and it had never happened. How on earth could this be happening to me? There is no way! I have always been a fan of baseball and have watched every World Series as far back as I can remember, and I can vividly recall watching many on-field celebratory scenes on TV, specifically Kirby Puckett and the Minnesota Twins in 1987 and 1991, the Red Sox in both 2004 and 2007, and many of the recent Yankee victories. Now, as I numbly ran onto the field and into the pile, I had a hard time believing that I was part of something of that magnitude. My next thought as I made my way out from the pile was that we were going to have to sprint off the field and into the safety of our clubhouse as soon as possible because all forty-six thousand Phillies fans were going to storm the field. But I looked around and realized that this wasn't the case, and the celebration continued on the field and then in the clubhouse.

At that moment Brad Lidge was being interviewed on TV, and I heard later that he went out of his way to thank Ruiz and me for helping him have a perfect year. I thought it was great of him to remember us in the midst of all that craziness.

More champagne. I still didn't have goggles, but this time it was out of superstition. I would have felt terrible if I had brought goggles and the team had gone on to lose. The sting in the eyes was a small price to pay to win it all. If only champagne regrew hair—by now I would have a full head of it!

★ THE PARADE ★

No more "P" word. We could actually say the word *parade* without worrying about superstition and jinxes. This was something we'd been hoping to be able to have for a long time, for the fans and the entire Phillies community. The on-field celebration with forty-six thousand fans in the seats was incredible and almost indescribable, but nothing could prepare us for the emotion, energy, and elation from what felt like two and a half million people. I wore sunglasses the entire day and I am glad I did, because from the moment we started down Broad Street and headed toward the Sports Complex, I was nearly overcome with emotion more times than I could count, almost wiping away tears several times. It was five hours of pure adrenaline and emotion, and none of us had ever experienced anything like it. I agree with Cole Hamels, who said, "One thing I can't wait to do is go down Broad Street for that parade again and again and again."

When I got on the plane and headed back to Fargo with my family, I still had a hard time comprehending the situation. Although I didn't get to play much throughout the playoffs, it truly was an amazing year for me personally. One of the many great things about the playoffs and especially the World Series is the fact that there is no ego and certainly no selfishness— just win! Every player, especially bench players, will say the same thing: If I get no at-bats and we win the World Series, I will be just as happy as if I get ten hits—and I felt that way 100 percent. I have been with the team during three playoff runs, two of which eventually fell short of the goal. For the first time, I was with a major-league team from the beginning of the season and I got to play a lot more than I or anyone else had ever expected, and at times I was catching four or five games a week.

It was never my goal to take Carlos Ruiz's job. In fact, we are great friends—have been since 2005—and believe me, I am his biggest fan, because I know how good he can be and how good he will be. No one was pulling for Carlos to have a good season more than I was, and somewhat for selfish reasons. If he has a great season, then the organization is less likely to worry about the catching situation and will feel content with both of us for, I hope, many years. But if he does not do well, it opens the door for the organization to try to upgrade the position, and the player most affected by that is me, because if they ever bring in another starting catcher I will be the odd man out. I was incredibly excited to see him do well in the playoffs for these reasons. As I said earlier, I will always know that nothing in my baseball life will ever be guaranteed and I will have to continue to fight for everything, just like everyone else. But in the meantime, I will enjoy the off-season knowing that I was part of an amazing season, and believe me, I need the rest, more mentally than physically. One of the by-products of watching from the bench was that my stress level went through the roof. When I am out on the field playing, especially behind the plate, I never have time to be nervous because there is always something happening, whether it is thinking about pitch selection, blocking a ball in the dirt, or simply catching the ball. But sitting helpless in the dugout during the most important games of the season caused a level of stress unlike anything I had ever felt in my baseball life—I guess that is what diehard fans must feel like on a regular basis. The only way I can describe my emotion was that it felt as if I were in the passenger seat of a race car going 250 miles per hour—I wanted to grab hold of the wheel, hit the brakes, and push the gas, but instead I was nervously rocking in my seat, hoping (and praying) for the best.

Well, the *best* happened!

Go Phillies!

ACKNOWLEDGMENTS

I WOULD like to start out by saying thanks to my wonderful family, especially my incredibly understanding wife, Marcia, and daughter, Casey. Their support ultimately made it possible for me to catch the big-league dream. Also, I need to acknowledge the rest of my family, including Marcia's side of the family. Not one member of either of our families ever questioned my career path, and they *never* uttered the common phrase heard by most career minor leaguers: "When are you going to get on with your life?"

I would also like to thank:

Doug Simunic and Jeff Bittiger for giving me every opportunity to make the RedHawks in 1996. It was Doug and Jeff who gave me a shot as a catcher, ultimately putting me on my path to the big leagues. Also, it was Doug who convinced me to sign with the Indians after the 1999 Northern League season. I hate to think about where I would be right now if he hadn't vehemently demanded that I accept the Indians' offer.

John Dittrich, the general manager of the 1996 Fargo-Moorhead Red-Hawks. He was one of the few people who truly believed that I would have success in the Northern League, despite my dismal stats in a lesser independent league. And even more important, John gave me a full-time job in the RedHawks' front office in 1997. Without this job, I would have had to give up playing baseball and would have had to look for a real job. As a result, I was able to make a career out of baseball.

All the individuals responsible for bringing the Northern League to Fargo in 1996. Gene Allen and Bruce Thom specifically come to mind. Witout the RedHawks, I would have ended up working in an office somewhere and playing softball on the weekends.

Bucky Burgau, my coach at Concordia College, for making baseball fun again and for making me feel I was worth something as a ballplayer.

Wade Beavers, for pushing me to transfer to Concordia College. He was the first person to see that I could become a successful hitter in college. He also created and maintains my website, www.chriscoste.com.

All of the teammates who believed in me throughout my college days and my eleven years in the minor leagues. It wasn't easy playing so long in the minor leagues, but their support, like my family's, made it easier to keep going.

Eric Wedge, my manager in the Cleveland minor-league system and the current manager of the Cleveland Indians, for telling me on many occasions, "I guarantee that you will play in the big leagues someday." Also, he stuck his neck out for me on many occasions and put me in the lineup when he probably wasn't supposed to.

Charlie Manuel, the manager of the Phillies, and the Phillies front office, not only for giving me a shot in the big leagues, but for sticking with me during my rough major-league start.

All of the Phillies fans and media for making me somewhat of a "modern-day Rocky." Since the first day of the 2006 spring training, Charlie Manuel has constantly said, "Chris Coste was born to play in a city like Philly" and "Chris Coste is definitely a Philly kind of guy."

All of the countless friends and fans in the Fargo area who "check the box scores daily" to see how I am doing.

All the photographers who contributed photos for the book, including Ken Carr, Julie's Photography, Miles Kennedy, and Rosemary Rahn.

Steve Harris, my literary agent, for guiding me through the entire book experience.

My agent, Pat Arter, for sticking with me through the tough years. As a result of his support and loyalty, he has become like an uncle figure, and I trust him as much as any member of my family.

Philip Bashe, for helping me transform this manuscript into an easier read. Although I wrote the entire book myself, he was able to add facts and help with research, and he also spent countless hours going through the manuscript, ultimately making it a lot more organized.

Last, and most important, I thank God every day for blessing me with such an awesome path in life. Chasing the dream isn't always pleasant, but day in and day out it is an unforgettable and priceless experience. I have crossed paths with thousands of unique personalities, and as a result, my life has been positively affected in more ways than I can count. This path has also taken me to more places than I would have ever imagined. I have had the opportunity to travel to almost every state in America, as well as Canada, Mexico, Venezuela, and Panama. Even if I had never made it to the big leagues, I would know that I am truly blessed!

CHRIS COSTE was an All-American at Concordia College in Moorhead, Minnesota, and played five seasons in various independent leagues before finally getting a shot with the Cleveland Indians' organization in 2000. From there, he moved to the minor-league systems of the Boston Red Sox, Milwaukee Brewers, and Philadelphia Phillies. Coste was awarded the 2006 Dallas Green Award for Special Achievement and the 2007 Media Good Guy Award in the Philadelphia area. He lives in Fargo, North Dakota, with his wife, Marcia, and their daughter, Casey.

✻ ABOUT THE TYPE ✻

This book was set in Caledonia, a typeface designed in 1939 by William Addison Dwiggins for the Mergenthaler Linotype Company. Its name is the ancient Roman term for Scotland, because the face was intended to have a Scotch-Roman flavor. Caledonia is considered to be a well-proportioned, businesslike face with little contrast between its thick and thin lines.